The

Blakeneys

BOOKS BY LOCHLAINN SEABROOK (alphabetized)

Abraham Lincoln: The Southern View - Demythologizing America's Sixteenth President

Aphrodite's Trade: The Hidden History of Prostitution Unveiled

A Rebel Born: A Defense of Nathan Bedford Forrest - Confederate General, American Legend

Britannia Rules: Goddess-Worship in Ancient Anglo-Celtic Society - An Academic Look at the United Kingdom's Matricentric Spiritual Past

Carnton Plantation Ghost Stories: True Tales of the Unexplained from Tennessee's Most Haunted Civil War House!

Christmas Before Christianity: How the Birthday of the "Sun" Became the Birthday of the "Son"

Everything You Were Taught About the Civil War Is Wrong—Ask a Southerner!

Nathan Bedford Forrest: Southern Hero, American Patriot - Honoring a Confederate Icon and the Old South

The Blakeneys: An Etymological, Ethnological, and Genealogical Study - Uncovering the Mysterious Origins of the Blakeney Family and Name

The Book of Kelle: An Introduction to Goddess-Worship and the Great Celtic Mother-Goddess Kelle, Original Blessed Lady of Ireland

The Caudills: An Etymological, Ethnological, and Genealogical Study - Exploring the Name and National Origins of a European-American Family

The Goddess Dictionary of Words and Phrases: Introducing a New Core Vocabulary for the Women's Spirituality Movement

The McGavocks of Carnton Plantation: A Southern History - Celebrating One of Dixie's Most Noble Confederate Families and Their Tennessee Home

UFOs and Aliens: The Complete Guidebook

To order or for more information, please visit the publisher's Website:
www.searavenpress.com

SEA RAVEN PRESS

Thought Provoking Books For Smart People

The *Blakeneys*

An Etymological, Ethnological, and Genealogical Study

Uncovering the Mysterious Origins of the Blakeney Family and Name

Second Edition

Lochlainn Seabrook

SEA RAVEN PRESS

Franklin, Tennessee

THE BLAKENEYS

An Etymological, Ethnological, and Genealogical Study

Second Edition

Published by Sea Raven Press
P.O. Box 1054, Franklin, Tennessee 37065-1054 USA
www.searavenpress.com • searavenpress@nii.net
Thought Provoking Books For Smart People

ISBN: 978-0-9827700-6-1

Library of Congress Catalog Number: 2010935440

The Blakeneys: An Etymological, Ethnological, and
Genealogical Study/Lochlainn Seabrook. Foreword by Ray H.
Blakeney. Includes biographical references and index.

Front and back cover design, book design and layout, by Lochlainn Seabrook
Front cover image: "The Blakeney Hotel," Blakeney, Norfolk, England
Front cover image copyright © The Blakeney Hotel—Used by permission
Typography: Sea Raven Press Book Design
Sketch of the author on "About the Author" page copyright © Tracy Latham

The paper used in this book is acid-free and lignin-free. It has been certified by the
Sustainable Forestry Initiative and meets all ANSI standards for archival quality paper.

Printed and manufactured in occupied Tennessee, former Confederate States of America

Dedication

Dedicated to the Danish Vikings from the 'Bleak Isle'
The de Blækneys

Epigraph

"It is a desirable thing to be well-descended,
but the glory belongs to our ancestors."

Plutarch

Contents

Notes to the Reader

Throughout this book, some readers will notice an emphasis on the so-called "negative" aspects of the Danish Vikings, and also of the physical characteristics of both the village of Blakeney, Norfolk, England, and of Scandinavia in general. And it is true that I do in fact, quite unfairly and subjectively, paint the former as a bloodthirsty and rapacious lot and the later two as "bleak" and "dismal" places.

This emphasis, however, has been both intentional and necessary, for it is absolutely essential in making my theories on the origins of the Blakeney family and name understandable (something that will become more comprehensible as the reader progresses through the book).

Meanwhile, let it be known that I am well aware of the many wonderful and positive contributions made by the Danish Vikings in the Middle Ages, many which have carried down into the present day (and some which I have noted herein). Indeed, two of these are the very focus of this book, for as we will see, the early Danes are the originators of both the Blakeney family and the Blakeney name.

Furthermore, I would also like it to be known that far from believing that Blakeney, Norfolk, and Scandinavia are "dreary" places, I—being of Anglo-Saxon, Celtic, and Scandinavian stock—am one who truly appreciates (perhaps more than most) the awe-inspiring natural beauty of these areas. In fact, I actually revel in what some refer to as "bleak" weather (that is, cold, damp, rain, snow, wind, and cloudy days) and "bleak" geography (that is, moorlands, fens, tundras, moraines, mountains, and ice-fields).

Many have asked me about not only my connection to the Blakeneys, but also about my own personal genealogical family history and my descent from European royalty. In an effort to answer some of these questions I have paused to comment on them (in footnotes) in the appropriate places.

Throughout the text I use 'single quote' marks for definitions and meanings, and "double quote" marks for actual quotations.

Lochlainn Seabrook
Franklin, Tennessee, USA
September 2010

Foreword

M r. Seabrook, a cousin of the Blakeneys, has done a great service in his excellent research of the Blakeney family name. Previous writers have always taken a very different view of its origin and meaning. Tracing it through time from the first written sources through changes to its present meaning is a fascinating journey.

The historical background, along with a scholarly and scientific approach, gives us a look at a name that, although always associated with black or dark, actually meant the opposite before Medieval times.

Blakeophiles (both Blakeneys and Blakeleys—and their variant spellings) should take a long look at Mr. Seabrook's research. Even within the Blakeney family itself the fact that it had original Norman roots is now completely revised through the author's Danish origin theory, which makes a great deal of sense.

We must, of course, remember that surnames became fixed and hereditary over a long period and were in common use from about the middle of the sixteenth century. The Danes named the area of Norfolk for its physical attributes and later, by a stroke of the pen, the letter *á* became the letter *a* (both are pronounced differently), changing the meaning from white to black!

As explained by the author, the pattern of family history can now be discerned through the differing threads of both heredity and environment. He records that the Blakeneys were of Danish Viking blood who settled originally in Norfolk, only to return generations later to affix, for a second time, the Blakeney name to the area.

Mr. Seabrook's book will, I hope, make you feel that a most useful contribution has been made to uncover the mystery of our name.

Ray H. Blakeney
Former President of the Blakeney-Blakley Family Association, and the author of, *My Help Comes From Above: Blakeney and Blakey - The History of Chambers Blakely and David Bleakney and Their Neighbours in the 18ᵗʰ Century*

Nova Scotia, Canada
January 2000

Acknowledgments

Special appreciation to my wife Cassidy and my daughters Fiona and Dixie, and also Ray H. Blakeney, Valerie Kinsella, Michael Nelson, Jean (Blakeney) King, and Sylvain Doucet, for their support and generosity during the writing of this book.

Introduction

To professional genealogists and amateur researchers alike, the Blakeney line has proven to be one of the most intriguing of all family groups. And for good reason.

Few family lines can be traced as far back, and few possess as many notable individuals and characters, ranging from governors, lords, barons, military heroes, surgeons, reverends, MPs, judges, barristers, and sheriffs, to outlaws, heretics, scoundrels, and outright scallywags!

The Blakeneys were present at such famous conflicts as the Battle of Hastings (the Norman Invasion of England), the Culloden Massacre, the English Civil War, the American Revolutionary War, and America's War for Southern Independence (where the majority of them fought with the Confederacy for the constitutional right of self-determination).

As this restless people spread out across the world, we find them settling in every corner of the globe, from Greece, India, Mauritius, Australia, and Africa, to England, Canada, Ireland, Scotland, France, and Cuba. In their wake, they left hundreds of thousands of descendants. Little wonder that the Blakeneys have been so earnestly and thoroughly studied over the years.

Yet, despite this intense scrutiny, two vitally important and unanswered questions remain: What does the name Blakeney mean? And where did the Blakeneys originate? In my opinion—and in the opinion of many others, I might add—these issues have never been resolved to anyone's real satisfaction.

Conventional wisdom has it that Blakeney is related to the word 'black,' and that the Blakeney families derive from England. However, according to Lochlainn Seabrook's new and exciting findings, in this case conventional wisdom couldn't be more wrong.

As both a Blakeney and a family history enthusiast, I certainly recognize the importance of traditional genealogy books, with their lengthy, and often tedious, lists of who "begat" whom. And yet, such books are designed more for research than for reading, and the authors typically offer little (or no) information on the one topic that so many of us Blakeneys are truly interested in: the origins of both our family and our family name.

What I've long sought is a book that provides not only an in-depth examination of this topic, but one that also relates it in a readable story format; one that can be read and enjoyed over and over.

Lochlainn's book seeks to correct this deficiency, and the result, I'm happy to say, is a riveting, edifying, and altogether surprising journey of discovery, from the mist-enshrouded period of the Vikings to the present day.

Thoroughly-researched, well-written, easy to read, and yet comprehensive in scope (with footnotes that are often as engrossing as the main text itself), Lochlainn has combined history with genealogy in a detailed and absorbing narrative of encyclopedic proportions.

In a word, *The Blakeneys: An Etymological, Ethnological, and Genealogical Study* is a must-have for anyone who is studying, knows, loves, or is her/himself a Blakeney.

Edith Blakeney
10th great-granddaughter of Launcelot Blakeney (circa 1555-1595)

General Explanations

ABBREVIATIONS

aft. = 'after'

b. = 'born'

b. c. = 'born circa' (that is, born around)

BCE = 'Before Common Era' (in the Gregorian Calendar, preceding the
       year 0)

bef. = 'before'

c. = 'circa' (that is, around or about)

CE = 'Common Era' (in the Gregorian Calendar, beginning in the year
       0)

d. = 'died'

ed. = 'editor'

f. = 'flourished' (that is, lived)

(fn) = 'footnote'

r. = 'reigned' or 'ruled'

DATES OF INDO-EUROPEAN
LANGUAGES & BRANCHES

• UNRECORDED

Prehistoric language: 10,000 to 7000 BCE

Proto-Indo-European: 7000 to 3000 BCE

Old European: 1st Millennium to about Common Era; a pre-Celtic, non-
       Germanic, Neolithic language spoken in the British Isles circa 4th
       Century BCE

• INDO-IRANIAN

Sanskrit: pre-1000 BCE; oldest known member of the Indo-European
       languages

• GERMANIC
Old Teutonic: identical to "Old German"
Old Saxon: to 12th Century
Old German: to 12th Century
Old High German: 750 to 1150
Middle High German: 1150 to 1350
Middle Low German: 12th to 16th Centuries
Early New High German: 1350 to 1650
New High German: 1650 to present

Old Scandinavian: to 1350 (can also include both Old Norse and Old
    Danish, as well as Anglo-Scandinavian languages, such as Anglo-
    Danish)
Old Norse: to 1350 (similar, and perhaps nearly identical to, Old
    Danish)
Old (or Early) Danish: 9th to 11th Centuries (similar, and perhaps nearly
    identical to, Old Norse)
Anglo-Danish: 9th to 11th Centuries

Early English: 450 to 7th Century (began with the Jute, Angle, and Saxon
    Invasion of England in the 5th Century)
Old English (also known as Anglo-Saxon): 7th to 12th Centuries (can
    include dialects such as Anglian and West Saxon)
    Four Dialects:
        1. Northumbrian
        2. Mercian
        3. West Saxon (spoken in Wessex, and referred to as "standard
            Old English"; *Beowulf* and the *Anglo-Saxon Chronicle*
            written in this dialect)
        4. Kentish
Middle English: 12th to 15th Centuries (held by some to begin with the
    Norman Invasion in the 11th Century, and to end with the death
    of Chaucer in the year 1400)
Modern English: 15th Century to present
American English: from 17th Century

THE BLAKENEYS

• CELTIC
Old Irish: 7th to 11th Centuries
Middle Irish: 11th to 15th Centuries
Modern Irish: 15th Century to present

Middle Scots: 1474 to 1730

Old (or Primitive) Welsh: to 1150
Middle Welsh: 1150 to 16th Century
Modern Welsh: 16th Century to present

• ITALIC
Old Latin: prior to Classical Period
Late Latin: 3rd to 6th Centuries
New Latin: 15th Century to present

Old French: 9th to 13th Centuries, and sometimes to the 16th Century
(can also include Norman French and Anglo-Norman)
Middle French: 14th to 16th Centuries
Modern French: 16th Century to present
Norman French: 9th to 11th Centuries
Anglo-Norman: 11th to 13th Centuries

• BRANCH UNKNOWN
Late Greek: 3rd to 6th Centuries
Middle Greek: 7th to 15th Centuries
Modern Greek: 15th Century to present

Auxilium Meum Ab Alto

"My Help Comes From Above"
Blakeney Motto

The
Blakeneys

1

The Singular Enigma

or many people the name Blakeney evokes images of a quaint English fishing village, while to others it elicits visions of splendid Irish castles. Some may think of Saxon rulers, though still others connect the name with Medieval French royalty.

The Blakeney name is indeed profoundly associated with these nations and peoples. However, its roots of origin lie further back—and further north—in a land that few ever associate with this particular family: Scandinavia, and more specifically, Denmark.

In this book I will offer evidence for this view, using chiefly comparative philology and linguistics, onomasiology, and onomastics (anthroponymy and toponymy), though history, ethnology, geography, archaeology, and cultural anthropology, will also play significant roles.

Most important of all will be the science of etymology, for knowing and understanding the meanings and origins of words and names provides valuable insights and information that cannot be gleaned from any other source.

In beginning our quest to find the origins of the Blakeney name and family we must observe a simple fact—one that in turn begs a simple question: the surname Blakeney appears in France *before* it appears in England or Ireland. Yet Blakeney is not a French word.

Where then did the Blakeney name and family originate?

Resolving this singular enigma, one that has plagued Blakeney researchers for decades, is the focus of this book.

2

Beyond Conventional Wisdom

Current notions of the origins and meaning of the name Blakeney derive primarily from John Oscar Blakeney who, in his 1928 book, *The Blakeneys of America and Some Collaterals*, wrote:

> The name Blakeney is thought to have originally been suggestive of dark, or black, and may have been applied to one who had a swarthy complexion, black hair, lived in a black cave, or dark forest, or dyed black the skins with which he clothed himself, or led his adherents into battle protected by a black shield, or carrying a black banner.

While Mr. Blakeney's explanation is, to a certain degree, informative, it neglects several significant items.

First, what he is defining here is the word 'black.' In fact, the original ancient meaning of the word *blakeney* was 'white' (or 'bleak'), while in the Middle Ages it meant 'yellow.' Only much later did it come to be associated with the color 'black.'

Second, Mr. Blakeney passes over the surprising reason why the words *blakeney* and black were connected to begin with, which, as it turns out, was the result of one of the more celebrated linguistic mistakes in the evolution of the English language.

Third, he does not delve into the fascinating (and often confusing) origins and development of the truly ancient word *blakeney*, which would have led him to the Blakeney families' actual land of origin. Although he admits that "there is evidence that [the name] came from the *North of Europe*" (my emphasis), he does not hazard a guess as to what region or nation this might be.

Fourth, Blakeney would not have been used originally, as Mr. Blakeney suggests, as a surname by people with, for example, dark complexions or black hair, or by those who lived in black forests. For one thing, as we just discussed, the original meaning of *blake* was not 'black,' it was 'white' (or 'bleak' or 'pale'), a meaning that was still in use until the 19th Century in northern England. But there is another equally important reason.

Long ago there were already-existing Old and Middle English surnames for such individuals (and their families). For instance:

• Someone with a dark complexion would have been surnamed either 'Black' (from the Old English word *blæc*), 'Blackman' (from the Old English words *blæc* and *mann*),[1] or 'Blackmore' (from the Old English and Middle English words *blæc* and *Mor* (that is, dark as a 'Moor').)[2]
• Someone with black hair would have been surnamed 'Blacklock' (from the Old English words *blæ* and *locc*).
• Someone living in a dark forest would have been surnamed 'Blackwood' (from the Old English words *blæc* and *wode*).
• Someone living near a dark stream would have been surnamed 'Blackbrook' (from the Old English words *blæc* and *broc*).
• A man with a dark beard would have been surnamed 'Blackbird' (from the Old English *blæc* and *beard)*.
• Someone who lived by a dark cliff would have been surnamed 'Blackcliff' (from the Old English *blæc* and *clif)*.

---

[1] The surname 'Blakeman' was later mistakenly derived from 'Blackman.'

[2] The surname 'Blakemore' was later mistakenly derived from 'Blackmore.'

THE BLAKENEYS

- Someone who lived by a dark knoll would have been surnamed 'Blackhill' (from the Old English *blæc* and *hyll*).[3]

Many more examples of this kind could be given.

The point is that while all of the above surnames are indeed related to Blakeney, that relation is distant. And in fact the *original* meaning of *blakeney*, as we will see, is not at all connected with either a person's physical characteristics or with anything black or even dark.

Of course, etymology and ethnology were not the focus of Mr. Blakeney's very fine work, which centers primarily on the genealogy of what I term the "American Southern Blakeney Branch" (which descends from Captain John Blakeney, 1732-1832).

Additionally, when we consider that, philologically speaking, the name *Blakeney* is a fossilized word[4] with a false etymology,[5] we should not be surprised that Mr. Blakeney was not aware of the authentic etymology of his own surname.

However, for those who are interested in a more detailed study of the origins of the Blakeney name and family, we will attempt, throughout this book, to pick up where Mr. Blakeney has left off; a task that will require us to go beyond mere conventional wisdom into the arenas of both science and fact-based speculation.

In the process we will not only uncover the original, and thus true, meaning of the word *blakeney*, but more importantly we will locate the genuine ancestral home of the very earliest Blakeney families.

---

[3] The surname 'Blakedown' was later mistakenly derived from 'Blackhill.'

[4] A fossilized word is one that may or may not still be in use, but whose original ancient meaning has become obsolete and forgotten. Often a new and completely spurious (or fabricated) meaning is later attributed to fossilized words and names, further obfuscating their true and original etymologies.

[5] A word comes to possess a false or erroneous etymology because of centuries of misunderstanding, mistranslations, mispronunciations, and misspellings. The result, typically, is confusion with other words with similar spellings, meanings, or pronunciations, but with which they possess no linguistic relationship. The name Blakeney is only one of many thousands of examples of this corrosive process.

3

The Core-word Blake: An Evolutionary Journey

n retracing the evolutionary steps of the word *blakeney* we must begin with its core word, *blake*, whose ultimate linguistic cradle is to be found in prehistoric times, some 7,000 to 10,000 years ago. The region in which this source-word originated is Asia, and more specifically India. For the ancient Vedic languages of India form the very wellspring of countless Indo-European (or Aryan) words, including thousands thought of as uniquely "English."

It is here that we find a proto-Indo-European, or possibly a Sanskrit, etymon or base-word: *phleg*, meaning 'burn,' and its later variant, *bhleg* or *bhlig*, meaning 'pale.'[6] We have no actual evidence for either of these words. Yet they are sound hypothetical reconstructions of unrecorded archaic words that once existed in what are now dead languages.

In fact, their actual existence can be inferred from later words

---

[6] From *bhleg* later emerged the Old English word *blegen*, in Middle English 'blain,' an inflammatory sore.

which must have developed out of them; fossilized words such as the ancient Greek *phlégein* and the Latin *flagrare*, both meaning 'burn' (note that from these we derive such Modern English words as flame, flagrant, conflagration, and fulminate).

In prehistoric Germanic speaking regions, *bhleg* gave rise to another hypothetical word from this period: *blangkaz* (the ultimate source-word for the English word blank), meaning 'white.' From this word emerged the Old German (or Old Teutonic)[7] stem-word *blaik*, meaning 'shining' or 'to shine,' which gave rise to the Old German word *blaiko*, 'shining,' 'white,' or 'pale.' This in turn gave rise to the Old German word *blaikjôn*, 'bleak.'

In ancient Scandinavia, the Old German *blaiko* gave rise to the Old Norse word *blá*, 'pale' or 'livid' (the core-word for such modern words as blah and blasé); after which developed the Old Norse *bleikr*, 'wan,' 'shining,' or 'white,' and the Old Norse *bleikja*, 'bleak'; in Old High German this evolved into *bleih*, 'pale' and *bleicha*, 'bleak.' From these developed the Old German word *blîkan*, meaning 'to shine.'

In early England,[8] the Germanic *blaik* gave rise to the Old English[9] words *blæc* or *blác*; that is, *blāc* ('bleak'), meaning literally not only 'pale,' 'wan,' and 'pallid,' but contrarily also 'bright,' 'shining,' 'flashing,' and 'glittering.' From *blác* came *blæco*, meaning 'paleness,'

---

[7] Teutonic, though now largely an obsolete term, still aptly describes the group of related Germanic languages that include English, Dutch, Frisian, German, Scandinavian (Danish, Faroese, Finnish, Icelandic, Lappish, Norwegian, and Swedish), the extinct languages of Burgundian, Gothic, Norn, and Vandal, and finally such derived languages as Yiddish and Afrikaans.

[8] English itself is a Germanic language, one belonging to the West Germanic language group, that is made up of the early German, Frisian, and Dutch languages. (This is why, grammatically speaking, Old English is similar to Modern German.)

[9] Old English, first written in runic letters, is the Germanic language ancestor that gave rise to both English and Scots. The original Anglo-Saxons, the Angles (in Old English, the *Engle*) of Angeln or Anglen (now in Schleswig), Germany—who began their invasion of England in the 5th Century—gave their name to both their language (originally Anglo-Saxon), English (or in Old English, *Englisc*), and their nation, England (from 'Angle's Land,' or in German, *Engle's Lant*; in Modern English, 'England'). In Old English, the language of the Angles (also known as Anglo-Saxon), the Angles themselves were called *Angelfolc* (the 'English people'), while England was called *Angelcynn* or *Angelðeod*. One Old English name for the Angles was *norðleode*; that is, the 'northern folk.'

then *blacian*, meaning 'to turn pale,' or *blæcan*, meaning 'whiten.' In northern England (though not in Scotland) *blác* was later written *blake*—where it meant 'yellow' until as recently as the 19th Century,[10] while in Old Saxon, *blác* became *blêc*, 'white.'

In Middle English *blacian* became *blakiken*; then *blaknen*; then *blacey* (in Modern English, blakey), sometimes meaning 'little fair-haired one.' *Blacey* then evolved into *bloc*, meaning 'fair-haired' or 'fair-complected,' while in southern England *bloc* was written *bloke* or *bloken*.

Long before that, however, in Old English the Old Norse word *bleikja* (that is, bleak) became *blæce*, then *bleche* (in Modern English, bleach), then *bleyke* (or *bleyken*), and then *blæyke* or *blayke* (or *blayken*), which became two words in Middle English: *bleke* (in Modern English, bleak) and the now obsolete *blake*, meaning mainly 'bleak,' but also 'pale,' 'colorless,' 'sickly,' 'pallid,' 'sallow,' 'wind-swept,' 'cheerless,' 'chilly,' 'wan,' 'livid,' 'hoary,' 'whitish,' 'ghastly,' 'barren,' 'foam-colored,' 'light-colored,' 'yellowish,' 'spark,' 'flash,' 'golden,' 'fair,' and 'dismal'; and more freely, 'purity,' 'innocence,' 'virtuous,' 'to whiten,' 'to whitewash,' 'to blanch,' 'to wash clean,' 'to boil or scald,' 'to foam,' 'to discolor,' 'to sanctify,' 'to purify,' 'to cleanse of stain,' 'to smooth out,' 'to make pale with fear,' 'to sicken,' 'to pall,' and 'having a sickly hue.'[11] (Evidence supporting these early definitions comes from an early form of the word *blake*, namely *blæce*, the Old English word for both leprosy and psoriasis;[12] we also have the Old English word for

---

[10] A Middle English word for yellow or yellowish, was *gaudi*, a word which (like *blác* to Blake) later became a surname, *Gaudi*, and which is related to the Latin *gaudium* ('joy'), the Middle English *gaude* ('ornament'), and the Modern English word gaudy ('cheap,' 'showy,' 'tasteless,' 'vulgar'). The modern variations of this surname, Gaudy and Gawdy, mean 'yellow-hair,' or 'yellow-complexioned.'

[11] Such words would never be confused with the Old English words *hwit* or *hwite* ('white,' 'bright,' 'glistening'); *hwitan* ('to whiten,' 'polish,' 'brighten'); or *hwitian* ('to whiten,' to 'become white,' to 'be white').

[12] There were two other Old English words for leprosy, both also related to the blake words: *blæcða* and *blæcðrustfel*.

candle or lantern: *blæcern*).[13]

All of these words find corollaries in such words as the Spanish *blanco* (in English, blank), meaning 'white' or 'blonde'; the Latin *blandus* (in English, bland), meaning 'smooth' or 'soothing'; the Old High German *blanch*, meaning 'white'; the Old French *blanc*, meaning 'colorless,' 'white,' or 'fair' (in Old French we also have *blanchart*, 'whitish'); and the Old English word *blæcan* (in Modern English, bleach), meaning 'to make pale or ashen.'[14]

From the early *blake* words we also derive such Modern English words as bare, blink, blight, and blaze (from the Old English word *blæse*, meaning a 'fire-torch'), this last which is spelled *flambee* in French (revealing its roots in the Latin *flagrare*, 'to burn to ashes').

In essence then, as *The Oxford English Dictionary* clearly states, the

---

[13] Many other Old English cognates give supporting evidence of the original meaning of *blác* or blake: *blachleor* ('with pale cheeks'); *blacung* ('to turn pale'); *blæcernleoht* ('lantern-light'); *blæco* ('pallor'); *blæcpytt* ('bleaching pit'); *blædre* ('blister'); *blatian* ('to be livid'); *blegen* (a 'boil' or 'ulcer'); *blican* ('glitter,' 'shine,' 'gleam,' 'dazzle,' 'sparkle'); *bliccettan* ('quiver,' 'to glisten'); *bliccettung* ('shining'); and *blician* ('to shine').

[14] Other French cognates with *blake* include: *blanc-bec* ('greenhorn,' 'youth'); *blanchaille* ('white-bait'); *blanchâtre* ('whitish'); *blanche* ('minim'); *blanchement* ('cleanly,' 'neatly'); *blancher* (a 'tanner'); *blancheur* ('whiteness,' 'hoariness,' 'cleanliness,' 'light,' 'purity,' 'innocence,' 'virtue'); *blanchiment* ('bleaching,' 'blanching,' 'washing'); *blanchir* ('to grow white,' 'to foam,' 'to whiten,' 'to wash,' 'to make clean,' 'to whitewash,' 'to boil,' 'to scald,' 'to plane down or smooth out'); *blanchissage* ('washing'); *blanchissant* ('grows white,' 'foaming'); *blanchisserie* ('bleaching-house,' 'laundry'); *blanchisseur* ('washerman,' 'bleacher'); *blanchisseuse* ('washerwoman,' 'laundress'); *blaser* ('to pall,' 'to sicken'); *blason* ('blazon,' 'heraldry,' 'proclaim,' 'display,' 'adorn'); *blasonner* ('to criticize,' 'to blacken'); *blême* ('sallow,' 'pale,' 'ghastly,' 'wan'); *blêmir* ('to turn pale'); *bléser* ('to lisp'); *blessant* ('offensive'); *blessé* ('wounded,' 'diseased'); *blesser* ('to wound,' 'to offend,' 'to gall,' 'to take offense'); *blessure* ('wound,' 'cut,' 'hurt'); *blond(e)* ('flaxen,' 'fair,' 'light,' 'sandy,' 'golden'); *blondin* ('a fair-complexioned person,' a 'spark'); *blondir* ('to turn light or fair'); *blondissant* ('yellowish,' 'golden'); and *bluette* ('spark,' 'flash,' 'flake of fire'). The French word *blasphème* (in English, blasphemy), meaning 'to offend someone's dignity,' 'wound someone's pride,' or 'whitewash someone's reputation,' is also a distant relative of *blake*. Many so-called "English" surnames derive from these early linguistic relations of *blake* as well. Among these are: Blain, Blaine, Blayn, Blayne, Blane (all from Old English *blegen*, 'inflammation'); Blaise (from Old English *blæse*, 'torch'); Blampey, Blampied (both from Old French *blanc* and *pied*, 'white foot'); Blamphin, Plampin (both from Old French *blanc* and *pain*, 'white bread,' i.e., a baker; and related to the Old English words *bacan*, to 'bake,' and *bæcere*, a 'baker'); Blanc, Blanck, Blank, Blanks (all from Old French *blanc*, 'white,' 'fair'); Blanche, Blaunch, Blaunche (all from Old French *blanche*, 'white,' 'fair'); Blanchard, Blanshard (both from Old French *blanchart*, 'whitish'); Blanchet, Blanchett, Blanket, Blankett, Branchett (all from a hybrid of Old French *blanc* and Old English *heafod*, 'white head'); Blanchflower, Branchflower (both from Old French *blanc flour*, 'white flower'); Blatcher (from Old English *blæcan*, 'to bleach'); Blaxter (from Middle English *blaker*, 'bleacher'); and Bleacher (from Old English *blæcan*, 'to bleach,' thus one who bleaches). Also, see the following footnote.

word

> " . . . blake was the direct phonetic descendant of the Old English word
> *blác*, 'pale,' a common Teutonic adjective . . ."

The Old English *blác*, however, ultimately derives from the Old Norse *blá* (which later evolved into the Old and Middle English words for 'livid' or 'pale': *blaa, blae, blay, blea, bley, ble, blee, bloo, blowe*), meaning 'pale,'[15] and *blá's* later Old Norse corollaries, *bleikr*, meaning 'wan,' *blaekno*, 'scorched pale,' and *bleikja*, 'bleak.' In Old English *bleikja* became *blæce*, and then *bleche*; in Middle English *bleche* became *bleyke*, then *blayke*, then finally *blake*, meaning 'bleak' (that is, 'pale' or 'dreary').

Let us keep these word-meanings in mind, for they will become increasingly relevant as our story unfolds.

---

[15] Many of these ancient Old Norse words have come down to us as "English" surnames. Examples are: Blaw, Blow, and Blowe, the earliest record of which was one *Randulf Bla*, in London in 1202. All mean 'livid' or 'pale.'

4

Medieval Confusion: How White Became Black

f *blake* began as a word meaning 'white,' 'pale,' and 'bleak' (and later 'yellow'), how, one might ask, did it eventually come to mean 'black'—as John Oscar Blakeney asserted—the sense in which it is so often mistakenly used today? There are two primary reasons.

In Medieval times the concept of colorlessness was viewed in two seemingly opposing senses: as something completely *pale*, and as something completely *dark*. Indeed, to this day, we might still define the word colorless as that which is either totally white or totally black.[16]

Contributing to this misconception of the definition of colorlessness, by the 12th Century—in England at least—we find two words existing side by side: *blac*, meaning 'white,' and *blac*, meaning 'black.'

---

[16] Note that technically both white and black are classified as colors, though they belong to the achromatic color group, for white reflects and transmits all colors while black neither reflects or transmits any color.

THE BLAKENEYS

Though in Old English, both words were written exactly the same (that is, as *blac*), originally they were pronounced quite differently: the former, meaning 'white,' was properly pronounced with a long 'ā' vowel, sounding like *'blake,'* with the 'ā' pronounced as in 'cake,' 'date,' 'fade,' 'drape,' etc. (this form was also occasionally pronounced with an 'ä' vowel, sounding like *'block'*); while the latter, meaning 'black,' was properly pronounced with a short 'a' vowel, sounding like *'black'* (with the 'a' pronounced as in 'mat,' 'map,' 'snap,' or 'patch').

As both words were originally spelled the same, throughout this book, to distinguish between the two words, I will employ the traditional modern spellings of the Old English forms, using an acute accent in *blác*, that is blake (meaning 'white,' 'pale,' or 'bleak'), and no acute accent in *blac*, that is black (meaning 'dark,' 'murky,' or 'swarthy'). Simply put:

- *blác*, with a long "a", is blake (rhymes with bake), meaning 'white.'
- *blac*, with a short "a", is black (rhymes with back), meaning 'black.'

The problem began with Medieval speakers, who often reversed the pronunciations of these two words, so that *blác* was sometimes pronounced 'black' and *blac* was sometimes pronounced 'blake.'

Combining such mispronunciations with both misspellings and misconceptions relating to color and colorlessness, it was inevitable that the words *blác* and *blac* would eventually become confused. And so they did, with the end result being that the two words began to be used interchangeably to mean both 'white' and 'black.'

Variant Old English spellings and pronunciations did not help the matter. In some Anglo-Saxon dialects, for example, *blác* ('white') was sometimes written and pronounced *blæc* ('black'), while *blæc* was sometimes written and pronounced *blác* ('blake'), subtle but important distinctions that were lost on the largely nonliterate and semiliterate population of the Middle Ages.

By the 12th Century, the period in which the spelling form *blake* ('white') first appears, confusion still reigned, this time with the Middle English word for 'black,' *blak*, which was also sometimes written *blake*, the final 'e' giving *blake* the contradictory meaning of both 'white' and 'black.'[17]

Similar problems developed with related Middle English words, such as *bloken* or *blokien*, 'to whiten,' and *blaken* or *blakie*, 'to blacken' (though eventually, *bloken* became obsolete and was replaced by such cognates as *bleyken*, *bleiken*, and *bleken*, all meaning 'to bleach'), and also with the Middle English words *bleche*, 'to turn pale,' and *bleeche*, to 'make dark.'

There was difficulty too with the Old English *blæcan*, 'to bleach white' (for example, using the Sun or chemicals), which was often used interchangeably with its Old English opposite, *blæcean*, 'to darken black' (for example, using soot or fire).

This bewildering exchange of spellings and meanings continued well into the 12th Century, at which time the Middle English *blaken*, 'to become pale,' was still being mistaken for the Middle English *bláken*, 'to grow dark.'

Early writers, like the English poet Geoffrey Chaucer (circa 1340-1400), contributed to this linguistic anarchy by using the word *blake*, which means 'white,' as a word meaning 'black.' He wrote the word 'blackberry,' for instance, as *blakebery* ('whiteberry'), when the proper spelling at the time would have been *blacbery* ('blackberry'). Though Chaucer was highly literate, his misunderstanding of *blake* illustrates the long-held puzzlement over the original meaning of the word, as well as the carelessness with which it was often used—even

---

[17] A parallel in Irish Gaelic is the word *blàr*, which derives from *bla*, the same Indo-European root-word from which the blake word-names derive. The Irish *blàr* means both 'peaty' (something dark in color) and 'white-faced' (something light in color), and is related to the Dutch *blaar* ('white mark on forehead'), and the Middle Dutch word *blaer* ('bald'). Another word, the Welsh *blawr*, which has the same origins as blake and *blàr*, illustrates the often baffling ambiguity of these words, for *blawr* means 'grey,' the color midway between white and black. We have a corresponding duality with the Old English word *asweartian* (cognate with the Old High German word, *swarz*, 'black'), which means both 'to turn livid' (i.e., bright) and 'to turn ashy' (i.e., dark). Then there are the Old English words *ablacian* and *ablican*. Though similar in spelling and pronunciation, the former word—which is related to the Old English words *ablæcan* ('to bleach,' 'whiten'), *ablæcnes* ('gloom'), and *ablæcung* ('pallor')—means 'to become pale,' 'grow faint,' or 'become tarnished.' The later word, however, means 'to shine,' or 'glitter.' These two nearly identical words, with their ambivalent and even opposing meanings, are early and direct ancestors to the blake/blakeney words, place-names, and surnames, and well illustrate the early foundation on which the confusion surrounding the surnames Blakeney and Blake later arose.

among the educated classes.

Indeed, the Medieval disarray surrounding the word *blake* is still with us today, as nearly all modern baby name books demonstrate. Under the entry for the forename "Blake" will typically be found one of the following contradictory definitions:

- 'fair or dark'
- 'fair-haired or dark-haired'
- 'fair-complected or dark-complected'

Under the entry "Blake" in one baby name book, for example, I found this curious definition: "Incongruously, this word can mean either 'pale-skinned' or 'dark-skinned.'" And under the entry for the name "Blakely" I found the following conflicting etymology: "May mean 'dark meadow' or 'pale meadow.'" (How many new parents bypass the forenames Blake and Blakely out of sheer bewilderment we will never know.)[18]

It is important to reemphasize here that the English word *blac* ('black') derived from a different evolutionary path than that of the English word *blác* ('white'). While both are certainly rooted in the ancient Greek *phlégein* (and the later Latin *flagrare*), it is the Old High German *blah* (or *blach*), 'black,' that gave birth to the Old English word *blæc* (*bleck*); this became, in Old Saxon, *blac*; then the Middle English *blak*, then *blaake*, then *blacke*, and finally the Modern English *black*.[19]

Moreover, it is vital to our discussion here to understand that the original English color-word for 'black' was not 'black' at all; nor did

---

[18] We have examples of Old English words that lie midway between *blác* ('white') and *blac* ('black'); words such as: *blæse* ('torch,' 'firebrand'); *blæsere* ('incendiary'); *blæst* ('blast' of flame, 'blowing,'); *blæstan* ('to blow'); *blæstbelg* ('bellows'); *blæstm* ('flame,' 'blaze'); *blæge* ('gudgeon,' 'bleak'); *blætan* (to 'bleat'); *blawende* ('blowing hard'); *blawere* ('blower'); *blawung* ('blowing,' 'blast'); *blæd* ('blowing,' 'blast,' 'breath,' 'spirit'); and *blat* ('livid' and 'pale'). Throughout the Medieval period, such ambiguous words helped further obfuscate the line that originally separated blake from black.

[19] There are many Old English words that are cognate to *blæc* or *blac* ('black'), all which illustrate this word's connection to the color black. We have, as just three examples, *blæcce* ('black matter'); *blæcfexede* ('black-haired'); and *blæcgymm* ('jet').

this initial word even contain the *bla* element. The word in question was *swært* or *sweart* (and later *swart*), which derives from the Old High German word for 'black,' *swarz*; in Modern German, *schwarz*; in Modern English, swarthy.

The original ancient meanings of *swært* are still current in the modern word *schwarz* itself: 'black,' 'swarthy,' 'gloomy,' 'evil,' 'dark.' Evidence supporting this fact can be found in its various cognates, such as *swearcian* ('to become dark'); *swearcung* ('darkness'); *sweartbyrd* ('dreary birth'); *swearte* ('evilly'); *sweartian* ('to become dark'); *sweartnes* ('blackness'); *sweartung* ('darkness'); and *swearð* ('swarth').

Indeed, the base-word *swarz* continues to be used in many Germanic-speaking nations to mean 'black,' even in those modern languages in which the original word for black came from the base-word *blac*. One example of this is Danish. In Early Danish 'black' was *blæk*, while in Modern Danish it is *sort*, akin to the Old High German *swarz* (note that the same phenomenon occurred in Danish with the word 'white'; in Early Danish it was *blá*, while in Modern Danish it is *hvid*).

In short, the early English word for 'black,' *blac*, descends directly from the Old High German word *blah* or *blach* ('black')—and so is linguistically related to such words as the Old Norse *blakkr* ('dark'); the Swedish *bleck* ('ink'); the Icelandic *blak* ('ink'); the Dutch *blaken* ('to scorch'); and the Danish *blæk* ('ink').

The Early English word for 'white,' however, which is *blác*, descends directly from the Old Teutonic word *blaik*, and its variations *blaiko*, *blaiki* (all meaning 'white,' 'pale,' 'shining') and *blaikjan* ('to bleach'), which in Old Norse became *blækno* ('scorched pale' or 'burned colorless'), and then *bleikja* ('bleak'), which in England then became *blæce*, then *bleche*, then *bleyke*, then *blayke*, and then finally *blake*, with the compound being *blakeney* (this form to be discussed at length shortly).[20]

---

[20] The confusion surrounding the blake words and names crosses language and national boundaries, as we can see from the words blake, blaker, and black. All derived from the same ancient linguistic ancestor, *phleg*, meaning both 'burn' and 'pale.' Yet, blake came to mean 'bleak' or 'pale,' while black came to mean 'dark' or 'scorched.' *Blaker*, however, never developed such black and white meanings, and in fact, still causes much confusion. As the Middle English word for 'bleacher,' *blaker* indicates a person whose job it is to figuratively 'burn' clothes 'pale'; while as the Dutch word for 'candlestick,' we have the suggestion of an item

The Blakeneys

Thus, while our ancestors thoroughly confused *blac* with *blác* (and in the process gave the latter, *blake*, a spurious etymology), we have the benefit of the modern science of onomastics, which reveals that the two words are quite distinguishable, and are in fact cousins, *not* siblings.[21]

whose object (i.e., the candle) has a flame that both 'burns' and is 'pale.' Furthermore, if we add the Dutch suffix *-en* to *blaker* we have the Dutch word *blakeren*, meaning to 'scorch' black, a word that is also directly related to the Dutch *blaken*, meaning 'burn' and 'blaze'; as *blakenvan*, to 'glow with'; and as *blakende welstand*, 'in the pink of health.' In all of these words we see the echoes of the ancient root-words that shared the dualistic meaning of both 'gleaming' and 'pale,' of both 'shiny' and 'bleak,' and of both 'flaming' and 'burnt.'

[21] Blakeney is far from the only example of a surname that has accrued a fraudulent etymology over the centuries. Another is Boniface, almost universally, and incorrectly, believed to mean 'beautiful face,' or sometimes 'well-doer.' In fact, the surname derives from the Latin word *bonifactius*, literally meaning 'good fate' (from *bonum*, 'good,' and *fatum*, 'fate'), or more freely, 'promising destiny.' We also have the curious example of the Irish surname *Ó hEachdhubháin* (in English, Aghoon), which means 'Blacksteed' (*each*: 'steed'; *dubh*: 'black'), but which has been mistranslated as the surname 'Whitesteed.'

11

5

Theories on the National Origins of the Name Blakeney

The questions we must ask now are, what are the national origins of the word blake, and how far back in time do we need to go to establish these origins?

In answer to the second question, we need only return to a point in time where Europe began to assume its current form. While there have been major shifts in her national boundaries over the millennia, Europe has retained the general ethnic lines of demarcation she now possesses since the beginning of the Common Era (the year CE 0). And since surnames were not used in Europe until, at the earliest, the year CE 900, and since manorial records and parish registers (our chief source of establishing early genealogical lines) did not come into usage until the 16th Century, it would be pointless to look back any further (such as to Neolithic times, when even ethnicity is difficult to trace with any precision).

Concerning the first question, there are several schools of thought as to the original nationality of the Blakeney family line.

One holds that it is Irish; another that it is French; another that it is Saxon; still another that it is Norman. I even know of some who maintain that it is American! The largest school, however, embraces the idea that the Blakeneys are of strictly English descent.

Unfortunately for their adherents all of these notions are incorrect.

The simple matter is that the word *blake* (including its compound variation, *blakeney*) is neither an American word, an Irish word, a Norman word, or a French word. In particular, it is not an English word.

Rather *blake* is a relatively modern English spelling of a pre-English word. For, as we have firmly established, primitive forms of the word *blake* are found in the language group that gave rise to English, and which existed long before England was a distinct nation. We are speaking here of the West Germanic language group, which in turn derived from Indo-European, which in turn emerged out of the proto-Indo-European language, a lost, or rather unrecorded, source language common to much of Europe and Asia prior to 3000 BCE (over 5,000 years ago).

Germanic-speaking peoples have been dated back to at least 1000 BCE (3,000 years ago), while English as a singular language cannot be said to have come into existence until much later, sometime after the 7th Century (1,400 years ago).[22] Since pre-historic Germanic is the parent language of English, it is here that we must start our search for the national origins of the name Blakeney.

---

[22] I view the "English" spoken in 5th- to 7th-Century England—often known as "Old English"—as a language perhaps more properly called "Pre-English." Indeed, the most accurate name for this language is not Old English at all, but rather *Anglo-Saxon* (named after the German peoples known as the Angles and the Saxons, who invaded England in the 5th Century). For it is a deeply Germanic language; one that is well nigh indecipherable and altogether foreign to the modern English speaker's ear.

6

A Prehistoric Germanic Foundation

lthough it is difficult to pinpoint the exact European soil in which the word *blake* first grew, it is not impossible. In fact, using etymology we can postulate a viable theory as to its emergence and development through time.

From what we have seen this emergence would have likely occurred in the heart of Europe, or what is now Germany, the root region from out of which all of the other Germanic languages spread out across Europe.

It is here indeed that we find the very oldest example of the word *blake*: the prehistoric Germanic *blaik*, meaning 'to shine,' and the resulting original adjective variously spelled *blaiko*, *blaikos*, or *blakko*, all meaning 'white,' 'pale,' 'bleak,' or 'scorched colorless.'

From the prehistoric *blaiko* evolved the Old Germanic words *blæko*, *blako*, *blak*, and *blaikjôn* ('bleak'), then in Old High German *bleicha* ('bleak'), which later in Old Norse gave rise to such words as *blá* ('pale'), *bleikja* ('bleak'), and *blækno* ('burned white'), and in Old English *blæc* ('pale'), and *blæce*, *bleche*, *bleyke*, and *blayke* (all meaning 'bleak'). Finally in Middle English, we find the spelling *blake*, which later became obsolete when it was replaced by the Modern English word *bleak* (that is, 'pale,' 'white,' 'dismal,' 'lifeless').

THE BLAKENEYS

Since the earliest known examples of the word *blake* are Old Teutonic (that is, Old German), it is more than apparent that the Blakeney name—like the Blakeney family itself—is neither Irish, English, Norman, or French in origin. It is Germanic.

The question now is, from which specific Germanic country did the Blakeneys originate, for there are a number to choose from? The Germanic-speaking nations are: Austria, Belgium, Denmark (which includes Greenland and the Faeroe Islands), England, Finland, Germany, Iceland, the Netherlands, Norway, Sweden, and Switzerland.[23]

We must bear in mind that none of these eleven countries existed under their present names in ancient times. Therefore it would be more accurate to speak loosely, in terms of Germanic *regions* rather than Germanic *nations*.

---

[23] While Afrikaans—the Anglo-Dutch language spoken in South Africa—is indeed a Germanic language, it is not listed here since there were no Germanic-speaking people in this region until the 17th Century. Therefore, it is not applicable to our story.

7

Scandinavia:

Land of

Extreme Contrasts

ur first clue as to the national origins of the Blakeney family line comes from the fact that *blaik* (blake) was to eventually carry the dual meaning of 'white' and 'black.' As we will shortly see, the earliest linguistic examples of this phenomenon occur in Old Norse, the homogenous language of the ancient Scandinavian peoples, the Danes, the Swedes, and the Norwegians—though linguistic studies show that Old Norse is primarily Danish in character.[24]

If we look closely at the traditional metaphors, stories, myths, allegories, and symbolism surrounding Scandinavia, something quite intriguing emerges. What we find is a region that has long been defined as a mysterious place of *extreme contrasts of lightness and darkness.*

On the one hand it was seen as a shadowy gloomy land due to the facts that:

---

[24] By the year 1000, regional differences in Old Norse began to arise, causing it to divide into two basic varieties. Consequently, *West Norse* was used in Norway and Iceland, while *East Norse* was used in Denmark and Sweden.

- at the time (that is, in ancient times), it was one of the last areas to be explored.
- for part of the year the region is largely covered in 'darkness' (due to the tilt of the Earth on its axis).
- it possesses 'ashen' lava fields, remnants of active volcanos.
- it possesses 'black' sand, also a result of volcanic activity.
- there were few people in this vast, largely empty territory.
- the weather is cold, rainy, grim, and wet much of the year.
- the 'bleakness' of the land, much of which is made up of large flat tundras, bogs, lagoons, infertile plains, sandy soil, craters, screes, moraines, swamps, quags, barren mountains, ice fields, fast, ice-cold, unfordable rivers, and deeply cut gorges.

Such traits have given the Scandinavian lands the nickname "the Black Lands" (that is, "the Lands of Darkness").

On the other hand, Scandinavia has also been associated with:

- the 'shining,' 'white,' 'bright,' 'blaze' of snow, ice, and glaciers, that cover the northern regions for so much of the year.
- the *Aurora Borealis* which 'burns' like a curtain of magic 'flames' in the night sky.
- the remaining part of the year when the Sun 'shines' 'brightly' both day and night.
- 'fiery' volcanoes, which produce 'burning' molten lava flows.
- steaming geysers and boiling mud pits.

Thus, this region has also been known as "the White lands," "the Land of the Midnight Sun," and also, as in Iceland, "the Land of Fire and Ice."

It is interesting to note that the ancient Romans feared these northernmost regions of extreme contrast, believing that only savage animal-like humans could survive there. Thus they referred to the Scandinavians (and those other denizens of the "far north," the Celts), as "barbarians," and called the lands of the former, *Ultima Thule*, roughly meaning 'the farthest known pieces of land, after which there is nothing.' In other words, 'the end of the world.'

THE BLAKENEYS

As we are about to see, it was from just such 'dismal' regions on the fringe of civilization that the excitable and bellicose ancestors of today's Blakeneys first sailed out to greet an innocent world.

8

Sea-Warriors
From Thule:
The Danish Vikings

or our purposes one Scandinavian people in particular stands out from among the others. This was the seafaring pirate society known as the *Wicings*, or Vikings (from the Old Norse *vikingr*, meaning 'warrior'), which flourished from circa 800 to 1050.

From among the Vikings—a group comprised of Norwegians, Danes, and Swedes—still another group stands out. They are first known to us from the historian Jordanes (f. 6ᵗʰ Century), who called them the *Dani*, for they took their name from the great European Mother-Goddess Dana. We are speaking here of a violent yet spiritual Goddess-worshiping people, the Danes, said to hail from a mysterious "island" in the north, known then as *Thule* (probably the great Scandinavian peninsula).[25]

---

[25] The great Goddess Dana also gave her name to the Greek *Danaids* and to the biblical Danites (Judges 18:11), as well as to the Rivers Danube, Don, and Dnieper. In Ireland, where she is known as the Goddess Danu-Ana, or Anu, she is still regarded as the ancestral "Mother of the Irish People"; which is why the ancient

THE BLAKENEYS

Though all of the Viking groups were exceedingly restless, energetic, and aggressive, the Danes could arguably be called the most Viking of the Vikings. For these tall, blond, narrow-headed, blue-eyed warriors were the first Scandinavians to land on the shores of the Netherlands, England, France, Spain, and Italy, where they laid waste entire cities, as they burned, pillaged, plundered, and looted their way across Europe.[26]

In his *History of the World*, the Spanish priest Paulus Orosius (f. 5th Century) notes, with barely concealed incredulity, that after capturing their enemies, early Scandinavian warriors (such as the Cimbri) would then follow

> a strange and unusual vow [in which] . . . they set about destroying everything which they had taken. Clothing was cut to pieces and

---

Irish called themselves, *Tuatha Dé Danann*; literally, the "people of the Goddess Dana." Note: the Old Irish words *túath* ('populus') and *túathal* ('left-hand') have given us the Irish surname *Ó Tuathail*—anglicized as O' Toole—the free translation which is 'the left-handed people.' This etymology shows us that this distinguished Leinster sept has its roots in the ancient Celtic Matriarchate. For matriarchal (or Goddess-worshiping) peoples perform their dances and rituals *widdershins*; that is, *anti-* or *counterclockwise* (also called "moon-wise," in imitation of the retrograde orbit of the Moon)—from right to left, rather than *clockwise*, from left to right, as patriarchal societies do. This is because, as ancient symbology reveals, the left side of the body is ruled by the Feminine Principle, while the right side is governed by the Masculine Principle. This practice, also known as "the Left-Hand Path" (or "the Female Way"), still flourishes in folk traditions the world over, and is far older than the Right-Hand Path ("the Male Way") of today's male-dominant religions and societies. Indeed, it has been preserved into the present in such places as modern Scotland, where it is still known as the marriage rite of "handfasting." Ancient Irish Druids are known to have danced widdershins around the temple of the Irish Mother-Earth-Goddess Tara. The custom of a man placing a wedding ring on a woman's *left* hand began as an effort to curtail the magical feminine powers that were once thought to originate in the left side of a woman's body. Also we will note that the practice of two people shaking their *right* hands to "seal a deal" is a relatively modern *male* invention. Earlier matriarchal peoples, who embraced the left-sided symbology of the Divine Feminine, shook each others' *left* hands when making pledges and promises. For more on the customs of ancient matriarchal societies, see my books, *Britannia Rules*, *The Book of Kelle*, and *The Goddess Dictionary of Words and Phrases*. Two Irish mountains in County Kerry still bear the name of the Goddess Dana as well, attesting to her widespread eminence among the ancient Celts: the Paps of Anu (i.e., 'the Breasts of the Goddess Anu'). Note that Ireland itself is named after another female deity; in this case, the Celtic Goddess Eriu. In Irish Gaelic the word Ireland is written *Erin*, a word that means: the 'land of [the Goddess] Eriu'. In Anglo-Saxon England (referred to in Old English as *Seaxland*; i.e., 'land of the Saxons'), the Goddess Dana was known as Black Annis; to the Angles she was Anna or the Blue Hag; to the Greeks she was *Danae* (mother of Perseus); to the Hebrews she was Dinah; and to the Russians, the Goddess Dennitsa. Dane's Hill in Leicestershire, England, is the site of one of the Goddess' ancient cave-shrines, still known as "Black Annis' Bower."

[26] Eventually, the Danes even managed to subdue and conquer one of their fellow Viking nations, Norway, which, temporarily, became a province of Denmark in 1536.

cast away, gold and silver was thrown into the river, the breastplates of the men were hacked to pieces, the trappings of the horses were broken up, the horses themselves drowned in whirlpools, and men with nooses round their necks were hanged from trees. Thus there was no booty for the victors and no mercy for the vanquished.

With such mindless savagery in their midst, it is little wonder that a special prayer, *A furore Normannorum libera nos* ("From the fury of the Norse deliver us!"), was inserted into the litanies of many European churches.

The 9th-Century Danish assaults on their European neighbors were said to have been of particular and "unsurpassed brutality." Men were callously put to the sword where they stood, women were carried off to become slaves and concubines, while children were mercilessly thrown upon stakes. Churches, businesses, and homes were ransacked, then burned to the ground, a Viking ritual called "blackening" (a word of significance that we will return to later).

Even the greatest most heavily defended cities were not safe from the rapacious Danes, whose devastation rained indiscriminately across Europe. Paris, France, fell as easily before this "unspeakable wave of slaughter" as Seville, Spain; Hamburg, Germany; Luna, Italy; and London, England, the next stop on our journey to discover the roots of the Blakeney family.

9

The Danish Vikings in 8th-Century England

According to the *Anglo-Saxon Chronicle* (composed about 891), the Danes began their initial raids upon England in the year 787. The most well-known of these early assaults occurred in 793, at Lindisfarne, in Northumbria (the Old English region of *Deira*), with much more decisive attacks following in 838.

Within one year, in 839, an immense well organized Danish Viking horde was despoiling nearly the whole of eastern England. In 851 the Danes spent their first winter on the island of Thanet, and in 865 a "great army" swept across the northeast, overthrowing the old kingdoms of Mercia, Northumbria, and the area of our focus, East Anglia.

As is the custom of invaders of new lands, the Danes brought more than mere military might to England. Also included in their "war chest" was something far less tangible than cannon, but no less sweepingly destructive: an arsenal of Danish cultural ideas, beliefs, practices, and customs. The purpose? As cultural anthropologists and comparative ethnologists well understand, few things can decimate a community or society, and bring it into total submission, as rapidly as the imposition upon it of a new and wholly foreign culture.

One of the more overwhelmingly deleterious aspects of cultural imposition is language, a tool long used to divide and conquer entire nations (one will recall the biblical tale of the "Tower of Babel," and those studies showing the many social problems that arise in modern bilingual countries).

The Danes, too, brought this cultural weapon with them to England, which they enthusiastically employed as they came ashore along her eastern coast. Here, using an ancient and popular custom of naming places in accordance with their usage, location, owner(s), and physical appearance, the Danes methodically bestowed Old Norse names on each of the towns they founded or conquered. In doing so they not only left hundreds of place-names to mark their passage (such as Lowestoft and Braithwaite), but they also printed an indelible Danish stamp upon the English world that would both permeate and undermine Anglo-Saxon society for centuries to come.[27]

---

[27] Other Old Norse (Danish) toponyms, or place-names, in England include *Kirkby*: 'Church Village'; *Whitby*: 'Hviti's Village'; *Corby*: 'Kori's Village'; *Scunthorpe*: 'Skuma's Outer Settlement'; *Derby*: 'Deer Village', *Fromby*: 'Forni's Village'; *Grimsby*: 'Grímr's Village'; *Romanby*: 'Róthmundr's Village'; and *Walesby*: 'Vals' Village.' All of these represent personal, probably masculine, Scandinavian names; except, obviously, Kirkby and Derby. But we will note that the Danes also coined many feminine place-names as well. Examples of feminine Anglo-Scandinavian English place-names that have come down to us are: Helperby (from a woman's personal name, *Hjalp*); Kenilworth (from a woman's personal name, *Cynehild*); and Wilbraham (from a woman's personal name, *Wilburh*). Anglo-Scandinavian place-names, or hybrid place-names—combining Scandinavian and English elements—include Welby, Durham, and Grimston, while some Old English place-names were later altered by Scandinavian influence, such as Keswick and Skidbrooke. Interestingly, however, English place-names with the words "Dane" and "Danes" in them are often not at all related to the Danish Vikings, and have no connection with Old Norse. Places such as Dane Court and Dane End, for instance, derive from the Old English word *denu*, meaning 'valley' or 'dale.' Likewise, there is the surname Dane or Danes, known as early as 1275, in, for example, the name of one *William de la Dane*. This surname also has no association with the Danes, as the meaning of this gentleman's name shows: 'William of the Valley.' Confusing the situation are the Old English words *dene* (also meaning 'valley' or 'dale'), which when spelled with a capital 'd' (giving *Dene*) means 'the 'Danes' (hence the Old English *Denemearc*, 'Denmark'), and *denn*, meaning a 'woodland pasture,' which has given us such place-names as Danehill, in Sussex County, England. We also have the old Celtic word *dane*, meaning 'trickling stream,' given to the River Dane, and which has given rise to such place-names as Davenham, 'village on the trickling river' (Cheshire County). There are a few authentic Danish-related examples of the word "Dane" in English place-names, however. Two such toponyms are Danby ('settlement of the Danes'), in North Yorkshire County, and Danby Wiske ('settlement of the Danes on the River Wiske'), also in North Yorkshire. As for English surnames using the word "Dane" we have several. The Old French word *daneis*, the Old English word *denisc*, and the Middle English words *danais* and *denshe*, all meaning 'Danish' (i.e., 'the Dane'), gave rise to the English forename and surname, Dennis (variations include: Denis, Denniss, Dennys, Dennes, Denness, Dinnis). From the Middle English word *denshe* specifically, we have the surnames: Dence, Denns, and Dench, which became Dens in Scottish. (Note that an alternate source for the name Dennis is the Latin masculine word *Dionysius*, while the Latin feminine word *Dionysia* has given us both the forename and the surname Denise.)

THE BLAKENEYS

To this day, for example, English place-names ending with the following suffixes or elements all have Old Norse origins: *-bec* ('stream'), *-beck* ('hill-slope'), *-bu*, *-by* ('village,' 'farm,' 'farmstead,' 'fortified place,' or 'town'), *-digue*, *-ey* ('island'), *-fell*, *-gill* ('deep narrow valley'), *-keld* ('stream'), *-mel* (sand-bank'), *-rigg*, *-scale*, *-sough*, *-skeith*, *-thorp* ('secondary village' or 'outlying village'), *-toft* ('site of a house') *-tot*, and *-thwaite* ('clearing' or 'paddock').[28]

By the year 840 the Danes had entered East Anglia in what is now Norfolk County—once the home of the British Iceni people, whose leader was the celebrated red-haired British Amazon, Queen Boudicca (d. 61).[29] Like the Paleolithic, Mesolithic, and Neolithic peoples who had inhabited the region long before them, the Danes too found the area to their liking. These latest invaders found something that their prehistoric counterparts did not, however; a deeply anglicized region that had been solidly unified, since 827, under the rule of the King of Wessex, Egbert (circa 775-839).[30] (Indeed, Egbert was the first ruler to place all English peoples under the leadership of a single sovereign.)

Yet the Danish Vikings were not easily dissuaded by such solidarity. Owing to their combative natures and land-hungry appetites, they no doubt viewed Egbert's Kingdom more as a trophy to be won rather than as a powerful domain to be avoided.

Thus it was that in 865, under the aggressive Danish leaders Inguar and Ubba (both f. 9th Century), violent battles began in earnest,

---

[28] The Viking Danes not only renamed, or Danicized, the English place-names they came upon. They often even renamed, by force, the English individuals who were brought under their rule, known as the Danelaw. Eventually, much of the English populace found it easier to simply adopt Viking names. Thus East Anglican records from 1095, for example, show that by this time some eight percent of the peasantry possessed purely Scandinavian names, many which have survived into the present day as modern "English" surnames. Among these we have: *Bóndi* (now Bond); *Rannulfr* (now Randolph); *Guðmundr* (now Goodman); *Bjorn* (now Barne); and *Svanhildr* (now Swannell). As early as the year 962 compound names comprising English and Danish names were appearing. Again, many of these hybrids are now mistakenly thought of as purely modern "English" surnames. Examples of this type of surname include: *Cytelric* (now Ketteridge); *Healfdene* (now Alden); *Tukka* (now Tuck); and *Walþeof* (now Waddilove, Wallett, or Walthew).

[29] Boudicca is my 40th great-grandmother.

[30] King Egbert is my 34th great-grandfather.

ending in 870 with the killing of the English king and saint, Edmund the Martyr (841-869) at the battle of Thetford (the Pagan Danes bound, tortured, and finally beheaded Edmund for refusing to renounce Christianity).

The 2,055 square-mile County of Norfolk now came under the complete control of the Danes, and by 878 it was absorbed into the large Danish administrative body known as the *'Danelaw'* (or in Old English, *Denalagu*; that is, the 'Law of the Danes'), the Anglo-Saxon name for those areas of England that had been colonized by Danish Vikings throughout the 9th Century, and which thereafter operated under Danish laws and customs instead of English ones.[31]

---

[31] The Danelaw, which covered that area of England ceded to the Danes by the English, comprised the regions east and north of an imaginary line drawn between London and Chester; that is, mainly eastern and northern England. This would have included the Danish settlements in Northumbria, East Anglia, and the southeast Midlands, as well as the five boroughs of Nottingham, Stamford, Derby, Lincoln, and Leicester (this last was known in the Romano-British period by the Celtic name, *Ratae*). Two of the more important geopolitical effects of the Danelaw on England were to open up the North Sea to continual trade with other nations, and also to divide the land into three basic regions: the Danelaw itself, English Mercia, and Wessex. And though the Danelaw lasted a mere fifty years, the Scandinavian impression it stamped upon England was still being felt several centuries later, as late as the Norman period (11th Century). The Danish influence in *northeast* Britain may be contrasted with the influence of the *Norwegian* Vikings, who conquered *northwest* England, and northern Scotland as well, in the 9th Century. Chief among the Norwegian leaders who invaded England was Ragnall O'Ivar, head of the Waterford (Ireland) Vikings. After taking Northumbria, O'Ivar crowned himself King of York, and ruled until 919, at which time he and the remaining East Anglican Danes reluctantly submitted to the rule of Alfred the Great's son, the King of the Angles (in Old English, the *Engle*) and Saxons (in Old English, the *Seaxan*), Edward the Elder (circa 870-924), my 31st great-grandfather. The impact of these early Norwegian forays, battles, and conquests has been preserved in the many Norwegian (*Norsk*) place-names that still dot northwest England. The Norwegian influence, however, was far heavier in Scotland than in England, particularly in the northern Scottish islands. The Norwegian Viking leader, King Harold I Haarfager, i.e., 'Harold the Fairhaired' (circa 850-932), had begun harrying the Pictish people of the Shetland, Orkney, and Hebrides Islands as early as the late 9th Century, while Norwegian farmers, principally from southwestern Norway, founded settlements there shortly after. The island of Iona herself was captured as early as 802, and within twenty-five years the Pagan Norwegians had extirpated nearly every Christian monastery in western Scotland. (A similar fate befell the Irish when the Danish Vikings sailed fearlessly up the River Liffey, into Dublin, and built a Pagan Temple to the Norse Goddess Frig (after whom the sixth day of our week, Friday, is named) in the middle of the city. According to Irish tradition, the Christian Church later built its own "temple" directly over the Danes sacred shrine, which is today known as St. Andrew's Church.) Besides Norwegian place-names (the word *firth*, cognate with *fjord*, for example, is Norse for 'an arm of the sea'), another lasting Norwegian impression in the northern Scottish isles—and also in Caithness and the West Highlands—was a variety of Norse called *Norn*. Once spoken widely in northern Scotland, Norn was first recorded in Shetland around 1485, with three sub-varieties having been eventually cataloged: Caithness Norn, Shetland Norn, and Orkney Norn. Norn is no longer spoken in Scotland, having finally died out in Caithness in the 15th Century, in the West Highlands and Islands in the 16th Century, in Orkney in the 18th Century, and in the Shetlands in the 19th Century, when Scots (also

THE BLAKENEYS

The fierce battles and raids of this period helped clear the way for the Danish Viking leader Guthrum (d. 890), who after establishing a large Danish settlement in Norfolk by 879, pronounced himself "King of East Anglia." For at least another century the area from the estuary of the Thames to the Rere Cross on Stainmore (eastern England) was considered "Danish England"—which is why, to this day, Norfolk County possesses one of the densest concentrations of Danish Viking place-names in the land.

Paradoxically, after being captured and destroyed by the Danes, the city of Norwich (which also operated as the county borough of Norfolk), went on to achieve tremendous prosperity under Danish rule. Indeed, it was known at the time as one of the most affluent shires in England. Additionally, what are now the nearby modern boroughs of Derby, Yorkshire, Leicester, Nottingham, and Lincoln, were taken over by the Danes shortly thereafter, forming what historians have referred to as a society "remarkable for its stability amid changing political conditions."[32]

In contrast to such peaceful successes, the zealous enthusiasm with which the energetic Danes ravaged England still amazes. Indeed, they eventually came within a single battle of achieving this goal. This occurred in 878, when the Vikings under Guthrum met (for the second and final time) their military equal in Alfred the Great (849-899), the

---

known as Lallans) and Gaelic began to be embraced. However, even now, as the 21st Century dawns, vestiges of Norn can still be heard in Scottish songs, poems, and proverbs, and the sea (fishing) language of the Shetland and Orkney Islands contains numerous Norn remnants as well.

[32] Even with the passage of several centuries, *and* the invasion and intrusion of new peoples (such as the Normans in 1066), the early Danes in England never truly assimilated into English society. Considered "a race apart" by their English contemporaries, the English Danes were known to jealously guard their ancient Scandinavian beliefs, laws, customs, and language in an attempt to insulate themselves from the Anglo-Saxon world around them. So intensely Scandinavian did the Danes remain throughout most of their stay in England that it was said that "the England which William of Normandy conquered formed a single monarchy, but it contained two races." Inevitably, however, the Danes, like all of England's other invaders before and since, merged with English society so completely that only their old place-names remain behind to reveal their once ubiquitous presence in northeast England. Nonetheless, some subtle traces remain. Tall, blue-eyed blonds/blondes are still not an uncommon sight in Norfolk County, the genetic inheritance of centuries of Danish influence in the area. And some say that the love of banqueting in Norfolk can be traced to a "Viking sense of feasting" left over from the days of the Danish Conquest of East Anglia.

King of the West Saxons and the fifth son of Ethelwulf (d. 858), the King-Bishop of Winchester.[33]

Here, at the Battle of Edington (Wiltshire County), Alfred's solid defeat of the Danes literally altered the course of English history. Had the Danes won, all of England—from Berwick-upon-Tweed to Lizard Point—would have eventually become a Scandinavian colony, with a Danish king ruling from the throne at Wessex.

But this was not to be, and by 879 such military losses and pressures had pushed the Danes further into areas such as the Anglo-Saxon Kingdom of East Anglia in Norfolk, where they set about exploring the county's ninety miles of coastline for inlets in which to harbor the *Norðsciphere* ('Danish fleet').

As they spread across the northern coastline of Norfolk, they eventually came upon the Old English seaside village of *Snytranléah* (Snitterly), situated a mile from the ocean, between Wells-next-the-Sea and Sheringham. The Danes must have been at once struck by both the area's overt 'burnt bleak' appearance and its ubiquitous watery ambiance.[34]

As is still true today in northern coastal Norfolk, both of these qualities, in turn, would have been accentuated by Snitterly's:

- 'gloomy' weather
- 'dark' surrounding waters
- 'white' chalk outcrops
- 'bland' windswept sand dunes
- 'ashen' heathlands
- 'livid' churning North Sea
- 'fair' beaches

---

[33] Alfred the Great is my 32nd great-grandfather; Ethelwulf is my 33rd great-grandfather.

[34] The 'watery' quality of Norfolk County is highlighted by the fact it has over 200 miles of navigable inland waterways alone, not to mention the North Sea and its bays and inlets. These waterways do not include the many hundreds of miles of non-navigable marshes, rivers (such as the Wensun, the Yare, the Ouse, and the Bure), river valleys, broads (lakes), creeks, and estuaries, not to mention the great Wash. Indeed, so wet is Norfolk that windmills, dykes, and ditches have long been used to drain the area.

THE BLAKENEYS

- 'colorless' mudbanks
- 'pale' weathered fens
- 'bleached' and silt-filled broads
- 'wan' and reedy sea-estuaries
- 'pallid' and desolate moorlands

All of these have long permeated the region which, in the minds of the people of the European Middle Ages (500-1500), would have imbued it with a raw, cold, windswept, and barren character, particularly in the harsher seasons.

As the Danish raiders gazed out from Snitterly toward the sea over the marshy wetlands, rivers, estuaries, and beach (today known as "Blakeney Beach"), they must have also noticed a colorless ('pale' or 'dark') strip of land offshore, which initially may have appeared to them to be an island.

It would have been quite natural—as was the European custom—for these new conquerors to have bestowed their own name on this *'bleakly'* area, just as they had in other regions of England; and that name would have been—in their own Scandinavian language—a combination of the words for 'bleak,' *blæyken*, and 'island,' *ey*.

While we can only postulate as to what the resulting Old Norse word might have been, it was probably *Blæykeney* or *Bleikjaey*; or possibly *Blaykeney*, *Blæknoey*, *Blæcaney*, *Blækaney*, *Blækney*, *Blækeneye*, or *Bleikenia*; all meaning the 'bleak island' (or more freely, 'dreary piece of solid ground in a fen,' or 'gloomy dry land in a wet marsh').[35]

Of course, this Danish place-name (technically a *topographical name*; that is, a place named after a physical trait or traits) would not have been recognized as legitimate by the conquered native English residents—who, in Old English, might have spelled Blakeney *Blæcan Eg*, *Blæcean-Eg*, *Blæceig*, *Bleykeig*, *Blaykeieg*, or even *Blakeniegland*,[36] all

---

[35] For more on the watery (and bleak) character of Blakeney, Norfolk, see Appendix A.

[36] For comparison, early Irish spellings of Blakeney might have been *Geal Ailén* ('Pale Island'), or *Tiamda Inis* ('Gloomy Isle').

meaning 'bleak island'; and more freely, 'cheerless watery place,' 'well-watered ground,' 'low-lying wet land,' or a 'dismal watery meadow' (in the Anglian dialect of the day, it may have been written *Blæce-Egland*).[37] And so the town continued to be known as Snitterly.[38]

But the Danish settlers who remained in Norfolk County would have used their own name for the area, *Blæykeney*, for several centuries afterward. And, as we will see, by 1242 it was known officially as *Blakenye*: 'Bleak Isle.'[39]

---

[37] Old German speakers living in England in the 9th Century might have called Blakeney, *Bleichauwa*, *Blaikjônaujô*, or *Blaikoaue*, that is, 'Bleak Isle.'

[38] We do not have a full and complete provenance for the place-name Snitterly; thus we do not know when the village was first given this name. But based on current data it is safe to say that it was either coined by the Danish Vikings who first landed in England in the late 8th Century, or it was already in existence by then. Either way, such antiquity would make it one of the oldest known place-names in England. With ancient toponyms such as this, it is usually quite impossible to know when they were first recorded, let alone when they were first coined—both which often occur centuries apart (for more on Snitterly, see Chapter 21).

[39] This spelling is curious since the more likely Middle English spelling of Blakeney would have been *Bleke-ey*, *Blekeie*, or *Blekenie*, 'Bleak Island.'

10

The Danish Vikings in 9ᵗʰ-Century France

n the mid-800s, while many Danish settlers chose to remain permanently in the 'bleak' Glaven Valley to peacefully till the soil, the more restless of the ferocious Norfolk Danes left the area for the enticing riches of France (where, for instance, a profusion of luxurious abbeys and cathedrals stood waiting, filled with valuable "plunder").

And so began the Danish invasion of France, which commenced on Easter Sunday, 28 March, 845, when the Vikings brazenly sailed up the River Seine and sacked Paris. From then on no village in western France was safe from the Danes, whose pirating expeditions also took them into the nearby Rhine country and Burgundy.

Their blood lust satiated for the moment, the Danes inflicted one final insult on the French: the dreaded *Danegeld* (from the Old English *Dene*, 'Dane,' and *geild*, 'payment'; thus meaning 'the Dane's Tribute'), an annual crown tax on native French citizens, used to pay off the Danish invaders. (In simple terms, under the *Danegeld*—or *heregild*, as it was also written in Old English—the vanquished handed over enforced payments, in money, services, and food, to their Danish conquerors in order to have their lives spared.)[40]

Though surnames had not yet come into fashion, as an invading people who came from the mysterious north (in French, *le nord*), the attacking Danes quickly came to be known in 8th- and 9th-Century Europe as *les Hommes-Noirs*; that is, 'the Black-men' or 'the Dark-men' (just as the terrifying and "barbaric" Celts were once known as "the People from the Darkness.") In Old France this figurative title would have been written '*les Noir Mants*,' or *les Noirmants*.[41]

Why were the Danish Vikings given this title?

---

[40] Despite their wide-ranging pillaging campaign across France, there is little archaeological evidence—beyond a few grave mounds, swords, spears, brooches, finger rings, smithy tools, and the remnants of a burnt ship—to mark the Danish Viking invasion here. Even linguistically the Normans made little impact on France. Indeed, while a few Norman place-names have survived in France, today there are no Norse words spoken in Normandy.

[41] The *Anglo-Saxon Chronicle* (9th Century) refers to the Danish Vikings as *Nordmanni* ('Norsemen') or *Norðmenn* (i.e., the 'men from the north').

11

Black Ships,
Black Lands,
Black Goddesses

he French may have coined the term *les Noirmants* on account
of the terrifying sleek *black* ships in which the Danish
sea-warriors sailed. Or perhaps they were so-called because
of the devastating Viking habit of 'blackening' towns, in
which cities were unhesitatingly and cruelly burned to the ground.

Maybe the name *les Noirmants* was meant to be an allusion to
Thule, the 'colorless,' 'dark,' and "hellish" northern lands from which
the early Scandinavians emerged. (We may conjecture here that there
are very ancient Indo-European links between the French words *noir*
('black') and *nord* ('north'), as the Anglo-French word *noreis* seems to
indicate: in Ireland *noreis*, meaning 'northerner,' was hibernicized to
noiréis, where it became an Irish synonym for those black demons from
the north, the Norsemen or Scandinavian Vikings.)[42]

---

[42] The Anglo-French word *noreis* (also spelled *norreis*) has given us two extremely popular surnames: the
English surname Norris (variants: Norriss, Norreys), and the Irish surname *Noiréis*. Though originally meant
to allude to a 'northerner,' that is, a Viking, as a modern word these surnames mean 'one who comes from

THE BLAKENEYS

For Scandinavia itself, like both Scotland and the Isle of Skye, takes its name from the great European Black- or Death-Goddess Skadi, also known as Scadi, Scota, Scotia, or Skuld, whose name means the 'Dark Lady.'[43] (Note that the Latin form of this Goddess' name, *Scotia*, derives from the Greek word *skotia*, a feminine Greek form of the masculine form, *skotios*, meaning 'dark' or 'shadowy.' *Skotios* in turn derives from the Greek *skotos*, 'darkness.' The Old English form of *scotia*

---

the north.' This makes them closely allied with the surname Norman (or Normand), which has the same meaning but different linguistic origins (in Old French).

[43] The Black-Goddess, or Death-Goddess, is an archetypal figure who appears in the religions and myths of nearly every known society. Memory of her ancient presence is never far away, even in modern Western cultures. One of the epithets for Demeter, the old Greek Black-Goddess, for example, was *Melanos*, meaning 'black.' In modern English this title has come down to us as the popular female name Melanie, or Melany ('dark'). The female name Dee derives from the Welsh word *Du*, meaning 'the Black One' or 'the Dark One,' a title-name given to many Celtic Black-Goddesses. Another of these is the Irish Gaelic *Dubhain*, in English Duana, a female Black-Goddess name meaning 'Little Dark One.' One of the most celebrated of all the Celtic Black-Goddesses is *Dubh Lacha*, a "dark" Sea-Goddess who gave her name to the Viking-Irish city of Dublin. Her name, which means 'black lake' or 'dark water,' contains the Irish adjective *dubh* (also spelled *duibh*), meaning 'black,' an element that has given us a host of common English and Celtic surnames. Among these are (identical surnames and variants are grouped within a semi-colon): Duf (Old Scottish), Duff (English), meaning simply 'black,' and *Ó Duibh* (Gaelic), meaning 'descendant of the black one'; Duffus (Anglo-Scottish), Dufis, and Dufus, from the Gaelic word *dubhais*, meaning 'one from the black place'; Duffy (Anglo-Irish), O'Duffy (Anglo-Irish), and *Ó Dubhthaigh* (Irish), meaning 'descendant of the black one'; Dugan (English), *Ó Dubhagáin* (Irish), and Duggan (Manx), meaning 'descendant of the black one'; Dolan (English) and *O Dubhshlain* (Gaelic), meaning 'black challenge'; Dunbabin (English) and *Dunbobbin* (Gaelic), meaning 'dark'; O' Doyle (Anglo-Irish), Doyle, Dowell, and Doole (English), and *Ó Dubhghaill* (Irish), meaning 'descendant of the black stranger'; Duncan (English) and *Donnchad* (Gaelic), meaning 'dark brown warrior'; MacDowell (English), MacDugall (Scottish), and *Mac Dubhghaill* (Irish); Dunn or Donne (English), meaning 'dark' or 'swarthy'; Dunnell (Modern English) and *Dunnwiella* (Old English), meaning 'dweller by the dark stream'; Dowd (English), O'Dowd (Anglo-Irish), and *Ó Dubhda* (Irish), 'descendant of the black one'; Dunning (English), 'the dark, swarthy one'; Donovan (English), O'Donovan (Anglo-Irish), and *Ó Donndubhán* (Irish), 'descendant of the dark brown one'; Doolan (English) and *Ó Dubhláin* (Irish), 'descendant of the black defiant one'; O' Diggin (English), Duigan (Anglo-Irish), Deegan, Deighan, and O' Deegan (Anglo-Irish), and *Ó Duibhginn* (Irish), 'black head'; O' Dilgan (English), *Ó Duibhleacháin* (Irish), Dullahan (Anglo-Irish), O' Dullaghan (Anglo-Irish), and *Ó Dubhlacháin* (Irish); O' Deeley (Anglo-Irish), Devilly (Anglo-Irish), O' Deffely (Anglo-Irish), and *Ó Duibhghiolla* (Irish), 'black lad'; Deeny, O' Deeny (Anglo-Irish), and *Ó Duibhne* (Irish), 'disagreeable'; Devoy (English), O' Deevy (Anglo-Irish), *Ó Dubhuidhe* (Irish), and *Ó Duibhidhe* (Irish); O'Degidan (Anglo-Irish), Dixon (English), and *Ó Duibhgeadáin* (Irish); Douglas (English) and *Dubhglais* (Gaelic), meaning 'black water'; Delaney (English), O' Delaney (Anglo-Irish), Delane (Anglo-Irish), and *Ó Dubhshláine*; O' Delargy (Anglo-Irish) and *Ó Duibhlearga* (Irish), 'black plain'; Dilworth (English), Deloorey (Anglo-Irish), Dilloughery (Anglo-Irish), Deloughery (Anglo-Irish), de Loughry (an Irish normanization), and *Ó Dubhluachra* (Irish); and Dooley, Dowley (English), and *Ó Dubhlaoich* (Irish), 'descendant of the black hero.' A *dubh* name that is not commonly known as such is Kirwan, or O Kirwan, a corruption of the double-'black' Irish surname, *Ó Ciardhubháin*, meaning 'descendant of the dark brown black one' (*ciar* meaning 'dark brown,' or even 'black').

was *sceadu*, 'shadow' or 'darkness,' from *scead*, 'shade').[44] Hence, Scandinavia (originally written *Scadin-auja*) literally means 'the Land of the Dark (or Black) Goddess.'[45]

Because the name Blakeney (often revealingly, but mistakenly, written 'Blackley' or 'Blacklee')[46] has been connected with the idea of darkness since the Middle Ages, it is illuminating to observe that the color black is an archetypal symbol of absolute emptiness and of the unknown; which is why unexplored areas (mostly northern ones) on ancient maps were often blackened in by cartographers.

Hence, there is good reason why one northern land, the

---

[44] Other Old English words that are related to this Black-Goddess' name include: *sceadiht* ('shady'); *sceadugeard* ('shady place'); *sceadugenga* ('wanderer in darkness'); and *sceaduhelm* ('darkness').

[45] The Goddess Skadi or Scotia was once widely worshiped. In modern Sweden countless place-names recall her memory, such as *Skadavé* ('Skadi's Temple') and *Skadalungr* ('Skadi's Grove'). One of ancient Ireland's early names was *Scotia*, after which one Celtic tribe, the Goddess-worshiping *Scoti* (i.e., the 'Scots'), named themselves. This same people later settled in what is now Scotland, transferring the name of their female Supreme Being onto the new land: Scotia, in English, 'Scotland' (i.e., 'the Land of the Goddess Skadi/Scota'). In Irish myth Scotia was an Ancestor-Goddess known as Scota; to the Celts in general she was Scath or Scatha; while in Asia she was called Kali Ma, the 'Dark Mother.' In Ireland Kali was known as Kele or Kelle, the Black Death- and War-Goddess from whom the Celts and the *Ó Ceallaigh* families (i.e., the O'Kelleys, Kellys, Kellies, MacKellys, and McKellys) took their name. The literal Irish translation of *Ó Ceallaigh* indicates that the bearer of the name is a "descendant of *Ceallach*," *ceallach* meaning the 'warrior-maiden,' a direct reference to the Black War-Goddess Kelle. Kelle's followers once performed rebirthing ceremonies in pits, while her favored sanctuaries were caves (symbols of the Goddess' life-giving womb). A pit or a cave thus came to be known in Irish as a *kill*, a word that has associations with the Old English word *celle* (a 'cell'), the Latin *cella* ('a small room'), and the Latin *celare* ('to conceal'). This is why, in Christian times, Kelle's *kill* became synonymous with a small private room or the hidden cell of a solitary person, usually religious in nature (such as a nun, hermit, or monk, in a monastery). One of Kelle's most important *kills* was located in what is now the city of Kill-Dare (Kildare), in County Kildare, Ireland, both which took their name from the Goddess' holy cave-shrine there. "Saint Kilda," whom the *Oxford Dictionary of Saints* asserts "never existed," was no doubt a christianization of this Pagan Black/Death/War-Goddess. (The adoption and christianization of Pagan deities has long been a popular Christian custom, one that serves two very practical purposes: 1) it helps attract Pagan converts, and 2) it eliminates rival deities and religions. For more information on this topic, see my book *Christmas Before Christianity*.) An associated English variation of the Celtic Goddess name Kelle is the Cornish word *celli* or *kelli*, loosely meaning 'a small grove of trees,' an allusion to the sacred groves in which the Goddess was also worshiped (modern Pagans still venerate her in such groves). Thus the town of Kelly, Devon County, England (recorded in 1086 in the *Domesday Book* by Norman scribes as *Chenleie*), would have been the ancient site of a major grove shrine to the Black Goddess Kelle (or Scotia or Skadi), as was the Swedish town of *Skadalungr*, whose meaning is 'Skadi's Grove'. (Note: in the year 1166 the Middle English spelling of the town of Kelly was *Chelli*.)

[46] For more on the topic of the confusion between the Blakeney surname and the Blackley/Blakely surnames, see Chapter 24.

Netherlands, for example, was given its name. The word nether comes from the Old High German word *nidar* (which gives us the English word nadir), meaning 'the lowest point' or 'down.' Early explorers assumed that this largely unsurveyed region was situated "down" below the Earth's surface in the inky blackness of Hell.

Indeed, the name Holland itself derives from the ancient Norwegian Underworld-Goddess who was worshiped by the early Dutch. In her Dutch form of the Goddess Skadi or Scotia, her name was Hol, Hel, Hell, or Helle; thus 'Hol's Land' or Holland.[47]

There was certainly another reason, however, for why the Danish Vikings were referred to as the 'Black-men.' This concerns the very character of the Vikings themselves.

---

[47] The Goddess Hol/Hel also gave her name to Helsinki, Finland; the Holderness Peninsula, England; Helgo, Germany; Holstein, Germany; Heligoland, Germany; Hollenstein, Austria; and Hollenstedt, Germany. She even gave her name to the Christian Underworld, still known today as "Hell"(early Christian authorities hoped that by giving the Underworld the Goddess' name, Hel, it would turn the masses away from Goddess worship out of fear. But the gesture had little effect, as Goddess worship is more popular now in Christian countries than it was in the Medieval period.) Many female human names derive from the Goddess Hel/Hol as well, including Eleanore, Elga, Ellen, Helen, Helga, Helma, Hilda, Hildagarde, Hildreth, Hilma, Holda, and Olga. Not surprisingly for a Goddess with omnipotent power and influence over millions of people, her name also entered the English language. Not as a Goddess name, but as the humble Old English word *holl* (or *hol*), which in Modern English became the words hole and hollow. All three words refer to a cave or den, and more particularly to an opening, crevice, or concave depression (i.e., in the earth, on a mountainside, in a tree, in a rock, etc.), and so are symbolic allusions to the female pudenda, which has long been referred as "the ultimate source from out of which all life flows." Around the world such natural features are still held to be sacred sites that honor the Female Principle.

12

Black Symbology & The Viking Mother-Goddess

ccording to the science of symbology, in Western societies at least, black has long been associated with evil, demonic forces, mourning, primal chaos, futility, pain, suffering, and most importantly to our discussion, with death.[48]

---

[48] Note that in many non-Western cultures, black is associated not with death, but with *life*, black being the color of the earth (i.e., dirt, clay, or loam), the life-creating "womb" of the great Mother-Earth-Goddess. Conversely, in such societies white is associated not with life, but with *death*, white being the color of bones. Despite its overt absence in modern Western society, this particular (reversed) color symbology was certainly at work, though perhaps unconsciously, during the Protestant Revolution in England. Associating all that was Catholic with Paganism, and thus with evil—including the Church's generous use of colors (particularly bright colors) in her stained-glass windows, wall paint, sacred attire, architecture, statuary, and iconography—the followers of the anti-papal King Henry VIII (1491-1547, my 8th cousin) broke into as many Catholic cathedrals and abbeys as possible, destroying their lovely (and artistically and historically important) stained-glass windows, paintings, and statues. They followed up this unthinking destruction by removing every last vestige of color from the churches themselves. This they did by "white-washing" the walls with great swaths of white paint. The result was great plain white rooms, quite empty of color (and everything else, for that matter), cleansed of the much hated "Catholic colors," and now "rendered suitable for Protestant worship." This vain attempt to "kill" off Roman Catholicism (Henry eventually completely separated from Rome, closed all Catholic monasteries, and instituted the Church of England—becoming its head), later became a powerful Protestant symbolic tradition, one that was carried to the Americas with the

But black also represents the *Female Principle*, for in terms of spiritual polarity feminine energy is negative and dark (and also wet and cool), while masculine energy, the *Male Principle*, is positive and light (and also dry and hot).[49] Hence, in Chinese cosmology the Yin aspect is considered female and is colored black (in opposition to the Yang aspect, which is considered male and colored white.)

This is also why in most early societies women were associated with night and the Moon (and its 28-day lunar cycle), while men were associated with day and the Sun.

And so we see the reasoning behind the traditional belief that the Moon is ruled by a female deity—or rather, that it is itself literally a Goddess (that is, the archetypal "Moon-Goddess," "Daughter-Goddess," or "Mother-Goddess"); and also why the Sun is believed to be ruled by a male deity—or rather, that it is a God itself (that is, the archetypal

---

first waves of Protestant European settlers. To this day this anti-Catholic tradition is still very much alive in the U.S., where—as anyone can clearly observe—the vast majority of Protestant churches (as well as most homes and businesses), possess all white walls, all white ceilings, and often even all white floors and furniture (sometimes drab "off-white" colors are used, though the intention, *and* the effect, are the same as when pure white is used). Such is the mania for white that I have even seen beautiful brick homes, natural stone walls, and rare redwood paneling painted completely over with white paint. The Georgian Period (1700s) briefly revived the ancient and innate human love of color; many examples of brightly painted interiors and exteriors remain from the tie, for example, of my cousin President Thomas Jefferson. Nonetheless, much of modern America continues to indulge in the practice of "white-washing" its architectural structures, a practice that, not surprisingly, turns out to be quite unhealthy. Contemporary scientific studies show that colors have profound positive affects on the human mind, body, and spirit, which is why so many of America's hospitals, prisons, stores, restaurants, government buildings, and schools, are being repainted in all manner of colors (from calming and healing pastels to energizing primary colors). As such, color therapists and Feng Shui consultants alike recommend painting the walls of homes and office buildings various specific colors, all in an effort to resuscitate the "dead" energies caused by the extravagant overuse of white paint. (It is interesting to note the child's inherent love of color, which eventually only dies away when its "inner child" is finally suffocated by the colorless adult world.)

[49] Note that the words "negative" and "positive" here do not refer to "bad" and "good." They refer to two neutral energies that act in opposition to one another, and yet which are one. Neither does the Female Principle's association with darkness represent evil, or the Masculine Principle's connection with light represent righteousness. All are but arcane symbols of oneness and polarity, like the symbol of infinity (∞), the Yin and Yang sign (☯), the Star of David (✡), and even the Christian Cross (✝; here the horizontal cross-beam represents Heaven or the Female Principle, while the vertical beam which pierces it represents Earth or the Female Principle); each indeed possesses deep significance related to both spirituality and biology, with opposites interacting in unison, as a single energy system. (Along these lines, those of a mystical turn may enjoy pondering the following biblical passage: Isaiah 45:7).

"Sun-God" or "Son-God," or "Father-God").[50]

The Mother-Moon-Goddess of the Danish Vikings was named Frīg (or Frigga), Freya, or Frejya. Frig's sacred day in the old Pagan lunar calendar was the seventh day of the week (now our sixth day of the week), known in Old High German as *Frīatag*; in Old English, *Frīgedæg*; both words meaning 'Frig's Day,' now corrupted (in Middle English) to "Friday." (Frig's Latin counterpart is the Roman Goddess Venus, which is why in Italian Friday is still written *Venerdì*, from the Latin *dies Veneris*, meaning 'Venus' Day.')

Frig herself, like most goddesses, not only governed many aspects of life (such as fertility, the sea, the Earth, the Underworld, virginity, motherhood, the stars, cats, and poetry), but she also functioned in a multitude of capacities (such as the Goddess of Love and the Goddess of Birth).

The two aspects that are of most interest to us, however, are her roles as Death-Goddess and Warrior-Goddess, in which she also served as head priestess and leader of the Valkyries, the wild-eyed, helmeted, and violent "corpse-maidens of war," who were said to instigate battles in order to eat the slain. (Additionally, it is revealing to note that two of Frig's titles were the "White Lady" and the "Flaxen ['pale']-haired Matron of Heaven and Earth, who was in existence before the Beginning.")

The symbology of the color black is profoundly associated, not only with the Vikings' Death-Goddess Frig, but also with the invading Danes themselves, as well. For it is clear from the writings of ancient historians that this particular group of Vikings was seen by the English as a bloodthirsty, reckless, heartless, defiant, and fierce people; in every way quite mad (little wonder that the word *berserk* is Scandinavian in origin).[51] Indeed, one historian has called them "utterly hateful, faithless,

---

[50] Hence pre-Christian Pagan Sun/Son-Gods, such as Sol and Helios, were referred to as "the Sun of Righteousness," a title later appended to Jesus (Malachi 4:2; see also Hebrews 1:7-8). See my book, *Christmas Before Christianity*.

[51] The word berserk derives from the Old Norse word, *berserkr*; literally 'bear' (*bjorn*) and 'shirt' (*serker*); loosely meaning 'an invulnerable Scandinavian warrior who becomes frenzied in battle.'

cruel and enemies of civilization and the arts of peaceful life."

13

The Black Devils
of Bleak Isle

rom the above it is obvious why the French referred to the Danish Vikings as the 'Black-men.' It was not for the color of their skin, their shields, their hair, their complexions, or their banners. It was because in the eyes of non-Scandinavians, they were Goddess-worshiping Pagans (that is, literally deranged worshipers of darkness and death), who fomented evil, pain, misery, and mourning upon the righteous God-worshiping Christians of England, Wales, Ireland, Scotland, and now France.

(Revealingly, in Old English, the very word Christian (written *cristen* or *cristnan*), had two meanings: 1) a member of the Christian faith, and 2) anyone who was *not* a Pagan Dane. The same dualism can be found in the Old English word *hæðen*, which means both 'heathen' and a 'Dane'.)[52]

It was true too that the Danes had invaded France from that desolate and gloomy area of Norfolk County, England, which the Danes had themselves called *Blæykeney* (the 'Bleak Island'). Furthermore, their own native land, Scandinavia, was long considered a vast dark and barren

---

[52] Hence, the Danish army was not known (as it should have been in Old English) as the *Denischere*, but rather as *Hæðenhere*; that is, the 'Heathen army.'

island by explorers, one known as "Thule."

As is still true today, early Western societies figuratively envisioned their enemies as the "bad guys," as "wearing black hats," while they themselves were the "good guys" who "wore white hats." Thus Irish writers referred to the Danish Vikings who ravished their towns as *Dubb-Gaill* (*dubh*, 'black,' and *gall*, 'foreigner'); that is, the 'Black Foreigners,' or 'Black Strangers.'[53]

Welsh annalists were far less charitable in their choice of words. In Wales the Danish hordes were called the "Black Devils"; the "Black Pagans"; the "Black Host"; the "Black Gentiles" (that is, the evil non-Christians), which in Welsh is written: *y Kenedloed Duon*; and also the "Black Norsemen," in Welsh: *y Normanyeit Duon*.

In one old Welsh manuscript, *Breuddwyt Rhonabwy*, the Welsh refer to themselves as "the pure white troop," while they speak of the Danes as "the pure black troop."

Thus it is plain that the Danish Vikings were associated, from the beginning of their violent campaigns in Europe, with the color black, with the 'Bleak Island' in Norfolk, with the worship of the Black Death-Goddess, and with the 'dark' mysterious "island" of 'pale' and 'shining' contrasts: Thule (Scandinavia).

To most Europeans they were, in a word, *la Blaca Deofles de Blaken Ey*; that is, "the Black Devils of Bleak Isle."

---

[53] This derogatory Irish nickname for the Danes later became an Irish surname, *Ó Dubhghaill*, which literally translated means 'descendant of *Dubhghall*.' In England *Dubhghall* became the surnames O' Doyle, Doyle, Dowell, and Doole. The Celtic surname *Mac Dubhghaill* (in English, MacDowell), is also derived from this name, as is the Scottish surname MacDugall. Despite these modifications the original meaning of 'Black Stranger' or 'Black Foreigner' remains, with the logical meaning of *Ó Dubhghaill* being: 'descendant of the Danes.' The surname Doyle is common in Leinster, Ireland, where the sept is considered to be Old Norse in origin. Other surnames possess the Irish *dubb* or *dubh* ('black'), as well, surnames such as the Irish *Ó Donndubhán* (in English, Donovan), literally meaning 'descendant of the dark brown one'; *Ó Dubhláin* (in English, Doolan), literally meaning 'descendant of the black defiant one'; and *Ó Dubhlaoich* (in English, Dooley or Dowley), literally meaning 'descendant of the black hero.'

14

Etymological Evidence of Old Norse Roots

ince we are at the point where the Danish Vikings have passed through England and are now in France, this is an appropriate time to address the beliefs that the Blakeney family and name are of either French or English origins.

To begin with, we will remember that though the core-word *blake* originally meant 'white' (as in 'bleach,' 'bland,' 'blank,' 'bleak,' etc.), it later came to mean both 'white' *and* 'black,' due to linguistic confusion in the Middle Ages.

Keeping this in mind, note that while the Old French word for 'white' was *blanche*, a word that is indeed distantly related to blake, the French word for 'black,' *noir*, is not. For Blakeney to be truly French in origin we would have to have an early French word that carried the dual meaning of both light and dark. And such a word does not exist in French.

Indeed, there is not a single French word that is even remotely similar to *blake*, in either meaning or spelling. Why? Because the word *blake* derives from the *Germanic* language branch—which includes Old Norse and Danish, while French belongs to the *Italic* language branch—which includes such languages as Italian and Spanish.

This same argument holds true for those who maintain that

Blakeney is English in origin. We have seen that the oldest English color-word for 'black' was *sweart* (from the German word for 'black,' *swarz*; and akin to the Latin word for 'dirt,' *sordes*), not the color-word 'black,' which is a modern form.

We will also recall that the earliest English word actually linguistically related to 'black' itself was *blác* (pronounced with a long "a," 'blake'), which meant 'pale,' 'colorless,' or 'white.' Only much later, sometime around the 12th Century, was *blác* confused with the new Middle English word for 'black,' *blac* (pronounced with a short "a," 'black'), which had by then come into use, replacing the Early English[54] word for 'black,' *sweart*.

Thus, to find a word that possesses the oppositional meaning of both 'white' and 'black,' we have had to turn to the Vedic or Aryan languages, where we find the ultimate stem-word, *bhleg*, carrying the dual meaning 'to turn pale,' and 'to burn.' This was absorbed into the Old Germanic languages, giving us such pre-English dualistic words as *blaiko* and *blaekno*, both meaning 'to shine' (something light) *and* 'to burn' (something dark).

Another linguistic example of this phenomenon is the Old Teutonic word *blik* (meaning 'pale'), which later became a base-word for both the English blank ('white') and black ('dark'). In ancient Scandinavia *blik* became *blika*, from which derived the Old English word *blician* ('to become pale'), then *blican* ('to gleam'); then the Middle English word *blikien* ('to shine,' 'twinkle,' 'glisten,' or 'glitter').[55] (These words find corollaries in the Middle Dutch word *blijken* ('to look'); the Old Saxon word *blikan* ('gleam'); the Old Slavonic *bliskat* ('to sparkle'); the Swedish *blicka* ('to glance'); the Dutch *blikken* ('to twinkle' or 'turn pale'); and the German word *blicken* ('to glance').)

Other evidence of the Norse (Danish) roots of the so-called

---

[54] The philological term, 'Early English,' encompasses not only both Old English and Middle English, but also includes the most primitive forms of the language, which date back to around the year 450, the beginning of the Anglo-Saxon Period in England.

[55] The English surname Blick derives from the Old English *blician* ('to shine' or 'glitter'), whose earliest known record is in 1185, in the surname of a gentleman called *Aluin Blic*.

"English" name Blakeney can be seen in the obsolete English word *bliken*, which also possesses the double meaning of 'to turn pale,' and 'to shine.' The Old Norse spelling of *bliken* was *blikna*, which later, in Middle English, became *blykne*, only a short step from *blakeney*. And due to differences in spelling and pronunciation in Old England (pre-12th Century), and also to confusion over the definition of the word colorless, the words *blik* and *blikien* ('bleach'; that is, 'white') were confused with such words as *blæc* and *blacian* ('black').

In the ensuing linguistic chaos, with the Danes' Old Norse language supplanting and/or combining with Anglo-Saxon, dozens upon dozens of variations emerged, including: *blaak*, *blayke(n)*, and *blake(n)*, and then finally the compound *blakeney*, in the Middle Ages. There are no comparable words in any other Indo-European language branch dating from the period in which the words *blake* and *blakeney* arose and evolved.[56]

Hence, from whatever direction we choose to look, etymology always leads us invariably back to an ancient Germanic origin, and ultimately, to one of Scandinavian—and more specifically, to one of *Danish*—character, for the Blakeney family and name.

---

[56] There is another Old English word besides *blác* that possesses the dual meaning of both 'light' and 'dark.' This is the word *scima* (pronounced "SKY-ma"). While it carries the meanings of 'light,' 'brightness,' 'ray,' and 'splendor,' it also carries the meanings of 'gloom' and 'dusk.' And we have a relative of *scima*, the Old English word *scimian*, which means both 'to shine,' 'glisten,' and 'be dazzled,' and also to 'grow dusky,' 'dim,' and 'shadowy.' These two words are not, however, related to, or even distantly associated with, the blake words.

15

Emergence of the Normans in 10th-Century France

hile the Welsh called them "the Black Devils," and their 9th-Century French name may have been *les Noirmants* ('the Black-men'), in 10th-Century France the conquered natives eventually began to refer to their Danish invaders from the north (in Old French) as *les Normants*; (in Modern French, *les Normands*) that is, the Normans—literally the 'Norse-men' or 'North Men,' or more loosely, 'the Men from the North.'[57]

(Note: we must sharply distinguish the *Northmen* from the *Normans*, for the former were fierce, independent, Norse-speaking, Danish, Goddess-worshiping Pagans, while the latter eventually became, in almost every way, benign, dependent, French-speaking, God-worshiping Christians, mere feudal vassals of West Frankish Kings.)

As the centuries passed, the Danes increasingly imposed

---

[57] In Medieval Latin 'Norman' was written *Nortmannus* or *Normannus*, while in Old English it was written *Norðmann*. Interestingly, in Scotland the Normans were considered "French," while in Ireland they were thought of as "English."

themselves upon French culture, creating, among other things, Normandy on the lower Seine in northwest France.[58] This momentous event occurred in the year 911 when, by treaty, the son of (the Holy Roman Emperor and King of Lorraine and Italy) Louis II (circa 822-875), the French King Charles III (the Simple) (879-929), ceded Rouen and adjacent territories to the Danish chieftain and Viking leader, *Hrolf the Ganger* (that is, 'Rollo the Walker' or 'Rover'; circa 860-931).[59] This made *Hrolf* the first duke of the new province, after which he immediately set about to strengthen the Norman duchy.

We will note here that as the Danish *Hrolf* is commonly known as "the ancestor of Norman dukes, kings, and crusaders," there can be little doubt that a number of modern Blakeney families descend from him, just as in general all Blakeneys—being first recorded in Normandy (a Danish province in France that was founded by the Viking Danes), ultimately descend from Danish "blood" (which is itself Germanic in origin).

One result of the new Danish intrusion in France was the merging of the Old Norse and Old French languages. This created a variety of Old Northern French called *Norman French*, that was fully adopted by the Normans in the 10th Century—and which later found its way to England after the Norman Conquest in 1066. Here in England, for a time at least, it largely displaced the Old English of the day, which had been built upon the Germanic West Saxon dialect.

(Note: Since the Normans were comprised primarily of Danes who had brought an Anglo-Saxon heritage with them from England to France, it would be more technically accurate, though perhaps more confusing, to refer to this language as Anglo-Danish French.)

Sometime in the late 9th or early 10th Century, a small Norman group of "the Black Devils" (or *les Diables Noirs*, as the French may have

---

[58] In Medieval Latin 'Normandy' was written *Northmannia*. In Modern French it is *la Normandie*; the French still refer to the Channel Islands as *les îles Normandes*: 'the Islands of the Normans.'

[59] The reason *Hrolf* was called "the walker" was that, according to legend, he was so gigantic that no horse could carry him. *Hrolf* is my 30th great-grandfather.

called them), following the common practice of the day, began to use a collective toponym, (place-name) to identify themselves.

Drawing from a large reservoir of old Danish legends, military stories, and family tales—and even from their own savage reputation across Europe, this particular Norman group seized upon the topographical place-name given by their Viking ancestors in England to the colorless region in Norfolk County that they had called *Blæykeney* (or *Blækney*, *Blaekeneye*, or *Bleikenia*).

In Norman French this compound word-name may have perhaps been *de Blakenia*, or *de Blacenheye*; or possibly *de Blaekeney* or *de Blaekney*. With the preposition '*de*', the literal meaning would have been: 'the people from (or of) the bleak island.'

De Blaekeney was not yet a surname. At this point it was still closer to a clan name (that is, i.e., the name of a tribe or dynasty), or more specifically, what I call a *toponymic group name*: a name, adopted by a group of people, that is taken from a place-name that purposefully denotes its area of origin or habitation, and which helps it to distinguish itself (often pridefully) from other groups from other specific cities or regions. Examples of *toponymic group names* would include the names of many modern day sports teams, such as the "Tennessee Titans," the "Glasgow Rangers," or "Manchester United."

In the case of this particular Norman group of Danish blood, the group name *de Blaekeney* would have had the advantage of signifying several things simultaneously:

1) It indicated that this group had arrived in France from 'the *bleak*' moorlands of East Anglia, England; and more specifically, from the area of the Norfolk village of *Blæykeney*, 'Bleak Isle' (originally known as *Snytranléah*, that is, Snitterly).

2) Since the name possessed the dual meaning typically associated with Scandinavia (namely, 'of the blackness and the whiteness'; or more freely, 'the white/pale snow country of the shining/burning sun'), it also indicated that they were a Norse people from Thule.

3) And finally, because it conveyed a 'dark' or 'black' aspect, the word

81

reminded the world that these were a people not to be trifled with; a people who were, in fact, the proud descendants of those old worshipers of the Black Death-Goddess, the high-spirited, vigorous, and potentially violent "Black Devils": the Vikings of Denmark.

16

The Norman Invasion: Birth of the De Blakeney Surname

y the year 1000, about the same time surnames first began to come into fashion in Europe (though mainly only among the urban wealthy classes), at least one prosperous and influential Norman family that descended from the Black Devils' group—the *de Blaekneys*, adopted the epithet as its personal surname. Thus was formed the beginning of the ancestral Blakeney line, a family whose children were the beneficiaries of its first hereditary surname.[60]

---

[60] It is a convention that hereditary surnames did not appear in Europe until *after* the Norman Invasion of England. However, this is wholly inaccurate, for records from pre-Conquest Normandy clearly reveal that hereditary surnames were already in existence among the Normans *prior* to their assault on England. What is more, English and Scandinavian bynames were in use in England *before* the Norman Conquest as well. What the Norman Invasion of England did do, however, was to make surnames mandatory, since under King

In the Anglo-Danish French of the day the surname of these eponymous ancestors may have been written *de Blækeney*, or in latinized form as *de Blakenia* or *de Blacheneia* (Latin was the documentary language of the Medieval period, and so was used by scholars and scribes for recording data).

Unfortunately there are no written records from the 11th Century to corroborate this momentous event in the history of the Blakeney family line. And yet with the enormous amount of etymological and ethnological evidence we now have, it must be considered the most likely scenario. In fact, we can infer this very occurrence from historical events that followed shortly after this period.

Saint Edward the Confessor (1002-1066), King of England (r. 1042-1066),[61] had promised his cousin, William I, the Duke of Normandy (1027-1087),[62] the throne upon his demise. Just before his death in 1066, however, Edward recanted and chose his brother-in-law, Harold II (1022-1066),[63] as his heir instead—probably to spite Harold's father, Godwin (d. 1053),[64] the Earl of the West Saxons, Edward's arch nemesis. On January 6, 1066, Harold II was crowned King of England,

---

William's new feudal system the Norman government had to be able to distinguish between individuals with the same first names, nicknames, and occupations. In the late 11th Century, London, as just one example, would have contained dozens, perhaps hundreds, of men named *Johannis atte Kechene* ('John [who works] in the kitchen'). By surnaming such men *Kechene* (making "John Kitchen"), it was easier to identify each individual and their children, as well as keep track of the taxes they owed, their military service, etc. Indeed, this was one of the reasons why surnames first appeared among the well-to-do, for it was they who possessed the most numerous and the most valuable taxable items. Careful assessment was required by both the individual (who wanted to avoid paying too much tax) and the government (who wanted to ensure that the proper amount of tax was paid). Thus, by the mid-12th Century hereditary surnames were adopted by nearly the entire upper class of London (though they were not fully used by the London working classes until the 14th Century).

[61] King Edward the Confessor is my 28th great-granduncle.

[62] King William I the Conqueror is my 26th great grandfather.

[63] King Harold II is my 30th great-grandfather.

[64] Godwin is my 31st great-grandfather.

in effect making Edward the last of the Anglo-Saxon line.[65] Harold's reign was to be one of the shortest in English history, however.[66]

England's newest king had underestimated the outrage and humiliation that William felt on being passed over for the crown. Not content to suffer the ignominious fate that had been handed him, William devised a daring plan to oust Harold and place himself on the throne; a plan that would not only precipitate one of the world's greatest political events, but one that would also bring the Blakeney family and name out of the Dark Ages and into the light of recorded history for the first time.

On October 14, 1066, an infuriated William led his Danish Norman subjects into battle against England.[67] The Norman armies easily took the south,[68] vanquishing the Saxons and their new king, Harold II, at Hastings, England.[69] On Christmas Day of that year, with

---

[65] One of the more influential and intriguing people in English history, Edward the Confessor was not only a reluctant king, but also a man of accomplishment and stark contrasts. A celibate who married, and a deeply spiritual monasticist who often favored war as a means to punish enemies, Edward also founded Westminster Abbey, abolished the hated *Danegeld*, and became the first English king to implement the "royal touch" (in which a royal is believed to be able to cure the sick by touch alone). So great was his authority and so wide was his popularity that Anglo-Saxon judicial functions were later cataloged under the title, the *Laws of Edward the Confessor*, and in 1161, ninety-five years after his death, he was canonized, becoming "Saint Edward."

[66] Officially, Harold II, the 21st King of England, reigned for less than a year, from January 6 to October 14, 1066.

[67] William's southern victory was aided by a simultaneous invasion of northern England, headed by the Saxon Earl of Northumbria, Tostig (d. 1066) (my 30th great-granduncle), and the King of Norway, Harold III Haardraade, that is, 'Hard-Ruler' (1015-1066) (my 1st cousin). Though Tostig and Harold III defeated Morcar (f. 1066), the Earl of the Northumbrians, at York, King Harold II (circa 1022-1066), Tostig's brother, defeated the pair at Stamford Bridge on September 25, 1066, where both were slain. Harold II, meanwhile, lost his life at Hastings fighting the armies of William the Conqueror. All three men thus died during the Norman Invasion, with brother fighting against brother.

[68] King William's supporters included French, Franks, Celts, Bretons, Flemings, and of course, the Danish Normans. William was himself directly descended from the Danish Vikings who had landed in France only some 200 odd years earlier.

[69] Harold II actually died at Senlac, which lies about nine miles from Hastings. Legend has it that Harold, the last Anglo-Saxon King of England, was pierced through the eye with an arrow.

the blessing of Pope Alexander II (r. 1061-1073),[70] William was crowned king in Westminster Abbey. He ruled until his death in 1087, and has been known ever since as "William the Conqueror."[71]

By 1071 England was unified as an *Anglo-Norman* nation, and the Anglo-Saxons—who had been the ruling class up until this time, and whose dominance had held sway since the departure of the Roman legions in the 5th Century—became a conquered people.[72] (This, the Norman Conquest of England, would be the last time an invading foreign people would succeed in subduing England.)[73]

As Norman influences swept over England in the following years, her Anglo-Saxon character was permanently altered, so much so that to this day, 1,000 years later, the words "Norman," "Normand," and "Normandy," are still used in the United Kingdom as both "English" forenames and surnames (the first use of such a name in England was recorded in the year of the Conquest itself, in 1066, as the personal name of a man called "*Normannus*").

Among the sweeping changes brought by William I and the Normans was the introduction of a new language[74] (one that evolved into

---

[70] In England, after separating church and state and asserting his own governmental supremacy, William later refused to pay homage to Pope Alexander II, the very man who had given the King his blessing only shortly before, on the eve of the Battle at Hastings. The Pope could not have been too surprised, for William had never been completely loyal to the Catholic Church. In 1053, for example, thirteen years before he invaded England, William married a close relative (Matilda), despite clear Church injunctions against such unions.

[71] Ironically, after surviving some of the most dangerous and bloody battles in history, William the mighty Conqueror met his end quietly and without violence, when his horse stumbled, throwing the king to the ground. He had been riding triumphantly into his latest captured town (in 1087), Mantes, France.

[72] The time between the withdrawal of Rome from England in the 5th Century and the Norman Conquest in the 11th Century, is called the "Anglo-Saxon Period." What would later be thought of as English culture and English society began during this time.

[73] Despite the overwhelming encroachments of the Normans, the English people held onto their traditions, and in so doing were able to prevent England from becoming a French province.

[74] The Anglo-Saxon language was almost pushed into extinction as the Old Norse language of the Danes and the Norman French language of the Normans swept across England between the 9th and the 11th Centuries. Indeed, 85 percent of Anglo-Saxon's 300,000-word lexicon became obsolete under the new "English" of the Danes and the Normans. Despite this linguistic battering, Anglo-Saxon has held its ground into the present day: all 100 of the most commonly used English words are Anglo-Saxon.

Anglo-Norman);[75] a new family naming-system (which superseded the Old English nomenclature, and caused English names to be replaced with both French names and also with Norman forms of Scandinavian and Germanic names);[76] a new political structure (known as the feudal

---

[75] The French influence brought by the Normans to England can be seen in the fact that men such as King Edward I "Longshanks" (1239-1307) (my 21st great-grandfather)—the executor of the Scottish hero-chieftain Sir William "Braveheart" Wallace (circa 1272-1305) (my 10th cousin)—and the Norman Earl of Leicester, Simon de Montfort (circa 1208-1265) (my 2nd cousin), spoke only French in England well into the 13th Century. The blending of Anglo-Saxon and French, however, eventually aided in the development of what we now know as English. This process was assisted by King Edward III (1312-1377) (my 20th great-grandfather) who, in 1362, finally banned the use of French in English courts of law, allowing only Anglo-Saxon to be spoken (this decree was called the "Statute of Pleading"). The bubonic plague of 1348 also helped propagate the usage of English. It was during this time that thousands of French-speaking Norman priests, teachers, and tutors, fell victim to the horrors of the "Black Death" (in all, a third of England's population died). Their replacements were chosen from among the Anglo-Saxon populace, who henceforth taught their own language to England's youth. This opened the way for the widespread usage and acceptance of English, and in the 14th Century, Henry IV Bolingbloke of Lancaster (1366-1412) (my 2nd cousin), became the first English King to consider it his native tongue, while during the same period Geoffrey Chaucer (1340-1400) choose to write many of his works, not in the Romance Languages (Italian, French, Spanish, Rumanian, Portuguese, Provençal—including Catalan, and the Rhaeto-Romanic idioms), but in the East Midlands English dialect that was spoken in London at the time. With the development of printing, introduced by William Caxton (1422-1491) in 1476, the works of William Shakespeare (1564-1616), the publication by James I (1566-1625) (my 7th cousin) of the King James Bible in English in 1611, and Samuel Johnson's (1709-1784) *Dictionary of the English Language* in 1755, English inevitably rose to its current position as the standard language of England.

[76] After 1066, the change from English to French names occurred most rapidly among the cosmopolitan upper classes, such as those in London (city-dwellers tend to be quite trend-conscious), and slowest among the farming peasant classes (in which survival is more important than fashion). By the year 1100 it had become vogue for English parents to give their children French names, and by 1200 even the peasantry had begun to earnestly embrace this new fad. Thus, we can be very certain that many "English" individuals with so-called French forenames, were not really French at all, but rather were quite purely English. Indeed, in present day England many of the most popular forenames remain as vestiges of this Medieval trend. "English" names such as: Agnes, Alice, Maud, Geoffrey, Gilbert, Henry, Robert, Peter, and John, are actually Norman French, which is why they were the most favored names among the Normans themselves. On the topic of forenames and surnames it is enlightening to note that the French Bretons, too, cast their linguistic influence over England. The many Bretons who served in William the Conqueror's armies at Hastings were granted pilfered English lands as compensation. As they migrated across England, in their wake these emigrés from Brittany left a string of towns (such as Boston) and family surnames of purely Breton character. Breton names that have become "English" surnames in England include: Alan, Brian, Conan, Justin, Mengi, and Samson. Many so-called "English" surnames, too, can be traced to Breton immigrants in England. The old Breton surname *Judhael* was later variously anglicized as Jewell, Jekyll, and Joel, when it reached English soil. The "English" surname Brett itself is an anglicization of the French phrase *le Bret*: 'the Breton.' Lastly, we will note that the Anglo-Norman Invasion of Ireland caused changes in the Irish naming-system that were identical to the changes caused in England by the Norman Invasion. Thus, just as the English began adopting Norman and French names, and vice versa, the Irish began adopting Anglo-Norman names, while the Normans and the English began adopting Irish names (as well as the Irish language). By the beginning of the 13th Century most of the first names found in Dublin were French, while most of the surnames were English and

system); and new architecture (in the form of majestic Norman-styled cathedrals and castles).[77]

But the invasion also opened up England to France, which allowed thousands of Normans, seeking a better future, to emigrate to the new land. Among these emigrés would have been the immediate descendants of the "Black Devils,"[78] the *de Blækeney* family line, speaking their "native language," Norman French.[79]

Scandinavian.

[77] An example of the latter can be found in the city of Norwich, the "County Town" of Norfolk, which still retains a conspicuous imprint of the Norman Conquest. Norwich, with both its 800-year old Norman Castle and its ancient Norman Cathedral (built with stone from Caen, France), is still referred to by modern Britons as a "Norman town."

[78] We will note here an item of interest in connection with the name "Devils" bestowed on the Danish Normans: King William I the Conqueror had been born out-of-wedlock, and so was considered a "bastard." Such an "illegitimate" background would have connected William—and perhaps in the minds of the defeated English, *all* Normans—with evil, the color black, and, of course, the Devil. Indeed, William's own father, the French Duke, Robert I (d. 1035), was called *Robert le Diable*; that is, "Robert the Devil." (Robert I is my 27th great-grandfather.)

[79] Norman French, used in England from the 11th to 14th Centuries—and referred to in that land as *Anglo-Norman*—left a profound mark on the nation, and in a myriad of ways. Though in the beginning it was hereditary only to the Norman aristocracy, it gradually permeated English society, eventually becoming the language of law, literature, and the court. As far as its impact on English, Norman French softened the language's guttural inflections (the product of English's Germanic heritage), by smoothing them over with Gallic inflections. Hence, *after* the Norman Invasion of England, the town of *Scrobbesbyrig*, England, became Shrewsbury; *Dunholm* became Durham; and *Grontabricc* became Cambridge (in Romano-British times, Cambridge was known as *Duroliponte*, a Celtic word). This same normanization of English place-names occurred with the town of Snitterly, the original name of Blakeney, Norfolk (see below), as the 11th-Century *Domesday Book* reveals. The Normans also brought their manorial family names with them—one of them, as we have seen throughout this book, being *de Blaekenia* ('from Blakeney'; or more accurately, 'from the Bleak Isle')—which were appended to the names of their English manors. One result of this was a number of hybrid double-place-names, with both English and French elements or words, such as *Kynggestone Lacy* (modern Kingston Lacy) and *Suttone Curteney* (modern Sutton Courtenay). Other Norman names that became English would include the French surname of *Mucegros* (anglicized to Musgrove); *de Moubray* (anglicized to Mowbray); *de Melville* (anglicized to Melville; 'bad township'); and *de Paynel* (anglicized to Panell). (Norman names traveled to Scotland as well, where such Viking French appellations as Bruce, Colville, Cumming, Fraser, Hamill, Hay, Montgomery, Picken, Sinclair, and Turnbull, became "Scottish" surnames.) Among the place-names the Normans bestowed on England we have: *Richmond* ('strong hill'), *Pontefract* ('broken bridge'), *Beaumont* ('beautiful hill'), *Beaulieu* ('beautiful place'), and *Haltemprice* ('high enterprise'). Though the Normans blended into the general population of England and France by 1125, Norman French continued to be the principal language in England (while having a significant influence in Scotland, Ireland, and Wales) well into the 13th Century. British vestiges of Norman French can still be found in the Channel Islands, the seventy-five square-mile archipelago in the English Channel off northwest France.

17

Appearance of the Earliest Recorded Blakeneys

t is around this very time, the late 11th Century, that we find the first documented record of an historical Blakeney.

In chronicles from this period there is listed a Norman Frenchman (that is, a *Danish* Frenchmen) by the name of *de Blækenia* (no first name is given),[80] who was honored for his service at the Battle of Hastings in 1066.

As such, this individual, our first known recorded Blakeney, was born in Normandy probably sometime between 1020 and 1045. From here we need only travel back about eight generations before we find the Danish Viking ancestors of *de Blækenia* in Denmark. We may hypothesize, with great certainty then, that *de Blækenia's* 5th great-grandfather (who would have been born in the early 800s) was not only a native of Denmark, but was also probably one of the Danish Vikings who viciously invaded France in the mid-800s.

---

[80] This spelling is my own hypothetical reconstruction.

THE BLAKENEYS

Eleventh-Century records show that *de Blækenia* and his family had already emigrated from France and were living in Norfolk County, England, where he had been granted "considerable land" by King William I the Conqueror.[81]

Since the town of Blakeney, Norfolk, was not officially known by this name in the year 1066 (or indeed even in the following decades, and possibly centuries), we can be sure that *de Blækenia* did not take his surname from the town *after* moving to Norfolk County, as some have argued. Rather, it is abundantly clear that *de Blækenia* moved to England from Normandy *already* possessing this surname (a discussion of this intriguing topic follows shortly).

At this point four generations are missing from the Blakeney family records, bringing us forward in time almost 100 years, to the middle of the 12th Century. Here we find the next recorded Blakeney: *William de Blakenia* (the original spelling of his full name was probably *Willihelm de Blakenia*, or perhaps *Guillaume de Blakeneye*), born about 1150, probably in Norwich, Norfolk County, England. William is not only the earliest known Blakeney possessing a first- or forename (that is, a Christian name), he is also *the first clearly traceable Blakeney ancestor of today's American Blakeney families*. Sadly, there are no known records of William's descendants over the following four generations.

However, records do appear again in the 5th generation, beginning with William's 4th great-grandson, *Simon de Blakenia*, born about 1260, again probably in Norfolk County, England. Simon was followed by his son *William de Blakeneye* (b. about 1295, in Norfolk?), who later, in 1339, became the Governor of Norwich.

We have examples of other early Blakeneys from this time period as well, though their relationship to the main Blakeney line is not known with any certainty. One such individual was *Thomas de Blakenia*, who was living in Gloucestershire County, England, in 1201 (as we will see, there is a second and possibly even older town of Blakeney—first

---

[81] It is a royal custom, and indeed an ancient tradition, to give land confiscated from enemies or rebels to one's faithful followers, a topic we will later touch on in more detail, as the "English" Blakeneys were very much a part of this process in Ireland.

recorded in 1196 as *Blakeneia*—in Gloucestershire County, the town in which this particular gentleman may have lived). Blakeneys appear in the records of Gloucestershire County prior to 1201, as early, in fact, as the late 12th Century, during the reign (1189-1199) of the then sitting King of England, Richard I, *Cœur' de Lion*, that is, "the Lion-Hearted" (1157-1199).[82]

Shortly thereafter, in 1215, we have evidence of another mysterious *de Blakenia* individual, this one taking part in the formulation of the Magna Carta (that is, the "Great Charter") at Runnymeade, in Surrey County, England. Unfortunately his forename is not known; he was probably born between 1150 and 1180, however.[83]

Next, in 1258, we find mention of a *John de Blakenia* (more of whom presently) living in the Norfolk village of what was by then known as *Blakenye* (modern Blakeney).

In 1332 a *Peter de Blakenheye* appears in the civil records of Dorset County; while in 1389 we find mention of a *Richard de Blakenia*, who had associations with St. Giles Church in Norwich. The manner in which these individuals may be connected to the main *William de Blakenia* (b. circa 1150) line of Norwich, is also not known at this time.

Continuing on with the main Blakeney line (that is, the true and known descendants of *William de Blakenia*, b. about 1150), we have Governor William's son, *Nicholas de Blakeneye* (b. about 1315, and also Governor of Norwich), and then Nicholas' son *Nicholas de Blakeneye* (b. about 1340), the last Blakeney in the family to serve as Governor of Norwich (from 1386 to 1392).

During the 14th Century (by 1341, it would appear), the now thoroughly anglicized *de Blakeneys* began to drop the preposition '*de*' (French for 'of' or 'from') from their name, making it, for the first time,

---

[82] Richard I the Lion-Hearted is my 20th great-granduncle.

[83] The Magna Carta was the result of a revolt by an alliance of barons who wished to curtail the near unlimited powers of the monarchy, then headed by the King of England, John I (1166-1216) (John I is my 22nd great-grandfather). In June 1215 John was forced to sign this major British constitutional contract, which reconfirmed the feudal rights of the barons. As a result to this day the government of England remains a constitutional monarchy.

a proper Danish English surname: *Blakeney*.[84] Evidence for this comes from the earliest records of two men with this particular prepositionless spelling: *Roger Blakeney*—a member of Parliament in Great Yarmouth in 1341, and *John Blakeney*—a member of Parliament for Norfolk in 1447. (Note: the use of *Blake* as a surname is first recorded in 1219 in Yorkshire County, some 122 years earlier than *Blakeney* of Great Yarmouth).

A son of Governor *Nicholas de Blakeneye* (mentioned above and b. about 1340) was *John Blakeneye* (b. about 1365). John's son was *John Blakeneye* (b. about 1420), famous (or infamous) for having been driven from the court of King Henry VI in the year 1451.[85] This John's son was *Johannis Blakeney* (b. about 1455), buried at a church in Hunningham (or Honingham), Warwick County, England (in 1515, his wife Elizabeth was laid to rest next to him).[86]

In 1509 Johannis' son, *Thomas Blakeney* (b. circa 1485), appears (with his wife, also named Elizabeth) as the owner of Horford Hall Manor (in Norfolk County). The estate was later bequeathed to his son *John Blakeney* (b. about 1520), who became the "Lord of Horford Hall" in 1546 (and was married to Anne Giggs of Stewkey Hall, Sparham, Norfolk, b. about 1525).

Finally, in the reign of Queen Elizabeth I (r. 1558-1603), we come upon John's son, *Launcelot Blakeney* (b. about 1555-d. about 1600) of Sparham, Norfolk, whose two sons, *Thomas Blakeney* (b. about 1580-d. about 1655) and *Henry Blakeney* (b. about 1585) were given land in

---

[84] Prepositions (e.g., *de*, *le*, *at*, *by*, *in*, etc.) began to disappear from names quite early on. Though this phenomenon was once believed to have occurred after 1300, the *Domesday Book* reveals that by 1066 many families had already dropped these types of prefixes from their surnames.

[85] King Henry VI is my 3rd cousin.

[86] Another "John Blakeney" from this period was *John de Blakeneye*, who is mentioned in the records of "the Church in London" in 1392. Though he was a London merchant who had dealings with churches in Wiveton, Cley-next-the-Sea, and even Blakeney, Norfolk, it is believed that he was probably from Blakeney, Gloucestershire. While his connection to the main Blakeney family is unknown, as we will see, we have reason to believe that the Norfolk Blakeneys and the Gloucestershire Blakeneys are indeed related.

Ireland by Queen Elizabeth I (1533-1603)[87] in appreciation "for services rendered their country."[88] (For more on the genealogy of the Blakeneys see Appendix F: "A Blakeney Family Tree.")

According to one tradition the emigration of the Norfolk Blakeneys from England to Ireland was expedited by the fact that an unnamed Blakeney female (perhaps one of Thomas' and Henry's sisters) inherited "the greater portion" of the Blakeney property in Norfolk.

Did Thomas and Henry leave for Ireland in a fit of jealousy and anger? If so, as we will see, many Irish and American Blakeney families owe their existence to this early family dispute.

---

[87] Queen Elizabeth I is my 5th cousin.

[88] Though little can be proven from forenames, in Launcelot Blakeney's forename we may have possible evidence reenforcing my view that the Blakeneys are of Norman (Danish and French) origins: *L'Ancelot* is an Old French word meaning 'attendant.' The name is also spelled *Lancelott* in Old English, and has come down to us, in Modern English, as the surname Lancelot.

18

The American Southern Blakeney Line

hatever the reason Thomas moved to Ireland, we know that the village of Thomastown, County Kilkenny, Ireland, was named after him. He also bore two sons: *William Blakeney* (1629-1664) and *Robert Blakeney* (1625-1660).

William was granted land near present-day Kilmallock, County Limerick, where he not only became the first Limerick Blakeney, but where he also constructed a castle, later known as "Mount Blakeney Castle." The village in the area was also eventually named after William, and still thrives to this day as "Mount Blakeney." Sadly, only unrecognizable ruins remain of Mount Blakeney Castle.

According to my genealogical research, the beginnings of the American Southern Blakeney Branch—which starts with the Ireland-born *Captain John Blakeney* (1732-1832)—may be traced from William and the Mount Blakeney Line. For as tradition has it, Captain John was the son of one of William's grandsons—either, *Charles Blakeney* (b. about 1677), *Robert Blakeney* (b. about 1683), *George Blakeney* (b. about 1690), or most likely, *John Blakeney* (b. about 1705)—which would make

William Captain John's great-grandfather.[89]

    Captain John and his Irish wife Margaret (nicknamed "Peggy") left (County Galway?) Ireland shortly after the Irish Rebellion, emigrating to Granville County, North Carolina, around 1750. The couple later settled in Chesterfield County, South Carolina (in 1758), where they had seven children: Jane Blakeney, Mary Blakeney, John Blakeney, Jr., Thomas Blakeney, Robert (or William) Blakeney, Hugh Blakeney, and James Blakeney.

    To this day vestiges of Captain John and his family's influence still linger on in this part of South Carolina. The town of Pageland, for example, has a road called "Blakeney Street" that runs through its center, while just outside of town is a road called "John Blakeney Lane." Nearby, between the towns of Pageland and Dudley, lies the "Old Blakeney Cemetery," where Captain John and many of his relations are buried.[90]

---

[89] It is not yet known for certain which of William's grandsons was the father of Captain John Blakeney, or if perhaps someone else may have been his father. Resolving this important mystery remains one of the chief goals of many Blakeney family members and researchers.

[90] For directions to the Old Blakeney Cemetery of Chesterfield County, South Carolina, see Figure 29 in the Illustrations section.

19

The Anglicization of Ireland & the New England Blakeney Line

homas' other son, Robert, was granted the town of Gallagh, County Galway (near Tuam), by Lord Protector of the Commonwealth, Oliver Cromwell (1599-1658), in recognition of "his military services" (Cromwell gave Robert various lands in County Mayo and County Kilkenny, as well).

We will note here that Robert Blakeney's birthplace, Norfolk County, England was, as a whole, firmly behind Cromwell and the Parliamentary cause during the English Civil War (1642-1651), also known as "the Puritan Revolution."[91]   As a reward for their support

---

[91] The term "Puritan Revolution" derives from the fact that the followers of the Stuart king, Charles I (1600-1649), were primarily Catholics and Episcopalians, while his opponents were Puritans. The war itself, however, focused upon whether England should be ruled by a parliament or by a monarchy; essentially a

Cromwell divided up the spoils of war among his loyal followers, one of whom was Robert.[92]

Cromwell's practice of granting confiscated Irish lands to the English, however, was not what it might at first appear to be: a charitable act of generosity and gratitude toward his supporters.

In 1649 Cromwell's forces had violently subdued Ireland in a series of "appalling massacres" (he used the same extreme ruthlessness on the Scots, brutally defeating them at Dunbar in 1650). In an effort to further break down Irish morale, if not Irish society itself, Cromwell instigated a nefarious anglicization process in Ireland by handing over captured lands, homes, villages, and castles to his English defenders.

During the 17th and 18th Centuries, *undertakers* (that is, specially assigned English women and men who "undertook" to move English settlers onto land seized from the Irish) conferred countless "Irish" land grants throughout England, and even Scotland. In response the English descended in their thousands far and wide across the "Emerald Isle," for decades after an ever constant (and purposefully painful) reminder to the Irish that they were a "defeated people" (this sentiment is yet very much alive in Northern Ireland).[93] Robert and Thomas were two of just such

---

battle between royal supremacy and public democracy. Some have regarded the English Civil War as little more than a revival of the old and bitter Saxon hatred of the Normans, in which Cromwell's victory served as the "final Saxon revenge" for England's overthrow by the Norman Duke, William I the Conqueror, at the Battle of Hastings, England, in 1066.

[92] King Charles I, Cromwell's nemesis, however, was captured in 1647, and two years later he was tried and executed for his deceitful dealings with his opponents.

[93] English is still the dominant language in modern day Ireland (a nation that once spoke Irish), just one of the many vestiges of Cromwell's domineering presence in 17th-Century Ireland. This condition, which many would call an "aberration," is being offset to a small extent by the revival of not only the Irish language, but by Celtic culture in general. Irish-only television programs, for example, are on the rise, the Irish dance sensation, *River Dance*, sells out in cities around the world, and the Celtic Vision network (which airs *only* Celtic programs and films) was recently launched in the USA (Website: www.celticvision.com). Yet Cromwell was not the first Englishman to assault, and insult, Ireland. In 1166 growing tensions were exacerbated when King Diarmait (or Diarmuid, i.e., Dermot) Macmurchada (1110-1171) of Ireland (my 27th great-grandfather) invited English troops onto Irish soil to aid him in his attempt to win back his crown after he had been dethroned by fellow Irish nobleman and chieftains. In 1169, under the leadership of Robert Fitzstephen, the first Normans arrived in Ireland, coming ashore at Bannow Bay. In 1170, my 26th great-grandfather Richard de Clare, or Strongbow (d.1176), on King Macmurchada's invitation to join forces—with the added promise of marrying the Irish king's daughter, Eva Macmurchada—attacked Ireland,

THE BLAKENEYS

Cromwellian Englishmen to partake in this program, as is clear from the following. The town of Gallagh that had been awarded to Robert as part of Cromwell's grant, maintained its own castle, known as "Castle Gallagh." The Irish owners, the O'Kelly family, were violently dispossessed of the building and property, after which it was immediately turned over to Robert. Subsequently, both the castle and the nearby town of Gallagh were renamed after him, both being thereafter called "Castle Blakeney."

With the passage of time all traces of the castle have disappeared (much of it had been destroyed in 1504, before Robert came to own it, during bloody battles between rival Celtic families). The little village of Castle Blakeney (now written, in the modern way, as one word:

---

seizing Dublin and Waterford. Shortly thereafter, in 1172, Pope Alexander III (d. 1181) made my 23rd great-grandfather, King Henry II (1133-1189) of England, feudal lord of Ireland. By 1300 the Normans were governing nearly the whole of Ireland, and had, along with their fellow English invaders, so thoroughly overwhelmed Irish society that even many in England began to protest the disappearance of Irish culture. In 1366, to help counteract this "unnatural" blending of Anglo-Norman and Irish cultures in Ireland, the third son of King Edward III (1312-1377), my 3rd cousin Lionel of Antwerp (fl. 14th Century), the first Duke of Clarence, enacted several laws at a special parliament in Kilkenny. Known as the *Statutes of Kilkenny*, they prohibited the English and the Normans from adopting or practicing Irish customs (as such, the Anglo-Normans were not allowed to dress in the Irish way, to speak the Irish language, to take Irish surnames, or to marry Irish women and men). The edict had little, if any, lasting effect. Under the reign of the Queen of England and Ireland, Elizabeth I (1533-1603)—known as the "Virgin Queen" due to the fact that she never married or bore offspring (though she did engage in many affairs)—the aggressive anglicization of Ireland continued unabated. Indeed, at this time, during England's "Golden Age" (that is, the Elizabethan Period), despite England's many forays and conquests in various parts of the world, her only true colony lay in Ireland, where, as one historian aptly put it, opportunities for English settlers (i.e., invaders) to further enrich themselves at the expense of the Irish population were now taken advantage of more mercilessly than ever. As in earlier periods the Irish fought back, this time in a bloody rebellion under the Earl of Tyrone, Hugh O'Neill (in 1597). But to little avail. Thus, while England was experiencing her first true Renaissance, Ireland was experiencing one of its lowest points in history; and it was just at this exact time that the Norfolk Blakeneys entered the picture, when Irish lands, cities, and castles were given to *Thomas Blakeney* (b. circa 1580) and *Henry Blakeney* (b. circa 1585)—two sons of *Launcelot Blakeney* (b. circa 1555) of Sparham, Norfolk—by Queen Elizabeth I in appreciation "for services rendered their country." While many other examples of the forced anglicization of Ireland could be given, one other instance of note will suffice. In 1609, in yet another violent bid by England to win Ireland's favor, Protestants, mainly from Scotland (but also from England and Wales), were "planted" on Irish soil. This act, known as the "Ulster Plantation," had one motivation: to continue the centuries-old tradition of uprooting those native Irish who were hostile to the English Crown and replace them with British loyalists. While this plot also failed to completely anglicize Ireland, the Ulster Plantation, like Cromwell's later invasion, was responsible for turning many an English, Scottish, and Welsh surname into an "Irish" one. Among such families we have the Scandinavian (and later, Scottish) Neilsons or Nelsons (now partly Gaelicized in Ireland to Ó Néill, and fully Gaelicized to *MacNeighill*), and the Scottish Kyles (an anglicization of the Scottish surname *MacSuile*).

"Castleblakeney"), however, still remains.[94]

According to my research, the New England Blakeney Branch—which starts with Dublin, Ireland-born American Civil War veteran *Thomas Richard Blakeney, Sr.* (1841-1934)[95]—derives from Robert and the Castle Blakeney Line. For Robert was Thomas Richard Blakeney, Sr.'s 4th great-grandfather.

---

[94] For those interested in visiting the village of Castleblakeney, County Galway, Ireland, it is three miles southeast of Mountbellew, fifteen miles west of Ballinasloe, and thirty miles east of Galway City. Note that in 1837 the population of the town was 4,305. Today it is around 500. See Appendix C for information on the efforts, goals, and projects of the Castleblakeney Development Committee.

[95] Thomas R. Blakeney, Sr. emigrated to North America (perhaps via Canada) around 1847 or 1848, and settled in Watertown, Massachusetts (by around 1868). Thomas seems to have married at least three times and had at least six children between these three marriages. We believe the names of his wives were: Helen (or Ellen) Murray, Mary (or Catherine) Hassett, and Elizabeth Giroux. Among his known children were: John William Blakeney, Sr., Thomas R. Blakeney, Jr., Howard Blakeney, Albert Blakeney, and Margaret Blakeney. As with all of the Blakeney branches, I am also related to this the New England Blakeney line.

20

The Canadian Blakeney Line

pecial mention should be made here of the Canadian Blakeney Branch,[96] which began shortly after the American Revolutionary War (1775-1781). It was at this time that two of five Ireland-born Blakeney brothers living in America were forced to leave the country due to their loyalties to the British crown.[97]

(One of the three brothers who remained behind to fight for the American cause against Britain may have been *Captain John Blakeney* (1732-1832), the progenitor of the American Southern Blakeney Branch, and who on November 16, 1775, was elected "Captain of Militia" in South Carolina.)

---

[96] The Blakeney/Blakey Family Association of Canada continues to promote genealogical research into this particular Blakeney line. For more information see Appendix B.

[97] It is not known with any certainty where in Ireland these first Canadian Blakeney families came from. Some say they were farmers from Ulster, while others maintain that they were from the city, or perhaps the County, of Galway. There are many conflicting views. According to one tradition their parents were William (or David) Blakeney/Blakely (b. circa 1715?) and his wife Elizabeth Chambers (after whom Chambers Blakeney was named). William emigrated from Northern Ireland to Halifax, Nova Scotia in November 1782 aboard the *Earl of Donegal*, and died in South Carolina. A current theory is that William Blakeney may be the son of Edward Blakeney (1659-1703) and Deborah Stanton. I have not seen any proof of this view, however. More research is needed. Note that Edward is a son of Major Robert "the Soldier" Blakeney and Susannah Ormsby. Robert "the Soldier" Blakeney is a son of Governor Thomas Blakeney (b. 1584) and Sarah Hatton. (Thomastown, in County Kilkenny, Ireland, was named after Thomas.)

THE BLAKENEYS

The state in which these five Blakeney families were living at the time is not known. However, it may have been Pennsylvania, or perhaps (Charleston) South Carolina, the state (and city) from which the two Loyalist Blakeney families sailed in 1782.

Landing at Port Royal, Nova Scotia, aboard the ship *Argo*, in December 1782, one Blakeney family, headed by *David Blakeney*, remained in Nova Scotia, while the other, headed by David's brother, a Quaker named *Chambers Blakeney*, settled in Saint John, New Brunswick, across the Bay of Fundy (tradition has it that a third brother settled in Ontario, Canada, at this time). A land grant is recorded for this family on January 8, 1802, at the "Head of Petitcodiac," a region still inhabited by Blakeneys to this day.[98]

Another major Blakeney migration from Ireland and England to Canada occurred during the first half of the 19th Century, with families settling mainly in Ontario, where they had been given land grants following the Napoleonic Wars.

Shortly thereafter, during the late 19th Century, waves of Canadian Blakeneys, descendants of David and Chambers Blakeney, filtered down into the United States as well, locating chiefly in New England (many in the Boston area). These "New England" Blakeneys, however, are recent and only distantly related to the original New England Blakeney Branch (which began, as we have seen, with the Irish-born *Thomas Richard Blakeney Sr.* (1841-1934).)

---

[98] Chambers Blakeney (whose surname is also spelled Blakely and Bleakney), along with his brother David (who spelled his surname Bleakney and Bleackney), emigrated to America (South Carolina) from Belfast, Northern Ireland, in 1767. Ray H. Blakeney, the author of this book's Preface, is descended from this line.

21

Blakeney, Norfolk: Village of Obscure Origins

ince there is some debate as to both the name and the naming of the town of Blakeney, let us examine this topic more closely before continuing.

At present there are two completely opposing schools of thought concerning the name-origins of the town of Blakeney, Norfolk County, England, with a third lying midway in between.

The first states that "the Blakeneys take their name from Blakeney, a small seaport in the County of Norfolk . . ." This quote, from "Evidences of the Blakeney Family in England and Ireland" (written in 1872), assures us that in 1066, when the first Norman ancestors of today's Blakeneys arrived in Norfolk, England, the town of Blakeney was already known by that name. There is no explanation here as to how, why, or when the town was named, however.

The same sentiment is expressed in the *Burke's Peerage* entry on the Blakeney family (under "The Landed Gentry of Ireland"): "The Blakeneys came from Norfolk, where they held many manors and took their name from a small coastal port."

The Blakeney History Group too holds that "the surname Blakeney . . . derived from the placename . . ."[99]

The second theory maintains that what is called the town of Blakeney today, originally known by the Old English name *Snytraléah* (or, with the Old English genitive singular, -*n*, making *Snytranléah*)—or in Middle English, *Sniterle*, or in Modern English, *Snitterly*—was renamed "Blakeney" in 1258 by King Henry III (1207-1272),[100] in honor of a Norman named *John de Blakeney*, whose prosperous fishing company had so benefited the town of Snitterly in which he lived.

The third theory holds that the village of Blakeney, Norfolk, was known by both the name Blakeney and the name Snitterly simultaneously up until the 16th Century, and that Blakeney may have actually begun as the name of a small district of Snitterly, and only later became the name of the entire town.

The question before us is which of these theory is correct?

The answer is theory number one, though it should be emphasized that the Blakeneys did not take their surname from the village of Blakeney, Norfolk, *after* emigrating from Normandy to England, as is commonly thought. As we have seen (and as we will discuss in more detail), this occurred *before* the Blakeneys' Danish ancestors left England to invade France.

Historical records indicate that this particular village was already known as *Blakenye* (or *de Blakenye*),[101] in 1242 (the first known year in which this place-name was historically recorded), sixteen years *before* the place-name, according to theory number two, was allegedly changed from Snitterly to Blakeney.

---

[99] Unfortunately for modern researchers, the spellings of the original place-names are never given by the authors of these statements.

[100] King Henry III is the author's 21st great-grandfather.

[101] The preposition '*de*' was commonly placed before English (and French) place-names in England after the Norman Conquest. In addition, English and French names beginning with vowels were often combined with the preposition '*de*,' producing a single softened word. Thus the English name *de la Mer* ('dweller by the sea') became Delamere after the Invasion, while the French name *de Yseigni* (from the French place-name *Isigny-sur-Mer*—'Isigny on the Sea') became Disney.

THE BLAKENEYS

When then did the town first begin to be called 'Blakeney'? And who named it?

In answer to the first question we know it must have been between 1086 and 1242. For the town of Blakeney is *not* mentioned by this name in King William's famous *Domesday Book*,[102] a comprehensive national chronicle of land ownership compiled between 1086 and 1087.[103] This was 156 years before the place-name *Blakenye* first appears, and 172 years before the time of *John de Blakeney*. Thus it must have been sometime during this particular 156-year period that the city of Snitterly was renamed *Blakenye*, not in 1258.

And what of the etymology and background of the word Snitterly? Since this topic is related to our study of the Blakeney name and family, let us pause here to discuss it.

Snitterly is what is known as a *folk-name* (that is, it is a place-name derived from the name of a person) which, in this case, is a modern compound form, blending an Old English personal name, *Snytra*, with the Old English word for a 'woodland clearing,' 'meadow,' 'piece of ground,' or 'woods,' *léah*; hence the meaning of Snitterly: 'Snytra's woodland settlement.'[104]

---

[102] The book title, *Domesday* (pronounced DOOMS-day), has, intentionally or accidentally, a number of meanings: 1) The information collected in it was purported to be binding until 'Doomsday,' *domesday* being the Middle English spelling. 2) Originally, in Anglo-Saxon England, a *dome* or *doom* referred to a decree, law, ordinance, or judgement, hence the English affix *dom* (as in the word king*dom*), meaning a 'jurisdiction.' 3) The Middle English word *dome* also once meant 'judge.' 4) Lastly, the Old English word *dom* also has the meaning of 'assessment.' Hence we have the additional sense here of the 'Assessment Day Book.' Interestingly, both the word *dome* and the word *domesday* have come down to us as English surnames, the former, now Dome, meaning simply 'judge' (from the Old English word *dema*, 'judge'), the latter, now Domesday, meaning 'assistant (or valet) of a judge.' The Old English *deman* and the Middle English *demen*, or *dema*, written apparently sometimes erroneously as *dome*, also gives us both the word deem, 'to think,' 'to judge,' 'to believe,' and the word doom (from the Old English *dom*), 'to condemn,' or 'give judgement.'

[103] The *Domesday Book*, known among historians as a "monumental achievement" and "the greatest record in Medieval history," was undertaken to appraise and record the economic resources of England for taxation purposes. The value of the *Domesday Book* for researchers lies in the fact that its authors recorded not only the names of landowners and their possessions, but also England's 11th-Century place-names and their contemporary spellings, most of which we can be sure are of greater antiquity than the *Domesday Book* itself.

[104] The personal name *Snytra*, and hence the place-name Snitterly, probably both derive from the far older name of the Scandinavian Wisdom-Goddess, Snotra, an ancient female deity whose figure and religion were brought to England's shores by the Goddess-worshiping Norwegian and Danish Vikings in the 8th Century.

THE BLAKENEYS

The original spelling may have been *Snytraléah*, or, with the Old English genitive singular, *-n*, possibly *Snytranléah*. We may theorize that this Medieval gentleman, named *Snytra*, cleared the first forest or plowed the first field in the area. Or perhaps he had been the first official land owner of what is now the village of Blakeney.

Whatever the reason, the town was eventually named after him (this man's name, *Snytra*, is linguistically related to, or identical to, the Old English word *snytre*, 'clever' or 'wise,'[105] which was applied as a nickname to an erudite or sagacious person; later it became a legitimate personal name).[106]

A conundrum accompanies the town of Snitterly: if it existed at the time of the writing of the *Domesday Book*, why is it not mentioned in this work?

Actually, Snitterly does appear here, under the spelling *Esnuterle*.[107] The question is why?

The Pagan Danes may have set up a shrine honoring Snotra in or around modern Blakeney, after which they referred to the area as *Snotraléah* or *Snotranléah*; that is, '[the Goddess] Snotra's woodland settlement'; or perhaps *Snotraleg* or *Snotranleg*; '[the Goddess] Snotra's Island.' If so, *Snotraléah* or perhaps *Snotranleg* may have been the earliest spelling of what would later be called *Sniterle* or *Sniterleg* (in Modern English, Snitterly), which was by then a Middle English corruption of the original Anglo-Danish word.

[105] *Snytre* is in turn related to such Old English words as *snotor* or *snoter* ('ingenious,' 'clever,' 'prudent,' 'philosophical,' 'astute,' 'bright'); *snotornes* ('prudence,' 'erudition'); *snytro* or *snyttru* ('intelligence,' 'wisdom,' 'cleverness,' 'wisdom'); and *snyttrum* ('wisely,' 'cleverly'), all associated with, or actually derived from, the name of the "All-Knowing" Scandinavian Goddess Snotra.

[106] Though we have no definitive provenance for the village of *Snotranléah* or *Snytranléah* (Snitterly) showing when it was first named and its early development, there can be little doubt that it is a very ancient name, since both it and the Old English personal name, *Snytra*, seem to have originated in the name of the prehistoric Scandinavian Wisdom-Goddess Snotra. It is therefore unquestionably far older than the work in which it first appears (i.e., the *Domesday Book*). To begin with it is certain that *Snytranléah* is a pre-Conquest place-name rather than a post-Conquest one, for it was already in existence when the Norman scribes compiling the *Domesday Book* arrived in *Snytranléah* to record their findings in the year 1086. On the other hand, since this place-name does not appear in the writings of Bede (8th Century), in Old English charters and land-grants (from the 7th Century), or in the writings of Ptolemy (2nd Century), we can speculate that it most likely emerged in the late 8th, 9th, or 10th Century. Indeed, hundreds of English place-names are known to have been coined during the Anglo-Saxon period—from the 5th Century to the 11th Century. Snitterly was no doubt one of these. (Note that English place-names possessing the elements *eg*, *dun*, *feld*, *-inga*, *ham*, *-ingas*, and *ford*, are known to be among the oldest forms of English toponyms, and so would have certainly emerged in pre-Conquest Anglo-Saxon times.)

[107] Snitterly also appears in the *Domesday Book* as *Snuterlea*.

To answer this we must turn to the second and final volume of the *Domesday Book*, often referred to as "Lesser Domesday" or "Little Domesday."[108] The Lesser Domesday focuses specifically on the three counties of Essex, Suffolk, and—the county which concerns us—Norfolk.

When the French Norman scribes compiling the *Domesday Book* data came upon the town of Snitterly, or *Snytranléah*, as it may have then been written, they discovered, as they so often did with other English place-names, that it was difficult to spell and pronounce the combined consonants of the first two letters; that is, 'Sn.'

The dilemma was resolved by resorting to a common French practice: linguistic normanization (or linguistic francicization). Here, the entire word *Snytranléah* was softened and an '*e*' was appended to the beginning which, in 11th-Century Latin (the scribal or documentary language that the *Domesday Book* was composed in), resulted in the spelling *Esnuterle* (making the evolution of the name: *Snytranléah*, then *Esnuterle*, then Snitterly).[109]

Thus, from these facts we know that sometime in the 156 years between the writing of the *Domesday Book* in 1086 and 1242 (sixteen years before the time of *John de Blakeney*, in 1258), the town of *Snitterly* (*Snytranléah* or *Esnuterle*) was renamed "*Blakenye*." The question before us now is why, and by whom?

---

[108] By contrast, the first volume of the *Domesday Book* is called the "Great Domesday" or "Greater Domesday."

[109] This same process occurred with the Latin word *spiritus* ('spirit'), which after francicization became *esprit*. The Normans also softened surnames by aspiration, as in the case of the Old Norse word, *ásgautr* (in Old Swedish and Old Danish, *asgut* or *asgot*). In Old English this word became the surname *Ōsgod* or *Ōsgot*. In Normandy the usual spellings of this surname were *Ansgot*, *Angot*, and *Angood*, until Norman scribes affixed an inorganic '*h*,' forming *Hosegood*. To this day a common surname in England (variants: Hosgood, Horsegood), it is identical to the English surname Osgood.

22

Who Named the Norfolk Village of Blakeney?

ince the surname Blakeney is ultimately Scandinavian in origin, logic tells us that the most likely originators of the place-name *Blakenye* were themselves Scandinavians; and more precisely, Danes, the very ancestors of the Blakeney family. In fact, we have three pieces of evidence to support this view.

1) While the Anglo-Saxons of Norfolk County may have exceeded them in sheer number, politically speaking their Danish neighbors were the dominant ethnic group in this area between the 11th and 13th Centuries, the time period in which the village of Blakeney was officially named. In fact, England was ruled, during part of this time, by Danish kings (from 1016 to 1042).

2) Furthermore, by 1242, the year in which we first find the village name *Blakenye* in Norfolk County, the Danes had already been in England for close to 450 years. One could not overestimate the influence of the long-staying Danes on English society and culture during this period. Not only did they alter both the English government and the English language, but they also irretrievably altered the English landscape

by leaving hundreds of Viking (Scandinavian) place-names in their wake.

Adding to the already overwhelming impact of the Danish Viking invaders on England was the fact that after the year 870, immigrants from Denmark poured into northeastern England, thoroughly colonizing what are now the modern boroughs of Leicester, Derby, Lincoln, Nottingham, and Yorkshire.

3) Finally, *blake* is not an English word. As we have seen, it is a Middle Anglo-Danish spelling variation of the Old Norse words *bleikja*, *bleyken*, and *blayken* (all meaning 'bleak').

In short, in the late 8th Century Danish Viking invaders gave the name *Blakeney*, or as they would have spelled it, *Blæykeney*, to the area surrounding Snitterly on account of its bleak watery characteristics, and perhaps because of its island-like peninsula. This name was understandably not immediately accepted or recognized by the conquered English populace in the area—which is probably why both names were used side by side for several centuries thereafter.

However, when Norman *de Blaekney* families of Danish heritage (who had taken the place-name while still living in Normandy) began emigrating from France back to Norfolk County after the Norman Invasion (in 1066), the original Viking name for the town, *Blæykeney*, was proudly resuscitated, and by 1242 Snitterly was legally known (in Anglo-Danish form) as *Blakenye*. Over time, this was further anglicized and modernized to *Blakeney*.

23

Blakeney, Gloucestershire: England's First or Second Blakeney?

*O*f interest to Blakeney researchers and family members will be the fact that not only was there once a city called *Blackney* in Stoke Abbott, Dorset County, England (where some of the early Blakeney name variations may have derived), but there are also numerous Blakeney place-names in North America, including: Blakeney (Ontario), Canada; Blakeney Creek (British Columbia), Canada; Port Blakeney (British Columbia), Canada; and Blakeney (Red River County), Texas, USA.[110]

Of most utmost importance to our discussion, however, is the

---

[110] Blakeney/Blakeley researchers please note that there are two cities in the USA called Blakeley, one in Baldwin County, Alabama, and one in Sibley County, Minnesota.

existence of a second *English* town of Blakeney. Located in the County of Gloucestershire, it lies on the north bank of the Severn River, northeast of Chepstow and Lydney and southwest of Newnham and Gloucester.

Intriguingly, the Gloucestershire Blakeney place-name (spelled in latinized Middle English, *Blakeneia*) was first recorded in 1196, almost a half century before the Norfolk Blakeney name (spelled in Middle English, *Blakenye*, or *Blekeney*) first appears in 1242.

This reenforces the author's theory that the Gloucestershire Blakeney name too originally derived from Scandinavia, for the Danes were a major presence in the region early on, raiding the Bristol (Bristow) Channel[111] and Severn River areas beginning in 795. A major Viking attack was recorded at Pedridanmutha (near modern day Burnham-on-Sea) in 845, for example, only sixty kilometers from Blakeney, Gloucestershire.

Since Blakeney, Gloucestershire, like Blakeney, Norfolk, is located close to water—the Vikings' favorite mode of travel—it is therefore probable that it also has the same linguistic origins. We will remember that the water-loving Danes may have named Blakeney, Norfolk, for its 'bleak' watery landscapes and the strip of land offshore that may have appeared to them to be an island, or an island-like strip of land. Hence the name *Blæykeney*, *Blakenye*, or *Blakeney*, meaning 'bleak island' (or more freely, 'dreary watery meadow' or 'dismal dry ground in a marsh.'

During the Middle Ages the area in which the Gloucestershire town of Blakeney is situated may have been exceedingly marshy as well, and so, by 1196, was given the same name; in this case, *Blakeneia* (a latinized spelling from 1280 is *Blacheneia*).[112] Or perhaps it was named

---

[111] Until the 16th Century, Bristol was typically written "Bristow," the standard Medieval spelling.

[112] It is extremely common for a people to give different towns in their country the same name. Americans in particular are quite fond of this custom. For example, there are at least fifty towns in the U.S. named "Franklin" (after the slave-owning statesman and Founding Father, Benjamin Franklin), six of them alone in the state of Wisconsin. California has five cities named Franklin, New York has four, and Pennsylvania has three. I myself live in a Tennessee city called Franklin. Additionally sixteen U.S. states have counties named

for its proximity to the Severn River.

Over time these spellings would have been anglicized and modernized to "Blakeney," the form in use today for the cities of Blakeney in both Gloucestershire and Norfolk Counties.

We will note here that since, as we have seen, Blakeney families are documented in Gloucestershire County as early as 1189 (during the reign of King Richard the Lion-Hearted), we can be sure that the Blakeney place-name appeared long before 1196 in this region—perhaps hundreds of years earlier. For, just as the Norfolk Blakeneys did in that county, the Gloucestershire Blakeneys would have adopted their surname from the place-name.

Naturally we cannot ignore the possibility that the Norfolk place-name and the Gloucestershire place-name, *despite their modern identical spellings*, have two completely different origins and meanings. This phenomenon has occurred with other place-names, and is not as rare as one might think.

The common English place-name Langford, for example, can mean:

1) 'long river crossing' (from Old English *lang* and *ford*)
2) 'river-crossing of a man known as *Landa*' (from Old English *lang* and a personal name, *Landa*)
3) 'land [bounded by a] river-crossing' (from the Old English *land* and *ford*)

Since the place-name Langford is also variously found in Bedfordshire, Essex, Somerset, Oxfordshire, and Nottingham Counties, it is quite possible that it may have arisen at different times with different meanings in all five of these regions, and still eventually come to have the same spellings in Modern English. (The only method of uncovering the original meaning of each one of these identically-spelled place-names

---

Franklin. It is thus not surprising that England gave at least two of its towns (and perhaps more in the past) the name Blakeney.

would be to study their earliest recorded forms.)[113]

This phenomenon, in which a place-name has multiple origins and meanings, is also what may have occurred with the Blakeney place-names in Norfolk and Gloucestershire Counties. There is some support for this view.

On the one hand we have those who assert that the etymology of the place-name Blakeney is 'dark-colored island,' or perhaps *'Blæca's Isle'* (that is, the 'island of a man called Black'), while on the other there is the author's conviction that Blakeney means 'Bleak Island.' If both views are correct, then it is conceivable that the Gloucestershire Blakeney was founded on the former meanings while the Norfolk Blakeney was developed on the latter.

Despite this possibility (of a dual origin and dual meanings), I believe that it is remote and very unlikely. For copious circumstantial evidence (as laid out in detail in this very book) supports the idea that both Blakeney place-names emerged in the same general period of time (that is, the late 9th Century or early 10th Century), and that both were coined by Scandinavian invaders: the Norfolk Blakeney by Danish Vikings, the Gloucestershire Blakeney by Norwegian Vikings (or also possibly by the Danes).

More to the point, the earliest spelling forms of both the Norfolk Blakeney (*Blakenye*) and the Gloucestershire Blakeney (*Blakeneia*) indicate that the two toponyms derive from a single source (the Vikings) and therefore have identical meanings: 'Bleak Island.'

---

[113] A similar problem, of course, occurs in the field of anthroponymy. An interesting example of this is the "English" surname Barr, whose origins point to at least nine different possible sources of origin: 1) from Scotland, where it is a toponym (Barry); 2) from the Irish (west Cork) surname, *Ó Báire* (which is an abbreviation of both the Irish surname *Fionnbharr*, 'fair-head,' and the Irish surname *Ó Beargha*); 3) from the English surname Barry, Barrie, or Dubarry; 4) from the Old English word *barre*, meaning 'a gateway'; 5) from the Irish Gaelic word *bearach*, meaning 'pointed' or 'spear-like' (thus as a surname meaning a 'sharp person'); 6) from the Norman gentleman who settled in England, named *Philip de Barry*; 7) from the ancient hypothetical Celtic word *barr*, meaning 'hill-top'; 8) from Wales, where it is a toponym (Barry); or 9) from the Old French word *bari*, meaning a 'farm,' 'rampart,' or 'barrier.' (To complicate the matter, Barr has been adopted as a surname by various Jewish families, and hence is often mistakenly thought to be a Hebrew name.) As with the toponym Langford, however, Barr could have originated simultaneously from out of all of these sources, either at different times or at the same time, and still have arrived at the same modern spelling in each case.

24

The Origins Debate, & the Blackley-Blakley Problem

The fact that there are two towns in England named "Blakeney" tells us that there may have been two major Blakeney branches in England in the Middle Ages, the mere possibility of which has created a passionate debate among Blakeney researchers: where did the place-name Blakeney *first* emerge in England: Norfolk County or Gloucestershire County?

Would not common sense tell us that it has to be one or the other? As we will see, the answer to this question is no.

Let us now look at the three main theories concerning this topic.

Theory 1: Those who believe that the place-name Blakeney originated in Gloucestershire County maintain that—after adopting the Gloucestershire Blakeney place-name as a surname—Blakeney individuals from this area later moved east through London, and finally into Norfolk County, where the Norfolk Blakeney place-name arose, and with it, a second major Blakeney family branch, the Norfolk Blakeneys.

Theory 2: Those who hold that the place-name first emerged in Norfolk County contend the opposite; namely, that—after adopting the

Norfolk Blakeney place-name as a surname—Blakeney individuals from this region later migrated west, some of whom settled in Gloucestershire County, where the Gloucestershire Blakeney place-name arose, and with it, a second major Blakeney family branch, the Gloucestershire Blakeneys.

Currently we do not have enough information to prove or disprove either of these two theories. It is true that the name of Blakeney, Gloucestershire, was recorded (in 1196) forty-six years *earlier* than the name of Blakeney, Norfolk (first recorded in 1242). But this means nothing in itself, since records showing an older date for Blakeney, Norfolk, may have simply been lost or destroyed. Furthermore, place-names, like surnames, are always older than the date they are first recorded.

Theory 3: Of course it is entirely possible that Theory 1 and Theory 2 are both incorrect, and that the two Blakeney place-names arose independently of one another in the two different counties. How?

Norman families moving into the two already-established Blakeney villages would have adopted the Old Norse Viking place-names (that is, *Blæykeney*) as surnames, creating two separately emerging Blakeney branches: the Norfolk Branch and the Gloucestershire Branch. This phenomenon is not unheard of in the fields of onomastics and toponymy, and is more common than one might think.

While I am receptive to Theory 3, I presently side with Theory 2 since, as I have described in detail throughout this book, the Vikings were on the east coast of England (where Norfolk County is located) *before* they were on the west coast (where Gloucestershire County is located).

We must add to this the fact that we have knowledge of Norman *de Blakenias* (that is, Blakeneys) settling in Norfolk County shortly after the Norman Invasion in 1066, but no records yet of *de Blakenias* settling in Gloucestershire County at such an early date. From these two facts alone it would seem then that Theory 2 is the most probable scenario. We really do not know for sure, however.

Something that would help to decipher the point of origin of the place-name, and thus the surname, Blakeney, is to survey the telephone directories for the various counties of England. When the final tally of surnames is counted and plotted on a map, we should see a clear dispersion pattern emerge, showing the areas of both the heaviest and the lightest concentration of the name.

In the year 2000 I did in fact execute this exercise, and though it could not be considered a truly scientific study (for I researched only the spelling form "Blakeney," and none of this name's many other spelling variations), the results are quite provocative and are germane to our discussion.

Below is a complete list of the counties of England—along with some of the various unitary authorities—and the number of Blakeney surnames that appear in each. All were taken from "British Telephone's" *White Pages* and other assorted British telephone directories (Welsh and Scottish counties in which Blakeneys were found, have been included as well):

- Avon County: 0
- Bath and North East Somerset: 0
- Bedfordshire County: 1
- Berkshire County: 0
- Bristol (city of): 2
- Buckinghamshire: 7
- Cambridgeshire County: 0
- Cheshire County: 3
- Cleveland County: 0
- Clwyd County (Wales): 1
- Cornwall County: 1
- Cumbria County: 6
- Derbyshire County: 0
- Devon County: 2
- Dorset County: 1
- Durham County: 0
- Dyfed County (Wales): 2
- East Riding of Yorkshire: 0
- East Sussex County: 2

- Essex County: 1
- Glamorgan County (Wales): 2
- Gloucestershire County: 1
- Greater London: 15
- Greater Manchester: 1
- Gwent County (Wales): 2
- Hampshire County: 1
- Hartlepool: 0
- Herefordshire and Worcestershire County: 2
- Hertfordshire County: 1
- Humberside County: 1
- Isle of Man: 0
- Isle of Wight: 0
- Kent County: 6
- Lancashire County: 4
- Leicestershire County: 0
- Lincolnshire County: 1
- Manchester County (see Greater Manchester)
- Merseyside County: 1
- Middlesbrough County: 0
- Midlothian County (Scotland): 2
- Moray County (Scotland): 1
- Norfolk County: 0
- North Yorkshire County: 0
- Northamptonshire County: 1
- Northumberland County: 0
- Nottinghamshire County: 2
- Oxfordshire County: 4
- Rutland County: 0
- Shropshire County: 0
- Somerset County: 0
- South Gloucestershire County: 0
- South Yorkshire County: 2
- Staffordshire County: 0
- Stockton on Tees: 0

THE BLAKENEYS

- Strathclyde County (Scotland): 1
- Suffolk County: 0
- Surrey County: 3
- Tyne and Wear County: 3
- Warwickshire County: 0
- West Midlands County: 2
- West Sussex County: 3
- West Yorkshire County: 3
- Wiltshire County: 6
- York County: 0

While this list cannot definitively tell us whether the place-name Blakeney first emerged in Norfolk County or Gloucestershire County, it can tell us the most likely region of entry. And from the dispersal pattern that emerges here, we can be nearly certain that the Blakeney surname came into England with the Normans on October 14, 1066. For the heaviest concentration is found in England's southeast corner, in and around East Sussex, the County in which lies the city of Hastings, where the Norman Conquest was won against the Saxons 1,000 years ago.

The list reveals other intriguing features of the Blakeney name, as well. One surprise is that there are no Blakeneys presently listed in the telephone directories of either the town of Blakeney, Norfolk County, or the town of Blakeney, Gloucestershire County. The original Blakeney families that once lived here and took their surnames from these two villages, have evidently disappeared, either going extinct in the area or simply moving away. (Either that or they live there but have unlisted phone numbers.)

Another feature of interest is revealed by the pattern of county surname distribution. The Blakeney surname seems to have migrated upward from southeast England in a fairly direct line to the northwest, ending up in central Scotland. To picture this one only need visualize an upright arrow that is leaning to the left, with its "tail-feathers" in East Sussex County and its pointed "head" far to the north in Cumbria County. There are few, if any, Blakeneys surnames to be found outside this narrow north-south path, which is a perplexing curiosity that demands further research.

Exacerbating the debate over the English point of origin of the Blakeney place-name and surname are the *Blakley* families, said to be close relations of, or even identical to, the Blakeneys—with whom they share some of the same spelling variations (for example, Blakely, Bleakney, Blakney, etc.). And yet many of the Blakely families assert that they descend from the Saxons, not the Normans, and that their German ancestors hailed from Blackley, Lancashire County, England, not Blakeney, Norfolk, or Blakeney, Gloucestershire (strangely, no mention is made by these same individuals of the town of Blackley, just to the south in Greater Manchester, a place-name first recorded in 1282).

Blakley, like Blacklee, Blaikley, Blakeley, and Blakely, is indeed a variation of the surname Blackley, which early families adopted from the Lancashire town of the same name. But rather than lending support to the idea that the Blackleys/Blakleys are Blakeneys, instead this tells us the opposite; namely, that the Blackleys/Blakleys and the Blakeneys probably descend from two entirely different and unrelated family lines. Let us look more closely at this for a moment.

To begin with the meaning of Blackley is quite unlike the meaning of Blakeney. Blackley derives from the Old English *blac léah*, literally meaning 'dark woods' (and more generally, 'dweller by/of the dark woods'). Blakeney, on the other hand, is from the Old Norse *blæyken ey*, literally meaning 'bleak isle' (and more generally, 'dweller of/from the pale/bleak island').

If etymological proof is not enough then one must also consider the plain fact that the Blakeneys took their epithet from the topographical place-name of the same name; that is from the name of the village of Blakeney (possibly in both Norfolk County *and* Gloucestershire County), while the Blakleys (by their own admission) took their name from the toponym Blackley; that is, from the name of the town of Blackley, Lancashire County. The problem here is that the town of Blackley is quite far north of both Blakeney, Norfolk, and Blakeney, Gloucestershire, and the author has not been able to find any records

THE BLAKENEYS

showing Blakeneys in this region in the Middle Ages.

Lastly, the Blackleys/Blakleys assertion itself, that they are from Saxon stock rather than Norman stock, rules out the possibility that they were originally Blakeneys. For the etymological evidence on this topic is solid and overt: not only is Blakeney a Danish Viking name, but it is a name that appeared in Normandy (a Danish region) *before* it appeared in England (a Saxon region).

The Blakleys may have one piece of evidence, however, that points to a possible early connection with the Blakeneys; a linkage found in the earliest recorded root-spellings of Blackley and Blakeney.

The first known Blackley individual on record, for example, is *William de Blekelegh*, in 1301, while the first known recorded Blakeney is *Thomas de Blakenia*, 100 years earlier, in 1201. Both *bleke* and *blake* are actually Middle English spelling variations of the same Modern English word: "bleak."

The trouble here is that the spelling form *blake* has remained virtually unchanged for nearly 1,000 years, while the spelling form *bleke* is now both quite obsolete *and* extinct, and has been so for many centuries. Indeed, the surname Blakley itself has had many incarnations, showing a wide variety of spelling forms in the last seven centuries, from *William de Blekelegh* (in 1301) and *Robert atte Blakeley* (in 1337), to *John Blaklay* (in 1543) and *Mungo Blaikley* (in 1687), with other later spellings including *Blakely*, *Blakeley*, *Blacklee*, and *Blackley*.

Why the spelling of the prefix *blake*, in Blakeney, has persisted unchanged for so long, and why the prefixes *bleke*, *blak*, *blaik*, *black*, in Blakley have continued to evolve, remains a mystery. Whatever the answers, these facts do raise serious misgivings about the belief that there is a familial relationship between the Blakeneys and the Blakleys/Blackleys.

In summary, what we have here are two distinct words, *black* and *blake*, with very different roots, spellings, meanings, nationalities, and geographical areas of emergence. The blurring of the line separating the Blackley families and the Blakeney families is no doubt another example of the ancient confusion between the Old English *blac* ('black') and the Old English *blác* ('white')—the latter which is *bleikja*, *blæyke*, *bleyke*, or *blayken* in Old Danish, and *bleke* in Middle English.

This misunderstanding has been aided over the centuries by misspellings and mispronunciations, and by the fact that both families not only intermarried, but also adopted the various spellings of one another's surnames along the way. Thus, though the Blackleys/Blakleys began as a Saxon family line, in every way quite distinct from the Norman Blakeneys, the two are now hopelessly merged together, making precise genealogy into the Blackleys' distant past extremely difficult, if not impossible.

25

The Strongbow Theory

hile we are on the topic of the town of Blakeney, Gloucestershire, mention should be made here of the theory that the first Blakeneys in Ireland came not from Norfolk County, England, in the 16th Century, but from Gloucestershire County, England, in the 12th Century.

According to this view these first Irish Blakeneys would have traveled from Blakeney, Gloucestershire, to Dublin, Ireland, with *Richard Fitzgilbert de Clare*, also known as *"Strongbow"* (d. 1176; buried at Christ's Church, Dublin, Ireland),[114] the leader of the Cambro-Normans, the 2nd Earl of Pembroke and Strigul, and the Lord of Chepstow Castle (located near Blakeney, Gloucestershire).

Strongbow left Chepstow for Ireland between 1168 and 1170, to aid *Diarmait Macmurchada* (1110-1171),[115] the deposed King of Leinster, Ireland,[116] who asked (in 1166) for England's aid in regaining his throne against a confederation of Irish nobles (in return, Strongbow was to be allowed to marry King Macmurchada's daughter, Eva).[117]

---

[114] Lord Richard Strongbow is my 26th great-grandfather.

[115] King Macmurchada is my 27th great-grandfather.

[116] King Macmurchada, whose full name in English is written Dermot MacMurrough, assembled the now famous *Book of Leinster*, a compilation of ancient Celtic traditions.

[117] Eva Macmurchada (in English, Eve MacMurrough) is my 26th great-grandmother.

The Blakeneys

Strongbow's English forces, which went on to capture and subdue Dublin and Waterford, would very likely have included Blakeneys (and possibly Blackleys and Blackneys, who were Roman Catholic) conscripted from the local male population of Gloucestershire County.

There is evidence to support this hypothesis.

Records reveal that the Blakeney name can be traced back to as early as the 1300s in Dublin. This is centuries before the *Norfolk* Blakeneys appear in Dublin, or anywhere else in Ireland for that matter. In fact, the first recorded Blakeneys in County Limerick and County Galway date, as we will recall, from the 16th Century, some three hundred years later.

If it is true, then, that the Dublin Blakeneys derive from Blakeney, Gloucestershire (in the 1100s), then it is probably equally true that the County Limerick and County Galway Blakeneys derive from Blakeney, Norfolk (in the 1500s), my current view.

26

A Cryptic Tail: The Blakeney Suffix

he 'island' or 'marshy' aspect of the name Blakeney naturally leads us to reflect on the enigmatic ending, or suffix, '-ney' or '-ey,' in Blakeney (that is, Blake-ney or Blaken-ey), with which it seems to be connected.

The mystery surrounding the '-ney' suffix is due to the fact that we do not know when it was first used; and also because of the fact that both *blakeney* and its core-word *blake* have each evolved and devolved so many times over the centuries, resulting in a truly confusing myriad of spelling variations. Modern Blakeney researchers have helped further confound the situation by recording all of the early spelling forms as "Blakeney," while disregarding the original spellings (which would have been Middle English in form, spelling, and pronunciation).

We do know that the core-word *blake* first appears in this spelling form in English records as a surname around 1167, as *Walter le Blake* of Devonshire,[118] and that *Blake*, as a *prepositionless* surname, first

---

[118] The 12th-Century name *Walter le Blake* is intriguing. If literally translated it would mean 'Walter the Pale,' or 'Walter the Bleak.' This gentleman may have had a sallow complexion, or perhaps he suffered from albinism. Maybe the characteristic for which he was named was not physical, but psychological. In this case he may have been afflicted with one of the many varieties of depression, such as melancholia, which would have given him what others would have seen as a 'bland' personality.

appears in the records of 1219, as one *Adam Blake* of Yorkshire (note that these surname usages are no doubt far older than these two dates).

But the time in which the exact spelling "Blakeney" emerged is not known with any certainty, though our sparse evidence would suggest the 14th, or possibly the 15th, Century.

The original Old Norse spelling of the word-name *Blake* would have been *bleikja*, *blæyke*, *bleyken*, or *blayken*, all meaning 'bleak' (the Old Norse *bleikr*, a related word, meant 'wan' or 'pale'). In Old English *blæyke* became *blæce* while *bleyken* became *blácian*; then the Old English *bleche* became *bleyke*, while *blayken* became *blakien*, then *blayken* or *blaken*, which in Middle English became *blayke*, then *blake*. Where then did the '*-ney*' or '*-ey*' suffix come from? Several theories present themselves.

Theory 1: Since the *exact* spelling form, "Blakeney," appears first in England, the simplest explanation is that the suffix '*-ney*' was an anglicization of the Old Norse suffix *-ja*, or *-e*, found in the original Old Norse words for 'bleak': *bleikja* or *blæyke*, which then became *Blakeney*. This would have occurred in heavily Danish Norfolk County, either purposely, or through continued mispronunciations, misunderstandings, misdivisions, or misspellings of the original Old Norse form (that is, perhaps *de Bleikjaey* or *de Blæykeney*).

In the 8th and 9th Centuries many Danes in England went on to invade France, where they, along with a French population of Celts and Franks, became "the Normans." However, many more Danes remained behind in England, where, in 878, they instituted the Danelaw,[119] installing several Danish kings on the English throne between the years 1016 and 1042.[120]

---

[119] The Danelaw included, of course, all of Norfolk, the county in which the Old English village of Snitterly was located. Thus, from the year 878 until the Norman Conquest of 1066, Snitterly was considered a Danish town by Norfolk's main population, the Danes (though we can be quite sure that the local Anglo-Saxon natives saw the matter quite differently).

[120] One of the most significant Danish kings of England was Harthacnut (1019-1042), who ruled England from 1040 to 1042. His death in 1042 brought an end to Danish rule in England. English nobles (such as Earl Godwin of Wessex) then returned the throne to England by electing Harthacnut's half-brother, the Oxfordshire-born ecclesiastic, Edward the Confessor of Wessex (circa 1002-1066). (Edward and Harthacnut had the same mother: Emma of Normandy; but Edward's father was the English King Ethelred II "the

THE BLAKENEYS

One important Danish King—and the son of Harald Blaatand; that is, 'Harold Bluetooth' (d. circa 985)[121]—was Svend Tveskaeg; that is, 'Sweyn I Forkbeard' (d. 1014),[122] who first raided England in 994 and later defeated the nation in 1013.

Svend's 2nd son, the "good king," Canute II (in Danish, *Knud*), the Great (circa 994-1035),[123] went on to forge a great Anglo-Danish Kingdom, over which he ruled as King of England from 1016 to 1035. His empire encompassed not only England and Denmark, but also Norway, regions in Sweden, and even various Slavonic areas in the Baltic.

During his reign, Canute II—a man known as "one of England's most successful rulers"—created a type of government that was both respectful of past tradition and receptive to contemporary customs. Thereafter the term "Canute's Law" became a synonym for a stable and fair government.

One result of this profound Danish influence in England—in which the entire English court at York spoke Norse for several decades—was a new sub-language: *Anglo-Danish* (a variety of Anglo-Scandinavian), essentially a blending of Old Danish and Old English.[124]

Unready" (circa 968-1016), while Harthacnut's father was Canute II "the Great" (circa 994-1035).) (King Ethelred II is my 28th great-grandfather.) Edward was the last of the Anglo-Saxon line, after which the throne was officially taken over in 1066 by Harold III "Hard-Ruler" (1015-1066)—though Harold claimed to have been king since 1047, at the death of King Magnus I "the Good" (d. 1047)—the son of King-Saint Olaf II (circa 995-1030), who died shortly thereafter, on September 25, 1066, in the Battle at Stamford Bridge, England. As history has well recorded the throne was then occupied by the Duke of the invading Normans, William I the Conqueror. Note: Though Edward had taken a vow of chastity (being deeply spiritual), he later married Earl Godwin's daughter, *Eadgyth* ('Edith').

[121] Harald 'Bluetooth' is my 31st great-grandfather.

[122] Svend I 'Forkbeard' is my 30th great-granduncle.

[123] Canute II the Great is my 1st cousin (many times removed).

[124] Our Modern English language has retained numerous Old Danish (Norse) words from the period of the Danelaw, such as: window, law, weak, calf, hit, outlaw, knife, sky, wrong, skill, seemly, husband, egg, hustings, take, leg, birth, skin, brink, cast, ill, skirt, scare, bull, thrift, happy, low, scrape, lift, scrub, loose, rift, fellow, awkward, odd, race, call, sister, bylaw, kid, reef, crawl, bank, gape, trust, booth, ugly, drown, cut, riding, skull, want, down (feathers), gate, sark, they, their, them, though, same, and both. Modern English Scandinavian loan-words include: smorgasbord, ombudsman, ski, and tungsten.

Anglo-Danish was widely used by the Danes in England between the 9th and 11th Centuries, particularly throughout the Danelaw,[125] and as a Scandinavian-based language, actually rivaled English (in Britain) and Gaelic (in Ireland) until around the year 1200.

In this scenario the Norse word-name *bleikjaey* or *blæykeney* would have been anglicized, evolving into what many think of as the "English" form, *Blakeney*. Though if this is indeed what occurred, the spelling "Blakeney" would actually be an Anglo-Danish form, not merely an English one.

Theory 2: A second possibility is to be found in the suffix '*-ney*' itself. *Ney* is actually a proper word, in that it is a variant spelling of the word *nyr*, which is the Old Norse word for 'new' (which is also related to *nywe*, the Old English word for 'new'). Note that in Modern Danish (and Swedish) 'new' is written *ny*.

Thus, the '*ney*' element in Blakeney (also written *ny*, without the '*e*,' as in Blakeny) may have originally been added to *Blæyke* or *Bleyke* (Blake) to create a Norman French word-name-phrase meaning 'the New Blakes,' the free translation which would be 'the New Bleak-men'; that is, 'the new people from the bleak lands of the north.' The resulting word might have been written *de Blæykeney* or *de Bleykeney*.

Theory 3: Of course, '*ney*' may not have been the original suffix at all. And our focus on this aspect may only be due to the anglocentric belief that *blake* is an "English" core-word to which was later appended the suffix '*-ney*.'

In fact, it is likely that this is an illusion, since *blake* is merely a Middle English spelling of the Danish word for 'bleak,' *bleikja*, which was later sometimes written *bleyken* or *blayken*, both which already possess an '*n*' element. (We will remember that the Old English spelling of *blake* was *blác*, with no '*n*'.)

There are other possibilities, as well. As we have seen we have record of an intriguing ancient Old Norse word, *blikna*, meaning 'to

---

[125] Around 1130 William of Malmesbury (circa 1090-1143) publicly rebuked those "rough foreigners" in the north of England who spoke Anglo-Danish, maintaining that it was almost impossible for the native English to understand.

shine' or 'burn,' which is related to both the Old Norse word *blá* ('pale'), and the Middle English word *blace*, 'black.' If *blikna* was the original core-word of Blakeney, an '*n*' would not have been added to the core-word either since, again, it already existed as part of the word itself.

We know that the Middle English spelling of *blikna* was *blykne*. If this scenario is the correct one *blykne* would have later been corrupted or anglicized to *Blakeney*. Hence, the added suffix would have been '*-ey*,' or more accurately '*-y*,' not '*-ney*'; thus giving *blykne* + *y*, which evolved to *Blakene-y*. (This process would have been aided by such English dialects as Cockney, in which the '*y*' and '*e*' in *blykne* would have been pronounced as long vowels, sounding like "BLYKE-nee.")

Theory 4: One of the more conventional theories for the *-ney* suffix pertains specifically to the single letter *-n*, which was the Old English genitive singular (that is, possessive). Typically, the genitive *-n* was attached as a suffix to a personal name (for example, Ella), and as an affix to a place (for example, a farm or settlement) or a thing (for example, a river or grove of trees). Thus in Old English "Ella's woods" would have been written: *Aelfnléah* (*Aelf-n-léah*); that is, *Aelf* (Ella) - *n* (the possessive element) - *léah* ('woods').[126]

In the case of Blakeney, Blake would have been a man's name which, as this theory goes, in Old English was spelled *Blæca* or *Blaca*, meaning 'Black,' 'Blackie,' or 'Mr. Black.' Thus the formation of Blakeney derived from *Blæca*, followed by the genitive *-n*, and then by the Old Anglo-Norse *-ey* ('island'). The result would have been the hybrid name *Blæcaney* or *Blacaney,* meaning '*Blæca's Isle*', or in Modern English, 'Black's Island'; that is, 'the Island belonging to a man called Blake—or Black or Blackie.'[127]

---

[126] The literal, and the technically correct, translation of *Aelfnléah* would be: 'Elves' Woods,' or 'the Woods of the Elves.' Ella is a Modern English form of the Old English word-name, *Aelf*, meaning 'elf.' Feminine nicknames for Ella include: Ellen, Ellie, Elly.

[127] A name of similar, if distant, meaning is found among modern Irish surnames: MacAvinchey, or in Irish Gaelic, *Mac Dhuibhinse*, means a person from or 'of the black island.' (Note: In parts of Ireland, MacAvinchey has been incorrectly anglicized as the surname Vincent, which is from the Latin word *vincentius*, meaning

THE BLAKENEYS

While *blæca* or *blaca* does mean 'black,' and this spelling was certainly in use as a surname as early as the year 901 (see "Black" in the Blakeney surname dictionary below), *blaca* was *not* the original spelling of *blake*; for as their separate etymologies show, the two words have completely opposing meanings, the former being 'black' and the latter 'white.'

The problem with this theory then, and the reason I reject it, is due to the fact that *blake* ('white') did not come to also mean 'black' until very late. Though there was doubtless already some confusion between *blác* ('pale') and *blac* ('dark') before the 12th Century (that is, during the Anglo-Saxon period of Old English), it was not until many centuries later that in parts of the British Isles *blake* sometimes came to be mistakenly synonymous with black.

Between the 12th and 15th Centuries, for example, the Middle English word *Blacey* (an early variation of Blakeney, and now written Blakey), still meant 'fair-haired or fair-complected one,' as did *Blacey's* southern English counterparts, *bloc*, *bloke*, or *bloken*. And until only 100 years ago the very word *blake* itself meant both 'bleak' and 'yellow' in northern English dialects. Many other examples of this type could be given.

As we have seen, *blake* descends from *blác* (written *blac*, but pronounced "blake"), meaning 'white' or 'pale,' while black descends from *blac* (written *blac*, but pronounced "black") meaning 'dark' or 'scorched.' The earliest record in England of the surname *Blake* (in 1167, *Walter le Blake*; that is, 'Walter the Pale') and the surname *Blakeney* (in 1201, *Thomas de Blakenia*; that is, 'Thomas of the Bleak Island'), were spelled in just this manner. The same is true of the earliest recorded instances of the place-name *Blakeney* (in 1196, written *Blakeneia*; that is, 'Bleak Island').

From this we can clearly see that no known *authentic* Blake or Blakeney place-name, individual, or family has ever been spelled using the word *blæca* or *blaca* ('black' or 'burned'). The first five letters of the

---

'conquering one.')

surname have always been *blake* ('white' or 'bleak') for as far back as we have records.

In short, the problem with this particular theory is a misinterpretation (and mistranslation) of the word Blakeney, which supporters of this view assert is *Blæcaney*. It is true that *Blæcaney* means 'Black's Isle.' What is not true is that *Blæcaney* is an early spelling of "Blakeney."

Actually, the correct Modern English spelling of *Blæcaney* would be "Blackney," a rare name that died out in large cities such as Dublin, Ireland, by the early 1900s. Blackney place-names are even rarer, the one known English example being an obsolete toponym once located in Stoke Abbot, Dorset County.[128]

To reemphasize then, the probable *original* English spelling of the *place-name* Blakeney was *Blakeneia* (though the Danish Vikings would have spelled it *Blæykeney*), while the probable *original* English spelling of the *surname* Blakeney was *Blakenia*. Both mean 'Bleak Isle.'

The core-word *blake* itself derives from the Old Danish word *bleikja* or *blæyke*, meaning 'bleak,' 'pale,' 'livid,' 'pallid,' 'barren,' 'dreary,' 'to whiten,' or 'colorless.'

If we add to this the fact that the dative, or indirect object, of the word Blakeney is *blacan,* not *blac* or *blaca*, we can be quite sure that the -*n* element in Blakeney is not a genitive singular that was appended later. It was simply an inherent part of the original early Viking word, *blæyke*, which was also spelled *bleyken* or *blayken*—that is, *blacan* or *blaken*—from its inception.[129]

Theory 5: This neatly leads us to the fifth and last possible source for the '-*ey*' or '-*y*' elements in Blakeney—and in my opinion, the most

---

[128] The surname Blackney survives in England, but is uncommon, infrequent, and widely scattered. In the Winter of 2000, for example, a nationwide UK telephone directory search found only five Blackneys listed.

[129] The dative is an aspect of the case system of early inflected languages, in particular Latin and Old English, where it denoted the indirect object (which is the secondary goal of the action of its verb, and hence comes after the verb) of a verb and sometimes prepositions. Thus datives are, generally speaking, the forms of various elements, such as nouns, pronouns, adjectives, etc., which act as the grammatical recipients of some type of action.

likely one. This comes from the Old Norse word *ey* (in Modern Danish, *oe*), meaning 'island,' which would have been appended to *blaken* ('bleak') as a suffix. This would have formed *blakene* or *blakeney*, a compound place-name meaning 'bleak island.'

This is the very process that created the word Orkney: the Old Norse word *orkn*, 'seal,' was combined with the Old Norse word *ey*, 'island,' to produce the compound Orkn-Ey, then Orkney, meaning 'Seal Island.' Why not then for the word Blakeney—that is, Blaken-Ey? There is some possible evidence for this theory.

As mentioned earlier there is a colorless ('pale' or 'dark') arm of land jutting out into the sea off the coast of Blakeney, Norfolk. Today this peninsula is known as "Blakeney Point." In the 9th Century, however, it may have looked quite different. It may have been wetter and marshier, or at high tide it may have become almost, or completely, separated from the mainland.

Even though during the Middle Ages Blakeney Point may not have been a true island, such natural phenomena could have given it the appearance of being one. On the other hand, perhaps the experienced sea-faring Vikings knew that Blakeney Point was a peninsula, not an island, but merely enjoyed an occasional game of word play.

Either way, the fact that the village of Blakeney, Norfolk is known by this name today (that is, the 'Bleak Isle') tells us that at one time the people who named it—in this case the Viking Danes—believed that it was either very marshy, or that it was a literal island; or it may tell us that they were simply a society that was amused by fanciful linguistics.[130]

---

[130] It is elucidating to examine the Early English word endings for 'island.' These are *-ay*, *-ea*, *-ey*, and sometimes *-y*. All are derivations of the Old Mercian *-ēg*, and the Middle English *-ei* and *-ey*. These in turn derive from the Old English *-ig* or *īeg*, and the Old English *-ēa* (which derive from, or are related to, the earlier Old Norse word, *ey*), indicating a 'brook,' 'stream,' or 'river.' The original character of these words and suffixes was feminine, with the meaning being 'a place of water,' or 'a watery place.' For early societies believed that feminine nature spirits and goddesses governed bodies of water, from wells and creeks, to lakes and seas. We will note here that this linkage between the Divine Feminine and water is an ancient one, probably deriving from the sacrality attached to pregnant women's breast milk and amniotic fluid, the latter which is nearly chemically identical to seawater, the former which can appear similar to white sea foam. Hence we have the ancient Indo-European root-word *ma* or *mar*, meaning 'mother,' which in Old Latin became *mare*, 'sea.' Likewise, in ancient Egyptian, *mer* meant both 'water' and 'mother-love,' and in Modern

THE BLAKENEYS

French *mer* still means 'sea,' while *mère* means 'mother.' This connection between the word *mar*, water, and female energy gave rise to thousands of goddesses with names possessing the '*ma*' or '*mar*' elements: Maerin, Mar, Mara, Marah, Mare, Mari, Maria, Mariam, Mariamne, Marian, Maid Marian, Mari-Anna, Marica, Mari-El, Mariham, Marina, Marratu, Marri, Mary, Marzanna, Maya, Meri, Meri-Ra, Merjan, Merry, Miriam, the Moerae, the Morrigan, Myrrha, Myrrhine, Myrtea, and Wudu-Maer. We should not wonder that the traditional Pagan title of many of these goddesses, *Stella Maris* ('Star of the Sea'), was eventually appended to Christianity's own "Mary" (by the biblical scholar Saint Jerome in the 5th Century). The belief in the link between the Feminine Principle and water is still current in indigenous Pagan religions and among modern Goddess-worshipers, and many modern European rivers still retain the names of the ancient goddesses who are said to still rule them. In Great Britain alone a list of such rivers would include the following: the Mersey (ruled by the Goddess Belisama); the Dee (Goddess Aerfen); the Carrawburgh (Goddess Coventina); the Severn (Goddess Sabrina); the Clyde (Goddess Clutoida); the Briant (Goddess Briant); the Devon (Goddess Devona); the Wharfe (Goddess Verbeia); and the Wye (Goddess Vaga). (For more information on this fascinating topic, see the my book, *Britannia Rules: Goddess-Worship in Ancient Anglo-Celtic Society - An Academic Look at the United Kingdom's Matricentric Spiritual Past*.) As with the Old Norse word *ey*, these English suffix variations can also refer not only to islands, but to any watery areas, including peninsulas, marshes, fens, estuaries, broads, and swamps, or those regions on, near, or surrounded by streams, rivers, lakes, and oceans.

27

A Blakeney Surname Dictionary: Variations on an Anglo-Danish Theme

From the Middle Ages on, many English forename and surname variations of the Old Norse word-names *Bleikja*, *Blæyke*, *Blaken*, and the Old Norse place-name *Blæykeney*, developed, including: Blake, Blakely, Blakley, Blakney, Blakeny, Bleak, Bleakeny, Bleakney, and the most common variation, Blakeley.

Included in this list would be those families not generally thought of as related, such as those with the surnames Black and DeBlakeland, the former which has been confused with the surname Blake, the latter which is identical to the old Blakeney names.

Below is an alphabetized dictionary of English surnames that I have researched and compiled. This dictionary lists surnames that are either linguistically related to, confused with, or are members of the

Blæykeney / Blakeney family group of names, along with their etymologies and date of first appearance, where known. (Note: double-quotation marks around surnames direct the reader to entries dedicated to those surnames. For example: "Blakeman" means 'see the entry under Blakeman'.)

BLACAGH: An Anglo-Irish variation of the surname "Blake." It survives in County Connacht, Ireland. Its original meaning was identical to that of Blake, namely 'bleak.' However, as with so many of the other Blake/Blakeney spelling variations and forms, this meaning has been lost and erroneously replaced by the sense 'black.'

BLACK: from the Old English word *blæc*, then *blaca*, then *blac*, 'black'; thus as a surname meaning 'dark-complexioned' or 'dark-haired.' Mistakenly interchanged with the surname Blake from Medieval confusion between the Old English *blác*, meaning 'white' (derived from the Old Norse words *bleikr* (meaning 'white' or 'pale'), and the Old Norse *bleikja* (meaning 'bleak') and the Old English *blac*, meaning 'black' (deriving from the Old High German words *blah* and *blach*, both meaning 'black'). The confusion stems from the fact that in Anglo-Saxon times, both *blác* and *blac* were written the same (that is, as *blac*, without an acute accent, which is actually a modern scholarly convention), but were pronounced differently; the former as "blake," the latter as "black." Since we have no records of the pronunciations of the early Black surnames, we will never know whether they were truly Blacks or Blakes, though we do know with complete confidence that they were originally two very distinct and unrelated families. In England Black is sometimes an anglicized form of the Anglo-Celtic surname Duff (from the Celtic *dubh*, 'black'), while in Scotland, where the surname Black is linked to three Scottish clans (the MacGregors, the Lamonts, and the MacLeans), its Anglo-Gaelic form is *Macildowie*, from *mac gille dhuibh*, meaning 'child of the black lad.' Date first recorded: 901, as a personal name, *Wulfhun þes*

Blaca (that is, variously 'Wolf the Black,' 'Wolf's son, the Black,' 'Wolf, son of the Black,' or 'the Black Wolf'; or perhaps most freely, a nickname meaning, 'one who is dark and mysterious, like the wolf').

BLACKAH: from the place-name Blacker, in West Riding Yorkshire, England; or perhaps a corruption of the Old English word *blaca* ('black'), which has long been confused with *blác* ('white'). Date first recorded: 1475, in a surname, *Alice Blaca*.

BLACKBIRD: literally 'black beard,' from the Old English *blac* ('black') and *beard* ('beard'), though doubtlessly often confused with the Blake names where *blác* means 'white,' 'bleak,' or 'fair.' Date first recorded: 1066, in a surname, *Brunstanus Blachebiert*; we will also note the confused spelling, in 1279, of the name of one *William Blakebird*.

BLACKBORN: from the Old English *blac* ('black') and *burna* ('stream'), and so meaning a 'dark creek,' or 'black-colored stream.' Here we find the origins of the place-name Blackburn, Lancashire County, England. From the place-name was derived the surname Blackborn, whose variants include: Blackborne, Blackbourn, Blackbourne, Blackburn, and Blackburne. We have evidence of early confusion with the blake ('white' or 'bleak') words, as the earliest known instance of the name reveals. Date first recorded: 1206, in a surname, *Henry de Blakeburn*. Note that though the original literal translation of this full name would have been 'Henry of [that is, who lives by] the pale or light-colored stream,' the inaccurate connotation that was actually meant was 'Henry of the dark or black-colored stream.'

BLACKBORO: from the Old English *blac* ('black') and *beorg* ('hill'), giving 'dark hill.' The place-name, Blackborough, in both Norfolk County and Devonshire County, England, derives from these words, and the surname derives from the place-names. There is confusion here with the blake words, as can be seen in the earliest known instance of the name, and in the variations of the surname Blackboro, as well. These variants include: Blackborough, Blackborow, Blackbrough, Blagbrough,

Blakeborough, and Blakebrough. Thus while Blackborough means 'dark hill,' Blakeborough means 'pale or bleak hill'; yet the two word-names have been accorded the meaning of only the former. Date first recorded: 1201, in a surname, *Robert de Blakeberg* ('Robert of the fair hill').

BLACKBROOK: from the Old English *blac* ('black') and *broc* ('brook'), giving 'dark stream.' Another surname confused with the blake words, as we can see from the early spellings. Date first recorded: 1279, in a surname, *Gilbert de Blakebrok* ('Gilbert of the bleak or pale stream').

BLACKCLIFF: from the Old English *blac* ('black') and *clif* ('cliff'), giving 'dark precipice.' From these words derived the place-name Blackcliffe Hill, Nottinghamshire County, England; and from the place-name derived the surname, which like so many other black words, has long been confused with the blake words. Date first recorded: 1219, in a surname, *Robert de Blaclif* (concerning this specific surname, if the first element is—like Blake and Blakeney—from the Old Norse *blá* ('pale' or 'livid'), giving *Blá-Clif*, then we have 'pale cliff'; if the first element is from the Old English *bla* ('black'), giving *Bla-Clif*, then we have 'dark cliff'); and in 1289 we have one *John de Blakeclif* ('John of [that is, who lives by] the bleak or pale cliff'). Variations: Blackcliffe, Blackliffe.

BLACKDEN: from the Old English *blac* ('black') and *denu* ('valley'), giving 'dark valley.' Here lies the origin of the place-name Blackden Heath, Cheshire County, England; and from it came the surname which, along with its variants, Blagden and Blagdon, have been confused with the blake words. Date first recorded: 1275, in a surname, *Roger de Blakeden* ('Roger of [that is, who lives by or in] the pale valley').

BLACKE: a variation of "Black."

BLACKELL: from the Old English *blac* ('black') and *hyll* ('hill'), giving 'dark hill.' Often confused with the blake words, as is apparent from the old surname spellings. Date first recorded: 1327, in a surname, *Gilbert atte Blakehulle* ('Gilbert [who lives] at the pale hill').

BLACKELY: a variation of "Blackledge."

BLACKER: from the Old English *Blæchere*, a derivative of the Old English word *blæcan* (from *blac* or *blaca*, 'black') and the Middle English word *blaken* (from *blác* or *blake*, 'pale' or 'bleak'). *Blæcan* itself means 'to bleach'; thus, confusingly, a blacker is 'one who bleaches or blacks.' The Old English spelling of Blacker, *Blæchere*, meaning 'black-army,' is also related to the Middle English masculine word *blaker*, 'bleacher,' which gave rise to the surname Blaker (also written, in feminine form, Blaxter). Date first recorded: 1047, *Blakere*. See "Black," "Blaker."

BLACKERS: from the Old English *blac ears*; that is 'black arse.' One of the few black names *not* confused with the blake names. Date first recorded: 1189, as a pejorative nickname, *Walter Blachers* (perhaps meaning 'one who sits a lot'; that is, a lazy person). See "Black."

BLACKETT: as the earliest spellings of this surname show, we have here a modernized corruption and a mistranslation of the Old English *blác* ('pale' or 'fair') and *hēafod* ('head'), thus actually meaning 'fair head.'[131] Due to the confusion between the Old English *blac* ('black') and *blác* ('pale,' 'bleak,' 'white,' etc.), this surname has lost its original meaning. For as Blackett (in Old English *Blachēafod*) it has come to mean 'black head,' which in German is *schwarz kopf*. We will recall that the Old Norse *blake* is *not* related to the German word for 'black,' *schwarz*. Date first recorded: in 1301, in a surname, *Thomas Blakeheuede* ('Thomas Fairhead').

BLACKFORD: from the Old English *blac* ('black') and *ford* ('ford,' that is, a shallow body of water that can be crossed by wading), giving 'dark river-crossing.' These words gave rise to the place-

---

[131] The phrase 'fair head' has itself become a surname, Fairhead; from the Old English *fæger* ('fair') and *hēafod* ('head'). Date first recorded: 1279, in a surname, *William Fairhevid* ('William the blond-headed, or light-haired').

name, Blackford, Somerset County, England, which gave rise to the surname. Commonly confused with the blake words and names, as the early spellings show. Date first recorded: 1211, in a surname, *Robert de Blakeford* ('Robert of the [that is, who lives near] the bleak or pale river-crossing').

BLACKHALL: literally translated from the Old English as *blac* ('black') and *hall* (a 'corridor'), thus a 'dark passageway.' Both elements in this surname, however, are erroneous and have been confused with other words, the first element with the blake words, as can be seen in the early spellings. The word black ('dark') is a misunderstanding of the Old Norse word *blaken* ('pale' or 'bleak'), while the word hall is a misreading of the Old English word *halh* (a 'secret place'). Date first recorded: 1221, in a surname, *Robert de Blakehall*; and in 1332, *Ralph de Blackhale*. As can be seen from these two examples, the original surname was *Blakehale*, meaning a 'bleak hidden corner.' Variants of this surname: Blackale, Blackall.

BLACKHAM: a corruption of the Old Norse *blake* or *blaken* ('pale' or 'bleak') and the Old English *hamm* ('homestead'), giving 'bleak homestead' or 'dreary farm.' The original spelling of the place-name, which still exists, was thus Blakenham, Suffolk County, England. The surname Blakenham was derived from the place-name Blakenham, after which it was misunderstood and thus misspelled, Blackham. This confusion began early and is already evident in the *Domesday Book* in 1086, where Norman scribes misspelled the place-name *Blacham*, meaning 'dark homestead.' Date first recorded: 1135, in a surname, *Benedictus de Blakeham* ('Benedict of the bleak homestead').

BLACKHURST: from the Old English *blac* ('black') and *hyrst* (a 'sandy, hilly, thicket'), giving 'dark thicket on a knoll.' *Hyrst*, a common element in place-names—for example, Amherst (Nova Scotia, Canada), Chislehurst (Greater London, England), Hawkhurst (Kent County, England), etc.—is correct, though *blac* here was obviously confused with *blác* ('pale' or 'bleak'), as early spellings of the surname reveal. Date first recorded: in

1296, in a surname, *Robert de Blakehurst* ('Robert of [that is, who lives near] the bleak sandy thicket on a hill').

BLACKIE: from the Old English *de blæc hæg*; that is 'dweller from the dark low-lying land or island.' Or possibly from a nickname: "black-eye." Blackie is a Scottish diminutive of "Black," sometimes confused with the surname "Blaikie," which is a Scottish diminutive of the surname "Blake." Date first recorded: 1275, in a surname, *Henry Blackeye* ('Henry with the dark eyes,' or 'Henry from the dark island').

BLACKLEDGE: from the Old English *blac* ('black') and *læcc* ('a marshy creek'), giving 'dark stream'; but the first element has been confused with *blác* ('pale' or 'bleak'), as revealed in early spellings. Date first recorded in England: 1332, in a surname, *John del Blakelache* ('John of the bleak stream'); also found in Scotland. Variants: Blacklidge, Blacklege, Blackely, "Blackley." Blackledge is also a variant spelling of "Blakeley" and "Blakely," which while historically true, is etymologically incorrect.

BLACKLEE: a variation of "Blackley" (pronounced BLAKE-lee). Also see "Black."

BLACKLEGE: a variation of "Blackledge."

BLACKLEY: a topographical place-name, or toponym, that became a surname. From the Old English words *blac* ('black' or 'dark') and *léah* ('woods,' 'clearing,' 'meadow,' 'piece of ground,' or 'settlement'); thus *Blacléah*, the full meaning being: 'dweller by the dark woodland clearing.' According to modern day descendants of this surname, the Blackley families took their name from the town of Blackley, Lancashire County, England. But unfortunately for Blackley genealogists, the surname later became confused with Blakley, then Blakeney (see below). Date first recorded: 1301, as a surname, *William de Blekelegh*. (Blackley is pronounced BLAKE-lee.) As is true of so many of the Blakeney names and variations, there is some confusion surrounding the origins and meaning of the surname Blackley (no doubt due to the confusion between the words *blác*, 'white,' and *blac*, 'black'), which has been discussed in detail in earlier chapters. Astonishingly, with Blackley, however, we seem to have a record of how, where, and when this problem actually began. There is a second town of Blackley, this one in Greater Manchester, England. Though its original Old English spelling (that is, before the 12ᵗʰ Century) would have been, as we have seen, *Blacléah*, there is sadly no record of this. Instead, the town's first recorded spelling is in 1282, where, in Middle English, it was written *Blakeley*, which changes the original meaning of "Black Woods" to its opposite, "White Woods"! Centuries later, families whose ancestors had derived the surname from this place-name would have not only forgotten its original meaning, but would have begun confusing it with both the surname Blakeley and the surname Blakeney. It is currently my opinion that though Blackley is indeed now a variation of both Blakeley *and* Blakeney, the three names had different origins, and that because of this, the Blakeney and Blackley families were originally not related. See "Black."

BLACKLIDGE: a variation of "Blackledge."

BLACKLOCK: from the Old English *blac* ('black') and *locc* (a 'lock' of hair), giving 'black-haired person.' The usual mistake has arisen here due to the fact that early writers and speakers confused *bla* and *blac* ('black') with *blá* and *blác* ('white' or 'fair'), as early spellings of the surname indicate. Date first recorded: 1275, in a surname, *Peter Blakloke*; in 1332, *Adam Blakelok*; and in 1431, *Robert Blaykelok*. All of these surnames literally mean one with 'fair hair,' as the variants, Blakelock and Blaiklock, also show.

BLACKMAN: From the Old English *blac* ('black') and *mann* ('man'), giving Blackman, but also spelled "Blakeman," which aptly illustrates the ancient problem: if spelled *Blackman*, we have the sense of a 'dark-haired or dark-complexioned adult male'; if spelled *Blakeman*, we have the opposite meaning of a 'fair-haired, or fair-complexioned, adult male.' Early spellings of this surname confirm that there was much confusion here between *blac* ('black') and *blác* ('white'). Date first recorded: 1166, in a forename, *Blacheman filius Ædwardi* ('the dark man who is the son of Edward'); then in later surnames we have, in 1188, *Jordanus filius Blakeman* ('Jordan, son of the fair-complexioned man'); and in 1206, *John Blakeman* ('John the bleak man').

BLACKMERE: from the Old English *blac* ('black') and *mær* or *mere* ('pool,' 'lake,' or 'sea'), literally giving *blacmær*, 'dark water'; though as a surname the more free meaning is 'one who lives near the dark lake.' The place-name, Blackmore End, Hertfordshire, England, derives from this phrase, and the surname derives from the place-name. If this were the original spelling and meaning we would have here the English version of *dubh lacha*, Celtic for 'dark water,' the name of the old Irish Goddess Dubh Lacha, after whom the city of Dublin was named. Early spellings of the surname, as well as variant spellings, however, tell us that Medieval speakers and writers confused the Old Norse *blá* ('pale,' 'livid') and the Old English *blác* ('white,' 'bleak') with the Old English *bla* ('dark') and *blac* ('black'). Date first recorded: 1066, in an unspecified type of name, *Blachemer* ('black pool'); and again in 1275, in a surname, *William de Blakemere* ('William of [that is, who lives by] the bleak or pale pond or lake'). Variant spellings of this surname further emphasize the confusion: Blakemere ('bleak lake' or 'pale water'), and Blackmer ('dark lake' or 'black water').

BLACKMOOR: a variation of "Blackmore."

BLACKMORE: from the Old English *blac* ('black') and the Middle English *mōr* ('moor,' that is, a grassy, infertile, region of rolling hills and bogs), giving *blacmōr*, 'dark wastelands.' If the "moor" element derives from the Middle English *More* (for the Arabic-Berber inhabitants of Mauritania), and later *Moor*, then the meaning is 'dark-complexioned.' From these words are thought to have derived the English place-names, Blackmore (Essex, Hertfordshire, Wiltshire, and Worcestershire Counties), and Blackmoor (Devonshire, Dorset, and Hampshire Counties); from the place-names derived the surname. But how do we account for the place-name Blakemore, in Dorset? Early

143

spellings of both the place-name and the surname give us the answer. What they reveal is the 1,500-year misunderstanding of the definitions of the early words for black ('dark') and blake ('light'). Date first recorded: 1200, in a surname, *Baldewin de Blakomor*; in 1307, in a surname, *Nicholas de Blakemore*; and again in 1547, in a surname, *John Blakemore*. It is not until 1576 that we see the spelling Blackmore in one *Henry Blackmore*, showing that the original spelling was almost certainly Blakemore and that original meaning was thus 'bleak or pale wasteland.' The earliest recorded spelling of the place-name corroborates this, for in 1213 the town of Blackmore, Essex County, was called Blakemore. Reinforcing evidence comes from a variant form of the surname, and what was no doubt its original spelling: "Blakemore."

BLACKNEY: a rare and widely scattered surname that has been, and continues to be, confused with Blakeney and its many variations. Few Blackneys are left in Ireland (the name is said to have gone extinct in Dublin a century ago, though it is still found sporadically in County Carlow), and it survives only tenuously today in England. It means 'Black Island,' or 'New Dark Marshland,' or perhaps, if the -*n* is a genitive singular, 'Island belonging to someone named Black.' While undoubtedly this form began as a Germanic Anglo-Saxon family surname, quite distinct from the Danish Norman family surname Blakeney, misunderstandings, misspellings, time, and intermarriage between the two families have obscured the original line of demarcation. One place-name (Blackney in Stoke Abbot, Dorset County, England) may bear witness to the origins of this surname, but it is now obsolete.

BLACKSTOCK: from the Old English *blac* ('black') and *stocc* ('stump' or 'log'), giving *blacstocc*, 'dark stock of wood.' Again, confusion reigns here between the blake words and the black words, as early surname forms demonstrate. Date first recorded: 1296, in a surname, *William de la Blakestok* ('William of [that is, who lives near] the bleak or pale stump of wood').

THE BLAKENEYS

BLACKSTONE: from the Old English *blac* ('black') and *stān* ('stone'), giving *blacstān*, 'dark rock,' possibly indicating a crossroads. Early English place-names, such as Blaxton, West Riding Yorkshire, and Blackstone Ledge, Lancashire County, betray a problem, however. And indeed both early spelling forms and modern variants of this surname reveal the usual Medieval confusion over the meanings of *blac* ('black') and *blác* ('white'). Date first recorded: 1086 (in the *Domesday Book*), in a unspecified type of name, *Blackstan*; then in 1235, a gentleman forenamed William, who spelled his surname variously as *Blakeston*, *Blacston*, and *Blackstan*; though in 1275 we are back at blake ('pale') with one *Philip Atteblakeston* ('Phillip [who lives] at the bleak or pale stone'). Variants of the surname: Blackston, Blackiston, Blakeston, Blakiston, Blaxton.

BLACKSTRODE: from the Old English *blac* ('black') and *strōd* ('boggy ground'), giving *blac strōd*, 'dark fen.' Confusion between *blac* and *blác* ('white,' 'pale,' 'bleak') is apparent here as we can see from early spelling forms of this surname. Date first recorded: 1296, in a surname, *Simon atte Blakestrode* (Simon [who lives] at the bleak swamp').

BLACKTHORN: from the Old English *blac* ('black') and *þorn* ('thorn'), giving *blac þorn*, 'dark thorn.' Centuries of misunderstanding, misspellings, and misreadings have confused *blac* with *blác* ('white' or 'bleak'), and so the original surname was probably *Blácþorn*, 'bleak thorn.' Early spellings of the surname would indicate as much. Date first recorded: 1276, in a surname, *John de Blakethorn*; in 1379 we have *John Blakethorn*; and in 1442 we have *William Blakthorn*. All of these names are loosely translated as 'one who lives near the pale thorn bush.' Blackthorn, the modern form, however, has the opposite meaning: 'one who lives near the dark thorn bush.' Modern variant: Blackthorne.

BLACKWELL: from the Old English *blac* ('black') and *wiell* ('stream' or 'well'), giving *blac wiell*, 'dark stream.' The English place-names, Blackwell (in Derbyshire, Durham, and Worcestershire Counties), derived from these words and the surname derived from the place-names. 'Black well,' however, may not have been the original spelling or intended meaning, as early surname spellings seem to indicate. Date first recorded: 1012, in a surname, *Leofric æt Blacewellan* ('Leofric [who lives] at the dark well'); but in 1243, we have *Benedictus de Blakewelle* ('Benedict of [that is, who lives near] the pale well or stream'); and again in 1296, we have *Robert atte Blakewell* ('Robert [who lives] at the bleak well'). Variant: Blackwall.

BLACKWIN: from the Old English *blac* ('black') and *wīn* ('wine'), giving *blac wīn*, 'dark wine.' Based on some of the early spellings of this surname, however, the original spelling and meaning may have been *Blácwīn*, 'pale wine.' Date first recorded: 1125, in a forename, *Blacchewynus* ('Black wine') *Monachus*; but in 1198 we have *Blakewinus* ('Pale wine') *de Thornham*. Modern variant: Blackwyn.

BLAIKIE: a Scottish diminutive of "Blake," often confused with the surname "Blackie," which is the Scottish diminutive of the surname "Black." Date first recorded: 1600, as a surname, *Patrick Blaikie*.

BLAIKLEY: a variation of "Blakeley." See also "Blackley."

BLAIKLOCK: a variation of "Blakelock."

BLAKE: The Middle English monothematic core-word (meaning 'pale,' 'bleak,' or 'yellow') from which all the modern various spelling forms of Blakeney derive. From the Old English word *blác*, meaning 'pale' or 'shining,' then *blæce*, then *bleche*, which in Middle English became *bleyke*, then *blayke*, then *bleke*, then *blake*, 'bleak.' *Blác*, later confused with the Old English word *blac* or *blæc*, 'black,' derives from the Old Norse words *blêc* or *bleikr*, meaning 'white' or 'shining,' from *bleikja*, then *bleyken*, then *blayken* (all meaning 'bleak'), which derive from the Old Norse *blá*, meaning 'pale' or 'livid.' These Old Norse words in turn emerged from the Old Germanic word *blaik*, meaning 'shining,' or 'to shine.' *Blaik* derives from the ancient Latin *flagrare*, which derives from the ancient Greek word *phlégein,* both meaning 'burn.' These two words arose from two postulated Sanskrit base-words: *phleg*, meaning 'burn,' and a later variation, *bhleg* or *bhlig*, meaning 'pale.' Date first recorded: 1167, as a surname, *Walter le Blake* ('Walter the Pale' or 'Walter the Bleak'), of Devonshire County, England. As a singular surname (that is, without the preposition, *'le'*), date first recorded: 1219, *Adam Blake* of Yorkshire County, England. Diminutive but confused forms of Blake are 'Blackey' and 'Blacky.' The Anglo-Norman Blakes have been in Ireland long enough to be considered "one of the Tribes of Galway." Indeed, the Irish themselves maintain that the Blakes of Ireland are a true Celtic clan, one that descended from the Sheriff of County Connacht, Richard Caddell (in 1303), whose family line bestowed at least three Blakestown place-names in County Kildare. The surname Caddell (or Caudill) is indeed distantly related to the color-word 'black' (see my book, *The Caudills: An Etymological, Ethnological, and Genealogical Study*), and in early Ireland the name was spelled *le Bláca*, that is, 'the Black' (in certain parts of County Connacht, Ireland, the surname Blake is still spelled *Blacagh*, an Anglo-Gaelic form). This connection, however, that is, between the Irish Blakes and the surname Black (as well as the surname Caddell), while historically true, is yet another example of the age-old confusion between *blác* ('bleak' or 'white') and *blac* ('black'). Finally note that in the 17th Century many Irish families with the County Connacht surname *Ó Blathmhaic* (from the Gaelic word *blath*, 'fame'), anglicized their name to Blawick or Blowick, surnames that in turn sometimes metamorphosed (either accidentally or intentionally) into Blake. This example is given to illustrate the fact that not all families surnamed "Blake" are true Blakes in the genetic or hereditary sense, and to emphasize the care that should be taken when attempting to trace one's genealogy. (Note: an interesting surname and cousin of Blake is "Blick," which descends from the same ancient root-words as Blake ('white'). In the case of Blick, it derives from the Old English *blician* ('to shine' or 'glitter'), and was first recorded in 1185, in a surname, *Aluin Blic*.)

THE BLAKENEYS

BLAKELAND: an Anglo-Germanic form of "Blakeney," with which it shares the same meaning. See "DeBlakeland."

BLAKELY: a variation of "Blakeley." See also "Blackley."

BLAKELEY: also sometimes written Bleakley, this is an Old English compound, *blácléah*, from the Old English words *blác* ('pale,' 'white,' or 'bleak') and *léah* ('woods,' 'clearing,' or 'meadow'), together meaning 'dreary meadow,' or perhaps 'desolate piece of ground.' Later, after *blác* ('white') was confused with *blac* ('black'), *blácléah* became *blacléah*, which changed the meaning to 'dark meadow.' And so Blakeley is often confused with the surname *Blacléah* (Blackley), which has the opposite meaning. Despite the fact that the two surnames have different origins and meanings, due to misunderstandings, and also because of intermarriage between the two families, Blakeney is indeed now a variation of Blackley. The name was in Ireland by the 15th Century and continues to flourish in the Irish Counties of Antrim, Cavan, and Monaghan. See "Blackley," "Black," and "Bleakley."

BLAKEMAN: from the Old English words *blác* ('pale,' 'white,' or 'bleak') and *mann* ('man'), giving 'pale man,' or more freely, a 'fair-haired or fair-complexioned person.' Due to the Medieval confusion between *blác* ('light') and *blac* ('dark'), this surname has long been confused with its opposite, "Blackman" ('dark-haired or dark-complexioned person'). Hence, today many so-called Blackmans are actually Blakemans, while many so-called Blakemans are actually Blackmans.

BLAKENEE: a variation of "Blakeney," one used by 14th-Century "English" Blakeneys.

BLAKENEY: the subject of this book, it is a normalized, then anglicized, spelling form of a compound Danish Viking, dithematic, topographical place-name, deriving from the Old Norse *blæyken* ('pale' or 'bleak') and the Old Norse *ey*, meaning 'island.' Hence, *Blæyken-Ey*, then *Blaken-Ey*, then *Blakeney*; that is, 'Bleak Island.' No doubt the Danish Vikings coined the original place-name, *Blæykeney*, on account of the watery character of the land in and around Snitterly, the coastal Norfolk village they appropriated in the 9th Century, and which later became officially known as Blakeney. Confusion surrounds the surname Blakeney, primarily because it is a fossilized form whose original meaning ('bleak island') is obsolete and thus not generally known. Additionally, however, its core-word, blake (in Old English, *blác*, meaning 'white,' 'pale,' 'bleak,' 'fair,' 'glitter,' 'shine,' 'bleached,' etc.), has been mistakenly interchanged with a word that is both identical in spelling, though not in pronunciation, and with which it shares many of the same meanings: black (in Old English, *blac*, meaning 'black,' 'dark,' 'burnt,' 'sooty,' 'fiery,' 'blanched,' etc.). This confusion has imbued both the surname Blakeney and the place-name Blakeney with a false etymology, one wrongly linked to the color-word black. Correcting this erroneous etymology, which continues to stubbornly cling to the word-name Blakeney to this day, was one of my chief motivations for writing this book. See "Blake." True variants: Blakenee, Blakey, Blakeneye, Blakeny, Blaknee, Blakney, Bleakeny, Bleakney. False variants: Blackney, Blakely, Blakeley, Blakley.

BLAKENEYE: a variation of "Blakeney," one used by 14th-Century "English" Blakeneys.

BLAKENY: a variation of "Blakeney."

BLAKER: from the Middle English masculine word *blaker*, meaning 'bleacher'; thus indicating one who bleaches. Date first recorded: 1199, in a surname, *William de Blakestere*. Identical to, and thus having the same meaning as, the Middle English feminine surname "Blaxter." Blaker is often confused with "Blacker." (Note that the Dutch word *blaker* ('candlestick') is indeed linguistically related to the Middle English words *blaker* ('bleacher') and *blake* ('bleak,' 'white,' 'pale'). For the fire of a candle burns 'pale,' while the chemical constituents in bleach "*burn*" objects 'pale.')

BLAKESLEE: a variation of "Blakesley."

BLAKESLEY: a variation of "Blakeley." Some Blakesley family names, however, may derive from the place-name Blakesley, Northamptonshire County, England. (Note that the name of this town was recorded in the *Domesday Book* (1086) as *Blaculveslei*.) Date first recorded: 1199, as a surname, *William de Blakesle*. Variant: "Blaxley."

BLAKEWAY: from the Old English *blác* ('white') and the Old English *weg* ('way' or 'street'); thus 'pale or bleak road.' Here we have the same ancient confusion between *blác* ('white') and *blac* ('black'); hence the meaning itself, typically given as 'dark road,' is incorrect, though now generally accepted. Date first recorded: 1221, in a surname, *Hugo de Blakewey* ('Hugh of Pale Street').

BLAKEY: a corruption and/or shortening of "Blakeney." As such it has the identical meaning: 'Bleak Isle.' The original Old Norse spelling would have been *Blækeney*, which later devolved to *Blækey* in Old English. Mistakenly believed by some to have originally been a variation of both "Blackley" and Blakeney; due to Medieval and modern confusion, today it is. Date first recorded: 1388, in a surname, *Geoffrey de Blakey* ('Jeffrey of Bleak Island'). We also have the place-name, Blakey, North Riding Yorkshire County, England, where some Blakeys must have derived their surname.

BLAKLEY: a variation of "Blakeley." See also "Blackley."

BLAKELOCK: from the Old English *blác* ('white') and the Old English *locc* ('lock' of hair), giving 'fair-haired person.' Often confused with the surname "Blacklock," though this has the opposite meaning ('dark-haired one').

BLAKEMAN: from the Old English *blác* ('white') and the Old English *mann* ('man'), giving literally 'pale person'; or more freely, 'fair-haired or fair-complexioned person,' or perhaps 'bleak person' (that is, one who is perpetually sad or depressed). Blakeman is also sometimes a variant spelling of the surname "Blackman" ('dark-haired or dark-complexioned person'), causing genealogists much difficulty.

BLAKEMORE: from the Old English *blác* ('white') and the Old English *mor* ('boggy hill' or 'wasteland'), giving 'pale hilly bogland.' Often confused in both ancient and modern times with its opposite, "Blackmore" ('dark hilly bogland'), which includes the variant "Blackmoor."

BLAKINEY: an extremely rare variation of "Blakeney," found in the old Blakeney wills listed by John Burke. Example: 'Robert Blakiney, Esq., born 1660 in Gallagh, County Galway, Ireland' (*Burke's Wills*, A-K).

BLAKNEE: a variation of "Blakeney," one used by 14th-Century "English" Blakeneys.

BLAKNEY: a variation of "Blakeney."

BLAKSLEY: a variation of "Blakesley."

BLANKLEY: a corruption of the place-name, "Blankney," Lincolnshire County, England. Date first recorded: 1202, as a surname, *Simon de Blankeneia* ('Simon of the featureless island').

BLANKNEY: normally a place-name, not a surname, it has been included here because it seems to have given rise to the surname "Blankley," a distant cousin of "Blakeney." Blankney may be a nasalization of *blæca* ('black'), with the addition of the suffix *-ey*, meaning 'island.' If so, the second *-n* is the genitive singular, giving '*Blæca's Isle*'; that is, 'Black's Island.' If Blankney is not a nasalization of *blæca*, then we have *Blanca-n-ey*, meaning 'Blanca's Isle,' or 'the island of a person called Blanca.' More probably, however, the name derives from the town of Blankney in Lincolnshire County, England, whose etymology is formed on the word *blanc*, from the Old High German *blanch* ('blank' or 'white'), denoting something that is empty or nondescript. Hence the literal meaning of the place-name Blankney would be 'featureless island.' Blankney is listed as a place-name in the *Domesday Book* (1086) as *Blachene*; and is recorded again in 1157 as *Blancaneia*.

BLATCH: a palatal form of "Black," from the Old English *blac* ('black'). Date first recorded: 1164 as a surname, *Geoffrey le Blache* ('Jeffrey the Black').

BLATCHER: another variation of "Bleacher," and thus related to

"Blaker," and "Blakeney." Date first recorded: 1305, in a surname, *Robert le Blacchere* ('Robert the Bleacher'). See also "Blacker."

BLATCHMAN: a variant of "Blackman," also erroneously spelled "Blakeman," and thus often confused with the Blake name variations. Date first recorded: 1210, in a surname, *Stephen Blacheman* ('Stephen [the] Blackman'; that is, 'Stephen with the dark hair, or dark complexion').

BLAWICK: an Anglo-Irish form of the Irish surname *Ó Blathmhaic* (from the Gaelic word *blath*, 'fame'), originally from County Connacht, Ireland. It is included here because over the centuries it has sometimes mistakenly become "Blake." Its sibling form, "Blowick" (also confused with Blake), survives in Counties Mayo and Fermanagh, Ireland.

BLAXLEY: a variant of "Blakesley."

BLAXTER: the feminine form of, and identical in meaning to, "Blaker."

BLEACKNEY: an extremely rare variation of "Blakeney" used by some 18th-Century Irish and Canadian Blakeney families (for example, David Blakeney/Bleakney/Bleackney, of Belfast, Ireland).

BLEAK: a variation of "Blake" (and thus pronounced BLAKE), known in Northern Ireland, and sometimes confused with "Bleakney," a spelling form of "Blakeney."

BLEAKLEY: a variation of "Blakeley" (pronounced BLAKE-lee). See also "Blackley."

BLEAKNEY: a variation of the surname "Blakeney" (pronounced BLAKE-nee). See also "Bleackney" and "Blackley." Related to the surname "Bleak," which survives in Northern Ireland.

BLECKLEY: a variation of "Blakeley" (pronounced BLAKE-lee).

BLICK: a linguistic cousin of "Blake," this surname derives from the Old English *blician* ('to shine' or 'glitter'), which derives from the Old Norse *blika* ('to turn pale'), and this from the Old German *blik* ('pale'). All three of these ancient base-words aided in the formation of the *blake* words. Date first recorded: 1185, in a surname, *Aluin Blic* ('Alan [the] Bleak'; or more freely, 'Alan the melancholy one').

The Blakeneys

BLOWICK: an Anglo-Irish form of the Irish surname Ó Blathmhaic (from the Gaelic word *blath*, 'fame'), which emerged in County Connacht, Ireland. It is included here due to the fact that it has sometimes mistakenly transformed into "Blake." It is also spelled "Blawick."

CADDELL: from the early Norman French word *caudel* (a 'hot dark beverage'); included here because in County Galway, Ireland—where this surname is known from the 13th Century—it eventually became the surname "Blake." The reason for this curious transmutation is to be found, as the reader will have guessed by now, in the confusion between *blác* ('white,' 'fair,' or 'pale') and *blac* ('dark,' 'scorched,' or 'black'). Caddell is a Middle English form whose earliest ancestor words include the hypothetical Sanskrit *kal* ('dark' or 'burnt'), *Kali* (the name of the Hindu Mother-Goddess, whose name means 'dark'), the early Latin *calere* ('to be hot'), and *Cale* (the name of the Greek Fate-Goddess, whose name means 'fair'). These words, like the surname Caddell, are in turn related to such words as calorie ('heat'), cauldron (a large pot used for boiling), and caldera (a volcanic crater). The change from Caddell to Blake in Ireland probably occurred during one of this country's many periods under English or Norman rule, when it was safer, and at times even required by law, for an Irish person to possess an Anglo-Norman name. A logical choice for Irish Caddells would have been the Anglo-Norman surname Blake ('dark,' 'fair,' 'scorched,' etc.), which shares identical meanings with the surname Caddell ('dark,' 'hot,' 'fair,' 'burnt,' etc.). Surname variants: Cadell, Cadle, Cadwal (a Welsh form), Caudell, Caudill, Caudle, Cawdell, Cawdle, Cawdor (a Scottish form), Codill, Cordall, Cordell, Cordial, Cordill, Cordle, and Kaldel. (For a detailed examination of this surname, see my book, *The Caudills: An Etymological, Ethnological, and Genealogical Study.*)

De BLÁCA: an early Anglo-Irish spelling of the surname Blake, literally translated, 'of Bleak'; freely translated, 'dweller of the bleak region.' Owing to Medieval confusion between *blác* ('white' or 'bleak') and *blac* ('black' or 'dark'), *de Bláca* has also been confused with the surnames "Black," "Blawick," and "Blowick."

DeBLAKELAND: an Anglo-Danish Norman form of "Blakeney," with the identical meaning; literally one 'from/of the bleak land.' (*De* is French for 'of' or 'from'; *blake* is Germanic for 'pale'; and land (from the German, *lant*) is English for 'a region of open space.')

De BLAKNEE: an early variation of "de Blakeney," one used by 14th-Century "English" Blakeneys.

Le BLÁCA: an early Anglo-Irish spelling of the surname Blake, literally translated, 'the Bleak'; freely translated, 'dweller from the bleak region.' Owing to Medieval confusion between *blác* ('white' or 'bleak') and *blac* ('black' or 'dark'), *le Bláca* has in turn been confused with the surnames "Black," "Blawick," and "Blowick."

Ó BLATHMHAIC: an Irish surname (from the Gaelic word *blath*, 'fame'), which was anglicized to the surnames "Blawick" and "Blowick," both of which were, and continue to be, occasionally confused with the surname "Blake."

Surnames have not been the only casualty stemming from the confusion between *blác* ('white') and *blac* ('black'). As we can see from the list below, many place-names too began as *blác*/blake words only to end up as *blac*/black words. Among these we have:

BLACKAWTON (Devonshire County, England), meaning 'dark-soiled farm of someone called Afa,' was spelled *Blakeauetone* in 1281. This, the earlier spelling, would have given the opposite meaning: 'pale-soiled farm of someone named Afa.'

BLACKDEN (HEATH) (Cheshire County, England), meaning 'dark valley,' was spelled *Blakedene* in 1287. This, the earlier spelling, would have given the opposite meaning: 'pale valley.'

BLACKFORDBY (Leicestershire County, England), meaning 'farmstead on the dark river-crossing,' was spelled *Blakefordebi* in 1125. This, the earlier spelling, would have given the opposite meaning: 'pale river-crossing.'

BLACKLAND (Wiltshire County, England), meaning 'dark land,' was spelled *Blakeland* in 1194. This, the earlier spelling, would have given the opposite meaning: 'pale land.'

BLACKLEY (Greater Manchester, England), meaning 'dark clearing,' was spelled *Blakeley* in 1282. This, the earlier spelling, would have given the opposite meaning: 'pale clearing.'

BLACKMORE (Essex County, England), meaning 'dark bog,' was spelled *Blakemore* in 1213. This, the earlier spelling, would have given the opposite meaning: 'pale bog.'

BLACKTHORN (Oxfordshire County, England), meaning 'dark thorn[bush],' was spelled *Blaketorn* in 1190. This, the earlier spelling, would have given the opposite meaning: 'pale thorn[bush].'

BLACKTOFT (East Riding Yorkshire, England), meaning 'dark homestead,' was spelled *Blaketofte* in 1160. This, the earlier spelling, would have given the opposite meaning: 'pale home-stead.'

BLACKWELL (Durham County, England), meaning 'dark stream,' was spelled *Blakewell* in 1183. This, the earlier spelling, would have given the opposite meaning: 'pale stream.'

Other place-names continue to be spelled with the blake prefix, but their meanings have been confused with the Old English color-word *blac* ('black'), and so are now incorrectly defined in reference books pertaining to toponyms. Examples of this type of place-name include:

BLAKEMERE (Herefordshire and Worcestershire Counties, England), meaning 'pale-colored water,' is now incorrectly defined as 'dark-colored water.'

BLAKENHALL (Cheshire County, England), meaning 'pale recess of land,' is now incorrectly defined as 'dark recess of land.'

BLAKENHAM (Great and Little) (Suffolk County, England), meaning 'pale or bleached-looking homestead,' is now incorrectly defined as 'dark-looking homestead.'

BLAKESLEY (Northamptonshire County, England), meaning 'pale or bleak clearing,' is now incorrectly defined as 'dark clearing.'

The place-name Blakeney (Gloucestershire and Norfolk Counties, England) itself, a major focal point of this book, has lost its original meaning as well. Based on our comprehensive study, we have seen that it clearly means 'pale isle,' or 'bleak island.' However, the typical English place-name book gives the meaning as 'dark-colored island,' or even more inaccurately as 'boggy land of a man called Black.'

28

An Enduring Name, an Enduring Family

espite the process of language modernization and the ever increasing mobility of contemporary society, the specific spelling form *Blakeney* has remained essentially unchanged for some 700 years. If we discount the old European preposition, '*de*', the Blakeney spelling has been in existence for at least 1,000 years, reinforcing the fact that topographical names, like Blakeney, are among the oldest and most stable types of place-names in England.

Even after its 400- (or possibly 800-)[132] year sojourn in Ireland,[133] and its 250-year stay in North America,[134] the form Blakeney

---

[132] For more on the theory that the Blakeneys have been in Ireland since the 12th Century, see Chapter 25.

[133] Thomas and Henry Blakeney, sons of Launcelot Blakeney (of Norfolk County, England), were the first known Blakeneys from Norfolk to settle in County Limerick and County Galway, Ireland—in the early 1600s.

[134] In 1737 an (English) Irishman, Lord William Blakeney Blakeney, became the first *known* Blakeney to arrive on America's shores (though he did not remain). But we will note here that there may have been, and almost certainly were, Blakeneys in the Americas prior to Lord Blakeney. However, of these we currently have no record.

is still found all over the world, intact and spelled in the ancient way. [135]

Little wonder that this topographical word-name has endured for a millennium or more, and that philologists refer to such words as "linguistic fossils." The roots of the Blakeney name lie deep in the prehistoric linguistic soil of Asia (*phleg* and *bhleg*), with early forms having been documented in both ancient Greece (*phlégein*) and Rome (*flagrare*).

As it moved up through Europe, it was embraced by Iron Age Germanic-speaking peoples (*blaikos, blaiko, blaik,*), until it made its way through Scandinavia (*bleikja, bleyken, blayken, blaken-ey*), and on into England (*blác, blæce, bleyke, blayke, blaken*), then France—where it was first used as a surname (*de Blacheneia*), back to England (*de Blakenye, de*

---

[135] Though it is not necessarily rare for a surname to endure for a millennium, the durability and longevity of the name and spelling form Blakeney still astonishes; especially when we consider that throughout most of the last 1,000 years of European history surnames were not seen as immutable, legally binding and obligatory family designations, as they are today. Quite the contrary. Our Medieval ancestors looked upon surnames as little more than convenient and temporary labels that could, and often were, changed at the slightest whim. So low was the opinion of the surname that parents thought nothing of giving their children different surnames than their own. Even when the parents' surname was passed down (called hereditary surnaming), children would often freely alter the spelling. Thus it was not uncommon for each member of a 14th-Century family to have spelled its surname differently. (This custom was also practiced by American families of European descent well into the 19th Century. For example, one of my ancestral families, surnamed Jans (Dutch for 'John' or more literally 'John's', but pronounced "Yonz "), a Dutch/German family from Oberalben, Rheinland-Pfalz, Germany, that settled in eastern Kentucky, spelled their Americanized surname at least seven different ways in only one generation: Yonts, Yonce, Yance, Yontz, Younts, Younce, and Yants. Note: I have uncovered a total of nearly 150 different spelling variations of the Jans surname, which originally derives from the Dutch matronymic Janassen ('Jane's son') and the Dutch patronymic Janssen ('John's son'). Janassen/Janssen was later shortened to Janss, then Jans, which in America was pronounced and spelled phonetically as "Yonts".) The modern mind can scarcely comprehend the fluid nature of the surnaming system (as well as of surnames themselves) as it was engaged in by our Medieval relations. For one thing, there were no laws regarding name changes, so one could legally modify, drop, or add a surname as easily as changing clothes. Behind this indifference was the fact that the very idea of a hereditary family name was quite foreign to most people of this period. A surname was merely whatever an individual felt suited her or his particular needs at that moment. This helps explain the ease with which purely English families often adopted French surnames, and the nonchalance with which purely French families often adopted English surnames, after the Norman Invasion of England. It also helps us to understand why early Celtic families did not hesitate to adopt the name of their clan as their own; why families would sometimes change their surnames for money—as the Scottish Bissets did (when they changed their surname to Fraser); or why families would not hesitate to translate their surnames from one language or culture to another (as when the Scottish Maceachrains became the "English" Cochranes, or when the Irish MacSeáins became the "English" Johnsons). Hence, from almost any viewpoint the long survival of the Blakeney name and spelling form must be seen as something of a linguistic miracle.

Blakenia, Blakeney), Ireland, and finally to the Americas and beyond.[136]

When the Danish Vikings first set sail from the shores of Thule in the late 700s for England, little could they have known that they would be remembered for something other than their daring overthrow of lands as diverse as Ireland, Asia Minor (Antioch), Turkey (Constantinople), Wales, Friesland, Germany, Russia, France, and Sicily.

For after nearly fourteen centuries their violent sea-warring legacy still lives on in the names of not only thousands of families, but also in the names of dozens of roads, towns, peninsulas, castles, and mountains (and even pottery), around the world. All from two ancient and obscure Old Norse words meaning 'bleak' and 'island.'

---

[136] Obviously, the latter half of this lineage was not as simplistic as this portrayal suggests, nor could this have been the exact evolutionary path of the surname Blakeney. The name no doubt appeared in various non-European and non-Western countries before it emerged in the Americas, for example. However, I have used this time line for the convenience of the reader, who is most likely of Western heritage.

Appendices

Appendix A

THE WATERY CHARACTER OF BLAKENEY, NORFOLK

The following text, promoting Blakeney Point, Norfolk, illustrates the profound *watery character* of the area, reinforcing why, according to my theory, the early Danish invaders of East Anglia would have given the nearby village of Snitterly the name Blakeney; that is, *Bleak Isle*.

> "Blakeney Point is the name given to the five and a half kilometre sand and shingle spit on the north coast of Norfolk, close to the villages of Cley, Morston and Blakeney. Owned by the National Trust, the Point has a variety of seashore habitats, including dunes, salt marshes, mud flats and the shingle ridge.

> "A wide range of birds can be found on Blakeney Point. There is a large colony of Sandwich Terns, and Common, Arctic and Little Terns are also found there. Oystercatchers and Ringed Plovers can be found on the mudflats. Brent Geese are amongst the winter visitors.

> "Amongst the plants, sea lavender is one of the most striking, with its bright purple colour in July. At the end of the Point, Common and Grey Seals haul themselves out to bask in the sun when the tide goes out.

> "Ferries to the Point can be caught from Morston or from Blakeney, but the ones from Blakeney depend on the tide. It is also possible to make the walk out to the Point along the shingle ridge from Cley beach. A National Trust warden looks after the Point.

> "Blakeney Point has a range of coastal habitats. The

long shingle ridge has been built up by longshore drift. The mudflats are covered twice each day by the sea as the tide goes in and out. The sand dunes gradually build as droppings from the birds and other natural materials enable marram grass to establish itself and capture sand—until a storm comes and moves or destroys the dune. The salt marshes are covered by the tides and have their own special types of vegetation.

"Blakeney Point illustrates dunes in all stages of creation and destruction , from embryo dunes beginning to form around driftwood, seaweed and vegetation, through to 'grey' dunes which have been established for many years and decaying vegetation has begun to change the colour of the sand.

"On the salt marshes, the type of vegetation varies, according to how long a particular zone is under the water in the course of each day. Calm and sheltered areas allow vegetation to gather tidal mud and gradually the vegetation itself begins to build up the marsh. Salt-pans can also be seen, where trapped tidal water evaporates, to build up a layer of salt.

"On the outside of the Point, the pebble ridge built up by the longshore drift can be seen. The drift naturally sorts sizes and types of pebbles. As with the dunes, dramatic changes can take place in times of storm. The whole coast of Norfolk is also affected by the many human factors, such as coastal defence works.

"There is an Information Centre for Blakeney Point at Morston Quay. There is restricted access to some areas on the point during the nesting season. The warden can be contacted from April to September on 01263

THE BLAKENEYS

740480, and from October to March on 01328
830401. If you are calling from outside the UK, dial
+44 and omit the initial 0, e.g., +44 263 740480."[137]

---

[137] Cited with the kind permission of *Anglia Multimedia* (Website: www.anglia.co.uk), who retains the copyright to the complete text.

Appendix B

Blakeney family members and/or Blakeney researchers may be interested in

THE BLAKENEY/BLAKLEY FAMILY ASSOCIATION (BFA)

whose objects are:

1. To develop, maintain and perpetuate the Association.

2. To pursue cultural purposes by collecting and disseminating information related to the Family. Collect and preserve literary, historical and genealogical records, documents and relics relating to the Family. Encourage reunions, gatherings and other functions to strengthen the bonds of kinship and to seek and foster kinship throughout the Family wherever they may be.

3. To acquire real and personal property and to use and supply such property to the realization of the objects of the Association.

Membership is open to all those whose surname is the same or similar to Blakeney, Blakney, Blakeny, Blakeley, Blakely, Bleakney, Bleakley, Blakley, Bleckley, Blackley, Blaikley, Blakeslee, and others.

Membership is open to any other person directly connected by marriage with or descended from a person of similar surname to the above or any other party interested in the family heritage. The members of the BFA do not all claim direct relationship to each other but rather consider themselves a *clan*.

The Blakeney motto is *Auxilium Meum Ab Alto*, "My Help Comes From Above." The BFA is responsible for assisting in the maintenance of monuments to Blakeney ancestors, such as plaques, memorials, stained glass windows, buildings and the promotion of literature and genealogies, as well.

For more information, contact the BFA at:

The Blakeney/Blakley Family Association
P.O. Box 2113
Dartmouth, Nova Scotia
Canada B2W 3X8

Appendix C

Blakeney family members and/or Blakeney researchers may also be interested in

THE CASTLEBLAKENEY
DEVELOPMENT COMMITTEE (CDC)

which is in the process of restoring the ancient Parish Church of Castleblakeney, Ireland (the village of Castleblakeney was originally known as Castle Gallagh).

The Parish Church of Castleblakeney appears to have been built in Killasoolan, Ireland, sometime in the 15th Century. It was later moved stone by stone (using carts and horses) to Castleblakeney under the direction of one Robert Blakeney in February 1711.

Note: This "Robert Blakeney", as well as an "Edward Blakeney", are listed as members of "the Church Vestry and Church Wardens" in the Church records of 1711. Who were they? It would appear that this particular Robert is Colonel Robert Blakeney, born about 1672 in Castleblakeney, died May 5, 1733, who married Sarah Ormsby. Robert was the son of John Blakeney (b. 1649 in Castleblakeney) and Sarah Persse. Concerning this particular Edward, he appears to be Robert's uncle, Lieutenant Edward Blakeney, born in 1659 in Castleblakeney, who married Deborah Stanton. Edward was the son of Sheriff Robert Blakeney and Elizabeth Rogers.

Today's Castleblakeney Development Committee began restoration on the church on April 8, 1999. When they began, the church was barely recognizable, having no floor, no windows, and no roof.

For more information on the CDC and their efforts, goals, and achievements (and how you can help), please contact:

Valerie A. Kinsella (Treasurer)
Gallagh
Castleblakeney Heritage Centre
County Ballinsloe, Ireland

(The CDC, along with the Castleblakeney Heritage Centre, welcomes both visitors and contributions.)

Appendix D

THE BLAKENEY HOTEL
Blakeney, Norfolk, England

Planning a trip to Norfolk? Please consider a stay at the beautiful Blakeney Hotel (pictured on the cover of this book).

CONTACT INFORMATION
The Blakeney Hotel
The Quay, Blakeney
Nr. Holt, Norfolk NR25 7NE
Tel: +44 (10)1263 740797
Fax: +44 (10)1263 740795
Email: enquiries@blakeneyhotel.co.uk
Website: www.blakeney-hotel.co.uk

The Blakeney Hotel, in Blakeney, Norfolk County, England. Our English Blakeney ancestors—who were Danish emigres from 11th-Century Normandy—named, then later took their surname from, this pleasant village near the North Sea. It is from here that our earliest traceable English Blakeneys derive (in the mid 1100s).

Appendix E

Article on
Lord Baron William Blakeney Blakeney (1672-1761)

From the Stirling Library, Stirling, Scotland
(author unknown)

LORD WILLIAM BLAKENEY BLAKENEY (1672-1761), the defender of Minorca, was an Irishman of English descent, and was born at Mount Blakeney in the county of Limerick in 1672. His father [Captain William Blakeney of Mount Blakeney, Ireland] was a fairly wealthy country gentleman, and represented the borough of Kilmallock in the Irish House of Commons for many years, and expected his eldest son to lead the same life as himself.

But young William Blakeney caught the martial enthusiasm of the Revolution period, and organized a small military force in 1690, when only eighteen, out of his father's tenants, with which he kept the

Repparees at bay, and defended the paternal estate. He was permitted to join the army in Flanders as a volunteer, and won his ensigncy at the siege of Venloo in 1702.

He served throughout the campaigns of Marlborough as adjutant of his regiment, and is said to have first exercised regiments by the beating of drums and waving of colours, and even to have once exercised the whole allied army in this way before certain German princes.

After the peace of Utrecht came a long period of peace, during which promotion went by favour and by court or parliamentary influence, which Blakeney did not possess, so that he was an old man of sixty-five when he was at last promoted colonel in 1737. During this long period he always remained with his regiment, taking a fatherly interest in both officers and men, and never going on leave or running after promotion.

This long neglect was said to be due to the misrepresentations of Lord Verney; but the Duke of Richmond, when appointed colonel of his regiment, at last took notice of him, and obtained him a command in the expedition to Carthagena, with the rank of brigadier-general, in 1741.

His services were highly appreciated, and by the aid of the same powerful patron he was promoted major-general in 1744, and made lieutenant-governor of Stirling Castle. The Scottish insurrection of 1745 gave him his opportunity.

The highlanders besieged Stirling Castle, and Blakeney, to keep them from joining the main body, allowed them to raise siege works for some weeks. When, however, these siege works became formidable, he ordered a sudden attack on the highlanders, who were utterly defeated and lost three hundred men.

His good service was not forgotten by George II, who promoted him major-general in 1745, lieutenant-general in 1747, and lieutenant-governor of the island of Minorca. He at once went to Minorca, and as

Lord Tyrawley, the governor, preferred stopping at home, Blakeney was left in chief command for ten years.

He earnestly pressed for more men, and for money for repairs. But the ministry of Pelham and Newcastle grudged money not spent in maintaining their parliamentary majority, and neglected his entreaties.

On the breaking out of the Seven Years' War in 1756 an expedition was hurriedly despatched from France under the debauchee Duc de Richelieu and Admiral la Galissonniere against Minorca. The French government well knew how the defences of Minorca had been neglected, and that a rapid attack before reinforcements could reach the garrison must be successful. Blakeney knew also that without reinforcements he could not hold out long, but determined to wait resolutely for those reinforcements.

When Admiral Byng retreated all hope was lost, and Blakeney after seventy days defence of an almost indefensible fortress, surrendered on the honourable terms that his garrison was to be transported to Gibraltar, and not made prisoners of war.

The gallant defence of Minorca had greatly excited the minds of the English people, and the veteran of eighty-four, who had never gone to bed for seventy days, was as popular as Admiral Byng was execrated.

After giving truthful evidence at Byng's trial as to the state of Minorca, Blakeney received great honours from George II, and was made a knight of the Bath, colonel of the Enniskillen regiment of infantry, and finally Lord Blakeney of Mount Blakeney in the peerage of Ireland.

He was M.P. for Kilmallock 1725-1757. His popularity continued unabated; a statue of him by Van Nost was erected in Dublin; and when he died, on 20 Sept. 1761, at the age of eighty-nine, he was buried, amidst general mourning, in Westminster Abbey.[138]

Blakeney was a soldier of the soldiers, always living among them, enjoying his punch as well as any of them, and beloved by them. In his family relations he was always exemplary; he used to live on his pay, and to allow his brothers to live on his estate of Mount Blakeney. One brother swindled him grossly; but he made no change in his arrangements, and merely transferred his estate to another brother.

---

[138] My note: Lord Blakeney's statue no longer stands. It was violently torn down during the Easter Week Rebellion of 1916, a famous insurrection proudly known to Irish Republicans as *Éirí Amach na Cásca*. This act is not surprising. Many native Dubliners viewed the Blakeneys as foreigners, invaders, and usurpers of Irish land, honor, and pride. (This same view is still held by many toward Yankees, that is, Northerners, in America's Southern states.)

Appendix F

A BLAKENEY FAMILY TREE
24 Generations

The Descendants of
Willihelm de Blakenia (William Blakeney)

(born about 1150)

IMPORTANT NOTES

This tree was compiled, edited, and written by Lochlainn Seabrook, based on:

- His own research
- *Burke's Landed Gentry of Ireland*
- John Oscar Blakeney's *The Blakeneys in America and Some Collaterals*
- "The Pedigree of the Blakeneys, 1277-1887," commissioned by William G. Blakeney in 1963 (England)
- Contributions from others (noted in bibliography whenever possible)

- Despite careful attention to detail, like all family trees, this one too is not only unfinished, but also contains errors, omissions, and a certain amount of unproven data. Therefore consider this tree incomplete and partially inaccurate. Please seek your own authentic documentation and supporting evidence.
- The individuals in this tree are *not* included in the Index.

WARNING!

This genealogical information is for private personal use only. Under no circumstances may any of this material be used for commercial or monetary purposes, which is strictly forbidden by law. For more information please contact the copyright holder, Lochlainn Seabrook.

KEY TO UNDERSTANDING THE FAMILY TREE

• The number in front of each name indicates the generation.

• A "+" sign in front of a name indicates the spouse (or mate) of the person listed above them.

• The numbers in brackets—for example, [127]—before some of the names should be disregarded as they are part of my personal filing system.

Descendants of William Blakeney
(Willihelm de Blakenia)

24 Generations

1 William Blakeney, (Willihelm de Blakenia) b: Abt. 1150 in Norfolk?, England Number of children: 1 Gender: Male (Notes: original spelling of his name was probably "Willihelm de Blakenia," or perhaps "Guillaume de Blakeneye"; he's the earliest traceable Blakeney; he descends from the Blakeneys of Normandy, who first settled in the town now known as Blakeney, Norfolk, UK).

...+_____ _____? b: Abt. 1155 Number of children: 1 Gender: Female

.2 _____ Blakeney b: Abt. 1170 Number of children: 1 Gender: Male

..+ _____ _____? b: Abt. 1172 Gender: Female

3 _____ Blakeney b: Abt. 1190 in Norfolk?, England Number of children: 1 Gender: Male

+_____ _____? b: Abt. 1195 Number of children: 1 Gender: Female

..4 _____ Blakeney b: Abt. 1215 in Norfolk?, England Number of children: 1 Gender: Male

..+_____ _____? b: Abt. 1220 Number of children: 1 Gender: Female

..5 _____ Blakeney b: Abt. 1240 in Norfolk?, England Number of children: 1 Gender: Male

..+_____ _____? b: Abt. 1245 Number of children: 1 Gender: Female

.6 Simon Blakeney, Lord of Bokenham Manor b: Abt. 1260 in Norfolk?, England Number of children: 2 Gender: Male (Notes: he may have spelled his last name "de Blakeney"; he was Lord of Bokenham Manor in 1277).

.+_____ _____? b: Abt. 1270 Number of children: 2 Gender: Female

.7 William Blakeney, Bailiff of Norwich b: Abt. 1295 in Norfolk?, England Number of children: 1 Gender: Male (Notes: he may have spelled his last name "de Blakeney", "de Blakney", "de Blaknee", "de Blakeneye"; he was Bailiff of Norwich from 1339 to 1355).

.+_____ _____? b: Abt. 1300 Number of children: 1 Gender: Female

.8 Nicholas Blakeney, Bailiff of Norwich b: Abt. 1315 in Norfolk?, England Number of children: 1 Gender: Male (Notes: he may have spelled his last name "de Blakeney"; he was Bailiff of

Norwich from 1364 to 1379).

.+_____ _____? b: Abt. 1320 Number of children: 1 Gender: Female

9   Nicholas Blakeney, Bailiff of Norwich b: Abt. 1340 in Norfolk?, England Number of children: 1 Gender: Male (Notes: he may have spelled his last name "de Blakenee"; he was Bailiff of Norwich from 1386 to 1392).

+_____ _____? b: Abt. 1345 Number of children: 1 Gender: Female

10 John Blakeney, Rector & Lord of Bodham Haxworth b: Abt. 1365 in Norfolk?, England Number of children: 1 Gender: Male (Notes: he was Rector & Lord of Bodham Haxworth in 1385).

+_____ _____? b: Abt. 1370 Number of children: 1 Gender: Female

..11 John Blakeney b: Abt. 1420 in Norfolk?, England Number of children: 1 Gender: Male (Notes: he was driven from the court of King Henry VI in 1451).

..+_____ _____? b: Abt. 1425 m: Abt. 1445 Number of children: 1 Gender: Female

..12 John Blakeney b: Abt. 1455 in Norfolk?, England d: 1515 Number of children: 1 Gender: Male (Notes: John has a memorial plate in Honingham Church).

..+Elizabeth _____? b: Abt. 1455 m: Abt. 1475 Number of children: 1 Gender: Female

..13 Thomas Blakeney, Lord, of Horford Hall b: Abt. 1485 in Norfolk?, England Number of children: 1 Gender: Male (Notes: he was Lord of Horford Hall in 1507, and also of Waterhouse Hall Manor and Buttorts Hall Manor).

..+Elizabeth _____? b: Abt. 1490 m: Abt. 1519 Number of children: 1 Gender: Female

.14 John Blakeney, Lord, of Horford Hall b: Abt. 1520 in Norfolk?, England Number of children: 3 Gender: Male (Notes: he was Lord of Horford Hall in 1546 and part of Stewkey Hall in 1551).

.+Anne Giggs b: Abt. 1530 in of Stewkey Hall, Sparham, Norfolk, England m: Abt. 1554 Number of children: 3 Gender: Female (Note: Looking for her ancestors)

.15 Launcelot Blakeney b: Abt. 1555 in Sparham, Norfolk County England? d: Aft. 1585 in England? Number of children: 2

Gender: Male

.+Grisell Cantroll b: Abt. 1560 in of Stanhorst (Norfolk County?), England. m: 1583 d: 1632 in Sparham, Norfolk County England Number of children: 2 Gender: Female (Note: Looking for her ancestors)

16 Thomas Blakeney, Gov. of Castle Neemund N. Ireland b: 1584 in Stanhow (Norfolk County?), England. d: Aft. 1655 in Mount Blakeney, Ireland? Number of children: 7 Gender: Male (Notes: the city of Thomastown, County Kilkenny, Ireland, is named after him).

+Sarah Hatton b: Abt. 1600 in England or Ireland? m: Abt. 1620 d: Aft. 1630 in Ireland? Number of children: 7 Father: Chancellor Hatton, Lord Mother: _____ _____? Gender: Female

17 [1] Robert "the Soldier" Blakeney, Major b: Abt. 1625 in County Limerick, Ireland, or Northern Ireland d: Abt. 1660 in Castleblakeney, County Galway, Ireland? Number of children: 4 Gender: Male (Notes: he purchased Castle Blakeney).

+Martha Bolton b: Abt. 1630 in Ireland Gender: Female

*2nd Wife of [1] Robert "the Soldier" Blakeney, Major:

+Katherine Kelk, Kelke b: Abt. 1625 m: Abt. 1645 Father: Colonel Kelk, Kelke Mother: _____ _____? Gender: Female

*3rd Wife of [1] Robert "the Soldier" Blakeney, Major:

+Susannah Ormsby b: Abt. 1625 in Tobervaddy, County Roscommon, Ireland m: Abt. 1647 in Ireland d: September 29, 1659 in Dublin (?), Ireland Number of children: 4 Father: Edward Ormsby, Captain Mother: _____ _____? Gender: Female Burial: St. Michael's Church, Dublin, Ireland

18 John Blakeney b: 1649 in Castle Blakeney, County Galway, or Dublin (?), Ireland d: 1691 Number of children: 6 Gender: Male

..+Sarah Persse b: Abt. 1650 in Roxborough, County Galway (?), Ireland m: 1671 in Ireland Number of children: 6 Father: Dudley Persse, Very Reverend Mother: _____ _____? Gender: Female

..19 Robert Blakeney, Colonel & MP, Castle Blakeney Line b: Abt.

1672 in Castle Blakeney (?), County Galway, Ireland d: May 05, 1733 Number of children: 8 Gender: Male (Note: the New England Blakeneys descend directly from Robert, who himself begins what has come to be known as the Irish "Castle Blakeney Line")

..+Sarah Ormsby b: Abt. 1682 in Tobervaddy, County Roscommon (?), Ireland m: Abt. June 22, 1702 Number of children: 8 Father: Gilbert Ormsby, Colonel Mother: _____ _____? Gender: Female

..20 John Blakeney, Colonel & MP b: Abt. 1703 in County Galway (?), Ireland d: July 21, 1747 in Abbert, County Galway, Ireland Number of children: 7 Gender: Male

..+Grace Persse b: Abt. 1700 in Roxborough, County Galway (?), Ireland m: Abt. 1720 Number of children: 7 Father: Henry Persse, Colonel Mother: _____ _____? Gender: Female

.21 [83] Robert Blakeney, Colonel b: Abt. 1720 in Abbert, County Galway (?), Ireland d: December 30, 1762 in Ireland? Number of children: 2 Gender: Male (Notes: Robert & Gertrude were cousins).

.+[82] Gertrude Blakeney b: Abt. 1734 in Ireland? m: May 28, 1752 in Ireland? d: April 21, 1757 in Ireland? Number of children: 2 Father: Robert Blakeney, Esquire & MP Mother: Deborah Smythe Gender: Female (Notes: Gertrude & Robert were cousins).

.22 [84] Grace Blakeney b: Abt. December 1755 in Abbert, County Galway (?), Ireland d: Aft. 1787 Number of children: 1 Gender: Female

.+[85] Thomas Lyon, Esquire b: Abt. 1755 in Watercastle, Queen's County (?) m: May 09, 1786 Number of children: 1 Gender: Male

.23 [86] _____ Lyon b: Abt. 1787 Gender: Female

.22 [87] John Blakeney, Lieutenant b: September 12, 1756 in Abbert, County Galway, Ireland? d: August 23, 1781 Gender: Male (Notes: he died unmarried).

.21 Martha Blakeney b: Abt. 1722 Gender: Female

.+M. Brown, Esquire b: Abt. 1720 Gender: Male

.21 Theophilus Bolton Blakeney, Captain b: Abt. 1725 in Abbert, County Galway (?), Ireland d: September 22, 1813 Number of children: 7 Gender: Male

.+Margaret Stafford (she probably descends from European royalty) b: Abt. 1750 in of Stephen's Green, Dublin (or Gillstown, County Roscommon?), Ireland m: December 1782 Number of children: 7 Father: John Stafford (Looking for John's ancestors) Mother: _____ _____? Gender: Female

.22 Bridget Blakeney b: Abt. 1783 in Abbert, County Galway (?), Ireland d: December 1866 Number of children: 7 Gender: Female

.+Richard Bligh Saint George, Baronet b: Abt. 1785 in Ireland? m: April 1807 d: December 29, 1851 Number of children: 7 Gender: Male

.23 _____ Saint George b: Abt. 1807 Gender: Female

.23 _____ Saint George b: Abt. 1808 Gender: Male

.23 _____ Saint George b: Abt. 1809 Gender: Female

.23 _____ Saint George b: Abt. 1810 Gender: Male

.23 _____ Saint George b: Abt. 1813 Gender: Female

.23 _____ Saint George b: Abt. 1815 Gender: Male

.23 _____ Saint George b: Abt. 1818 Gender: Male

.22 Grace Blakeney b: Abt. 1785 d: Abt. 1786 Gender: Female (Notes: she died young).

.22 Margaret Blakeney b: Abt. 1787 in Fitzwilliam Place, Dublin (?), Ireland Number of children: 1 Gender: Female

.+John O'Dwyer, Esquire b: Abt. 1785 in Dublin (?), Ireland m: 1817 in Dublin (?), Ireland Number of children: 1 Gender: Male

.23 _____ O'Dwyer b: Abt. 1818 Gender: Unknown

.22 Elizabeth Blakeney b: Abt. 1788 Gender: Female

.+Charles (de) Hugo, Captain b: Abt. 1785 in France? m: 1825 Gender: Male

.22 John Henry Blakeney b: January 06, 1790 in Abbert, County Galway (?), Ireland d: November 17, 1858 Number of children: 12 Gender: Male

.+Charlotte Ross Mahon b: Abt. 1790 in Ireland m: July 01, 1813 d: August 09, 1865 Number of children: 12 Father: Ross Mahon, Sir & Baronet Mother: _____ _____? Gender: Female

.23 Harriette Anne Blakeney b: 1815 d: March 06, 1903 Gender: Female

+William Henry Crossmaker b: Abt. 1830 in Westwood, Surrey County England Gender: Male

.23 Elizabeth Margaret Blakeney b: Abt. 1816 in England? d: February 14, 1892 Gender: Female

+Albenarle Cator, (or Cater), Esquire b: Abt. 1830 in Woodbastwick Hall, Norfolk County England m: April 24, 1834 d: May 01, 1868 in England? Gender: Male

.23 Sarah Blakeney b: Abt. 1817 d: October 30, 1905 Gender: Female

.23 Robert Blakeney, Major b: Abt. 1819 in Abbert, County Galway (?), Ireland d: June 20, 1902 Number of children: 5 Gender: Male

+Mary Sophia (Flower) Ashbrooke, Honorable b: Abt. 1830 in Ireland or England? m: Abt. 1860 d: April 17, 1886 Number of children: 5 Father: Viscount Ashbrooke Mother: _____ _____? Gender: Female

24 Henry Ross Blakeney b: April 02, 1862 in Abbert, County Galway (?), Ireland Gender: Male

24 Frederick Robert Blakeney b: May 16, 1863 in Abbert, County Galway (?), Ireland, or London, England d: March 29, 1914 in Victoria, British Columbia, Canada Gender: Male Burial: Ross Bay Cemetery, Victoria, British Columbia, Canada; web site: http://www.oldcem.bc.ca/

+Laura _____ b: 1873 in Ireland or England m: Abt. 1890 d: in Victoria, British Columbia, Canada Gender: Female Burial: Ross Bay Cemetery, Victoria, British Columbia, Canada

24 Frances Alice Blakeney b: Abt. 1865 in Abbert, County Galway (?), Ireland d: October 04, 1889 Gender: Female

24 Beatrice Maria Blakeney b: Abt. 1867 in Abbert, County Galway (?), Ireland d: April 27, 1899 Gender: Female

24 Ernest Cecil Blakeney b: June 29, 1869 in Abbert, County Galway

(?), Ireland Gender: Male

.23 Mary Gertrude Blakeney b: Abt. 1821 in England? d: July 03, 1893 Gender: Female

.23 Louisa Elizabeth Blakeney b: Abt. 1823 in England? d: March 20, 1894 Gender: Female

.23 Margaret Blakeney b: Abt. 1825 Gender: Female

.23 [2] John Blakeney, Lieutenant b: October 1826 in Abbert, County Galway (?), Ireland d: 1901 Number of children: 7 Gender: Male

+Francis "Fanny" Burke b: Abt. 1830 in Isserchleron, County Galway (?), Ireland m: Abt. 1850 Number of children: 5 Father: James Hardiman Burke Mother: _____ _____? Gender: Female

24 Frances "Fanny" Blakeney b: Abt. 1850 in Abbert, County Galway (?), Ireland d: March 17, 1931 Gender: Female

+Gilbert Mahon b: Abt. 1850 in Ireland m: March 19, 1895 d: January 02, 1947 Father: William Vesey Ross Mahon, Sir Mother: _____ _____? Gender: Male

24 John Theophilus Blakeney b: January 31, 1855 in Abbert, County Galway (?), Ireland. d: January 16, 1905 in Ireland? Gender: Male

24 Mary Blakeney b: Abt. 1857 in Abbert, County Galway (?), Ireland d: December 10, 1921 Number of children: 6 Gender: Female

+John Octavius Coussmaker, Reverend b: Abt. 1855 in Ireland? m: April 28, 1881 d: May 08, 1923 Number of children: 6 Gender: Male

24 Robert Edward Blakeney b: 1858 in Abbert, County Galway (?), Ireland d: Bef. 1941 in Ireland? Gender: Male

+Katherine (Everleigh) Batt b: Abt. 1860 in Cae Kenfy, Abergavenny, Monmouthshire, Wales m: 1897 d: September 22, 1941 Father: William Batt Mother: _____ _____? Gender: Female

24 Anne Blakeney b: Abt. 1860 in Abbert, County Galway (?), Ireland Gender: Female

.*2nd Wife of [2] John Blakeney, Lieutenant:

+Joanna Isabella Blake b: Abt. 1830 in The Heath, County Mayo (?), Ireland m: 1873 in Ireland? Number of children: 2 Father:

THE BLAKENEYS

Henry Martin Blake Mother: _____ _____? Gender: Female

24 Henry Robert William Blakeney b: Abt. 1875 in Abbert, County Galway (?), Ireland Gender: Male

+Aileen Mary Armstrong b: Abt. 1875 in Ireland? m: April 29, 1905 Father: George R. Armstrong Mother: _____ _____? Gender: Female

24 Ethel Frances Charlotte Blakeney b: Abt. 1877 Gender: Female

+Lucien Joseph Jerome b: Abt. 1875 in Ireland? d: April 23, 1943 Father: Henry Edward Jerome, Major-General Mother: _____ _____? Gender: Male

.23 Edward Blakeney b: Abt. 1831 in Cheltenham, Gloucestershire, England? d: Abt. 1910 in England? Number of children: 1 Gender: Male

+Mary Parker b: Abt. 1835 in England? m: Abt. 1855 Number of children: 1 Gender: Female

24   William Edward Albermarle Blakeney, Col b: Abt. 1855 in Camberley, Surrey County England? d: March 07, 1927 Number of children: 1 Gender: Male

+Mary Emily Long b: Abt. 1855 in Newton House, Clevedon, Somerset, England m: August 15, 1894 Number of children: 1 Father: William Long, Col. Mother: _____ _____? Gender: Female

.23 Anna Blakeney b: Abt. 1833 in England? Gender: Female

+Charles Morgan Norwood b: November 19, 1825 in Ashford, Kent, England Father: Charles Norwood Mother: Catherine Morgan Gender: Male

.23 Henry Blakeney, Col b: Abt. 1835 in England? d: August 11, 1884 Number of children: 1 Gender: Male

+Louisa Jane Hutchinson b: Abt. 1835 in England? m: July 27, 1865 d: December 14, 1872 Number of children: 1 Father: Francis C. Hutchinson, Dr Mother: _____ _____? Gender: Female

24   Herbert Norwood Blakeney, Col b: Abt. 1865 in England? d: December 20, 1946 Gender: Male

.22 Harriet Elinor Blakeney b: Abt. 1792 in Kilrush House, Freshford, County Kilkenny (?), Ireland Gender: Female

.+Arthur Saint George, Esquire b: Abt. 1790 in Kilrush House, Freshford, County Kilkenny (?), Ireland m: February 11, 1810 in County Kilkenny (?), Ireland d: 1853 Gender: Male

.22 Sarah Blakeney b: Abt. 1794 d: Abt. 1794 Gender: Female (Notes: she died young).

.21 Sarah Blakeney b: Abt. 1727 Number of children: 1 Gender: Female

.+William Persse, Colonel b: Abt. 1720 m: 1750 Number of children: 1 Gender: Male

.22 _____ Persse b: Abt. 1750 Gender: Unknown

.21 Mary Blakeney b: Abt. 1730 Number of children: 1 Gender: Female

.+Thomas Taylor b: Abt. 1730 in Castle Taylor, County Galway (?), Ireland m: June 19, 1759 Number of children: 1 Gender: Male

.22 _____ Taylor b: Abt. 1760 Gender: Unknown

.21 John Blakeney, Lieutenant b: Abt. 1733 in Abbert, County Galway (?), Ireland d: July 25, 1789 Number of children: 3 Gender: Male

.+_____ _____? b: Abt. 1735 in County Galway (?), Ireland m: Abt. 1755 Number of children: 3 Gender: Female

.22 Robert Blakeney, Captain b: Abt. 1755 in Abbert, County Galway (?), Ireland Gender: Male

.22 John Blakeney, Captain b: Abt. 1758 in Abbert, County Galway (?), Ireland d: July 10, 1815 in Louisiana, USA Gender: Male

.22 William Blakeney, Ensign b: Abt. 1761 Gender: Male

.21 William Blakeney, Colonel b: 1735 in County Roscommon (?), Ireland d: November 02, 1804 Number of children: 11 Gender: Male

.+Sarah Shields b: Abt. 1735 in Ouseburn, Newcastle-Upon-Tyne, England m: September 06, 1770 d: May 31, 1799 Number of children: 11 Father: Samuel Shields Mother: _____ _____? Gender: Female

.22 William Augustus Blakeney, Major b: 1772 in County Roscommon (?), Ireland d: September 03, 1848 Number of children: 6 Gender: Male

.+Sarah O'Dell b: Abt. 1770 in Ireland? m: Abt. 1790 in Ireland?

Number of children: 6 Gender: Female

.23 Sarah Blakeney b: Abt. 1790 Gender: Female

.23 Mary Blakeney b: Abt. 1794 Gender: Female

.23 William Augustus Blakeney b: Abt. 1796 d: Abt. 1797 Gender: Male (Notes: he died young).

.23 John Blakeney b: Abt. 1798 d: 1885 in Melbourne (Australia?) Number of children: 1 Gender: Male

+_____ _____? b: Abt. 1830 m: Abt. 1847 Number of children: 1 Gender: Female

24 Mary Sarah Blakeney b: 1848 Gender: Female

.23 Barbara Jane Blakeney b: Abt. 1800 d: 1824 Gender: Female

.23 [3] Edward Hugh Blakeney, Surgeon-Major b: Abt. 1829 in Dorking, Surrey, England? Number of children: 8 Gender: Male

+Caroline Miller b: 1826 in Hasfield, Gloucestershire County, England m: Abt. 1842 d: May 23, 1847 in Quebec, Canada Number of children: 3 Gender: Female

24 William Augustus Frederick Blakeney b: Abt. 1842 in England? d: 1884 Number of children: 2 Gender: Male

+Emily Courtenay (probably from a royal line) b: Abt. 1845 in England? m: Abt. 1863 d: 1926 Number of children: 2 Gender: Female (Note: Looking for her ancestors)

24 Sarah Blakeney b: Abt. 1845 in England? Number of children: 6 Gender: Female

+Richard Moon b: Abt. 1845 in Llanymynech, Montgomeryshire, Wales m: Abt. 1863 Number of children: 6 Gender: Male

24 Edward Henry Blakeney b: 1847 in England? Number of children: 1 Gender: Male

+Flora Constance Collier b: Abt. 1850 in England? m: September 01, 1875 Number of children: 1 Father: G. B. B. Collier, Captain Mother: _____ _____? Gender: Female

.*2nd Wife of [3] Edward Hugh Blakeney, Surgeon-Major:

+Charlotte Maria Weare b: Abt. 1830 in England? m: Abt. 1850 in England? Number of children: 5 Gender: Female

24 Charlotte Blakeney b: Abt. 1850 Gender: Female

24 Henry Weare Blakeney b: Abt. 1852 in England? Number of

children: 5 Gender: Male

+Constance Inman b: Abt. 1855 in Upton, Cheshire, England? m: Abt. 1873 Number of children: 5 Gender: Female

24 Robert Weare Blakeney b: Abt. 1854 d: 1876 Gender: Male

24 Hugh Theophilius W. Blakeney, Dr. b: Abt. 1856 Gender: Male

+Ellen M. Gosset b: Abt. 1850 Gender: Female

24 Barbara Edwins Blakeney b: Abt. 1860 Number of children: 4 Gender: Female

+William L. Batson b: Abt. 1850 m: Abt. 1875 Number of children: 4 Gender: Male

.22 Catherine Blakeney b: Abt. 1771 Gender: Female

.22 John Theophilus Blakeney b: 1774 in County Roscommon (?), Ireland d: March 31, 1856 Gender: Male

.22 Hargrave Blakeney b: Abt. 1776 in County Roscommon (?), Ireland d: Abt. March 12, 1778 Gender: Male Burial: March 14, 1778.

.22 Thomas Blakeney, Lt-Col. b: Abt. 1775 d: July 02, 1808 in Trincomalee, Ceylon Gender: Male Burial: (Notes: one record says he died in 1858).

.22 Barbara Blakeney b: Abt. 1777 Gender: Female

.22 Edward Blakeney, Right Honorable Sir b: March 26, 1778 in England or Ireland? d: August 02, 1868 Gender: Male (Notes: he was also RCB, Field Marshall).

.+Mary Gardiner b: Abt. 1780 in Twickenham, Middle Sex County England? m: May 05, 1814 in England? (Notes: they had no children). d: 1866 Father: Thomas Gardiner, Colonel Mother: _____ _____? Gender: Female

.22 Samuel Blakeney, Captain b: 1780 d: June 1803 Gender: Male

.22 Sarah Blakeney b: Abt. 1781 Gender: Female

.22 Robert Blakeney, Lieutenant b: April 30, 1782 in England or Ireland? d: January 10, 1810 in Off Barbados Gender: Male

.22 Henry Persse Blakeney b: Abt. 1785 in Cheltenham, Gloucestershire County England? d: January 07, 1823 Gender: Male

..20 Margaret Blakeney b: Abt. 1705 in Dublin (?), Ireland Gender: Female

..+Samuel Simpson, Esquire b: Abt. 1700 in Dublin (?), Ireland Gender: Male

..20 Dorothy Blakeney b: Abt. 1709 in Dublin (?), Ireland Gender: Female

..+Francis Persse, Esquire b: Abt. 1700 in England or Ireland? Gender: Male

..20 Letitia (Lettice) Blakeney b: Abt. 1713 Gender: Female

..+H. Hardy, Esquire b: Abt. 1710 in Dublin, Ireland, or England? Gender: Male

..20 George Augustus Blakeney, Captain b: June 07, 1716 in Distington, Cumberland County England? d: February 25, 1799 Number of children: 4 Gender: Male

..+Mary Dixon, or Drion b: Abt. 1730 in of Whitehaven, or Gilgarron, Cumberland County England? m: January 29, 1744/45 d: September 17, 1800 Number of children: 4 Father: John Dixon Mother: _____ _____? Gender: Female

.21 [4] Robert Blakeney b: Abt. 1745 in Whitehaven, Cumberland County England? d: November 06, 1822 Gender: Male

.+Margaret de la Brouf Edwards b: Abt. 1750 in Pentre Hall, Montgomeryshire, England d: February 14, 1828 in England? Father: Samuel de la Brouf Edwards, Reverend Mother: _____ _____? Gender: Female

.*2nd Wife of [4] Robert Blakeney:

.+Elizabeth Burrows b: Abt. 1750 in Whitehaven, Cumberland County England? m: Abt. March 10, 1780 d: February 14, 1828 Father: Robert Burrows Mother: _____ _____? Gender: Female

.21 _____ Blakeney b: Abt. 1747 Gender: Female

.21 _____ Blakeney b: Abt. 1750 Gender: Male

.21 _____ Blakeney b: Abt. 1752 Gender: Female

..20 Gilbert Blakeney b: Abt. 1718 in England? Gender: Male

..20 Robert Blakeney b: Abt. 1720 in Dublin (?), Ireland d: February 1799 in Ramsey, Isle of Man, England Number of children: 2 Gender: Male

..+Elizabeth Gill b: Abt. 1725 in Dublin, Ireland m: Abt. 1743 Number of children: 2 Gender: Female

.21 Robert Blakeney b: Abt. 1744 Gender: Male

.21 Elizabeth Blakeney b: Abt. 1750 Gender: Female

..20 William Blakeney b: Abt. 1722 Gender: Male (Notes: he died unmarried).

..19 William Blakeney, Mount Blakeney Line b: Abt. 1675 in Abbert, County Galway (?), Ireland Gender: Male (Notes: William gave rise to the 2nd Irish Blakeney line, the "Mount Blakeney Line," (circa 1625-1664?), one of whose sons' sons instigated the "American Southern Blakeney Line" (by way of the famous South Carolinian, Captain John Blakeney, b. 1732)

..19 Susannah Blakeney b: Abt. 1677 in Abbert, County Galway (?), Ireland Number of children: 1 Gender: Female

..+J. Colpays, Admiral b: Abt. 1675 in Ireland? m: Abt. 1697 Number of children: 1 Gender: Male

..20 _____ Colpays b: Abt. 1700 Gender: Unknown

..19 Mary Blakeney b: Abt. 1680 in Abbert, County Galway (?), Ireland Number of children: 1 Gender: Female

..+Thomas Taylor b: Abt. 1675 in Ireland? m: Abt. 1700 in Ireland? Number of children: 1 Gender: Male

..20 _____ Taylor b: Abt. 1700 Gender: Unknown

..19 John Blakeney, Captain b: 1681 in Distington, Cumberland County England? d: May 21, 1749 Gender: Male (Notes: he died unmarried).

..19 _____ Blakeney b: Abt. 1682 Gender: Female

..+_____ Ormsby b: Abt. 1680 in of Loughrea, Ireland Gender: Male

18 Charles Blakeney b: Abt. 1651 in Ireland d: 1685 Gender: Male (Notes: There is no mention of marriage or children in the Blakeney records for Charles).

18 [5] Robert Blakeney, Captain/Sheriff b: Abt. 1657 in County Galway, Ireland d: October 12, 1731 in Ireland? Number of children: 1 Gender: Male (Note: he may have spelled his last name "Blakiney")

..+Elizabeth Rogers b: Abt. 1655 in County Galway, Ireland? d: Abt. 1739 Father: _____ Rogers Mother: _____ _____? Gender: Female

*2nd Wife of [5] Robert Blakeney, Captain/Sheriff:

..+_____ (Macormack) _____? b: Abt. 1660 Number of children: 1
Gender: Female

..19 _____ Blakeney b: Abt. 1680 Gender: Male (Notes: he died
unmarried).

18 Edward Blakeney, Lieutenant b: 1659 in Castle Gallagh (now
Blakeney), County Galway, Ireland d: 1703 Number of
children: 6 Gender: Male (Note: Lochlainn's theory is that he
may be a son of Hatton Blakeney, born 1660)

..+Deborah Stanton b: Abt. 1675 in Galway (?), Ireland m: Abt. 1689
in Ireland d: Aft. 1697 Number of children: 6 Father: Thomas
Stanton, Captain & Esquire of Galway Mother: Deborah Morgan
Gender: Female

..19 Robert Blakeney (son of Edward, b. 1659) b: Abt. 1690 d:
February 18, 1766 Number of children: 5 Gender: Male

..+Elizabeth Marshall b: Abt. 1700 Number of children: 5 Gender:
Female

..20 Charles Blakeney b: Abt. 1720 in Ireland d: Abt. 1782 in Ireland
Gender: Male

..20 Edward Blakeney, Captain-Lieutenant b: Abt. 1723 in Parke,
County Galway (?), Ireland d: 1770 Gender: Male (Notes: he
died unmarried).

..20 _____ Blakeney b: Abt. 1725 Gender: Female

..+A. Wadman, Reverend b: Abt. 1720 Gender: Male

..20 [17] Simon Blakeney, Lieutenant b: Abt. 1728 in Parke or
Gortgariffe (?), County Galway, Ireland d: 1780 Number of
children: 4 Gender: Male Burial: 1780 Tuam Cathedral, Tuam,
Ireland. (Notes: Simon and Marcella were cousins).

..+[16] Marcella Blakeney b: Abt. 1736 in Ireland m: Abt. 1755 d:
November 29, 1781 in Ireland? Number of children: 4 Father:
Thomas Blakeney, Judge, Mother: Sarah Burke, Gender: Female
(Notes: Marcella and Simon were cousins).

.21 [18] Thomas Blakeney b: Abt. 1756 in Ireland d: 1769 in Ireland
Gender: Male Burial: 1769 Tuam Cathedral, Tuam, Ireland.

.21 [19] Edward Blakeney b: Abt. 1757 in Ireland d: Abt. 1758 in

Ireland Gender: Male

.21 [20] Elizabeth Blakeney b: Abt. 1759 Number of children: 1 Gender: Female

.+[21] James Bertragh b: Abt. 1755 in Manin, County Mayo (?), Ireland m: 1787 in Athlone, Ireland Number of children: 1 Gender: Male

.22 [22] _____ Bertragh b: Abt. 1790 Gender: Unknown

.21 [23] Sarah Blakeney b: Abt. 1765 Gender: Female

..20 Robert Blakeney, Sr. b: 1732 in Parke or Gortgariffe (?), County Galway, Ireland d: February 04, 1808 in Athenry, Ireland Number of children: 1 Gender: Male

..+Judith Ryland b: Bet. 1750 - 1772 in Clonburn, County Galway (?), Ireland m: Abt. 1787 Number of children: 1 Gender: Female

.21 Robert Blakeney, Jr., Captain b: 1788 in Galway, Ireland d: 1855 in Paxo, Greece Number of children: 7 Gender: Male (Note: He lived on the Greek island of Zante; He wrote a book called "A Boy in the Peninsular War," edited by Julian Sturgis)

.+Maria Giulia (Julia) Balbi, Contessa (royal family) b: Abt. 1806 in Venice, Italy m: 1823 in Corfu, Greece d: in Corfu, Greece? Number of children: 7 Gender: Female (Note: She's from an ancient Venetian family)

.22 Cecilia Blakeney b: 1824 in Kerkiras, Greece Gender: Female

.+John Gibson, Captain b: Abt. 1820 m: 1844 in Paxo, Greece d: 1846 in South Africa Gender: Male

.22 Robert Blakeney b: 1830 in Kerkiras, Greece d: April 09, 1886 in Corfu, Greece Gender: Male

.+Amalia Alexachie b: Abt. 1840 in Corfu, Greece or Santi Quaranta, Albania? Gender: Female

.22 John Henry Blakeney, Lieutenant b: 1832 in Kerkiras, or Zante, Greece d: September 17, 1869 in Corfu, Greece Gender: Male

.22 Mary Blakeney b: 1823 in Kerkiras, Greece Number of children: 9 Gender: Female

.+William Hugh Barton, Major b: Abt. 1830 m: Abt. 1848 in Paxo, Greece Number of children: 9 Gender: Male

.23 _____ Barton b: Abt. 1849 Gender: Female

.23 _____ Barton b: Abt. 1850 Gender: Female

.23 _____ Barton b: Abt. 1852 Gender: Female

.23 _____ Barton b: Abt. 1854 Gender: Female

.23 _____ Barton b: Abt. 1856 Gender: Male

.23 _____ Barton b: Abt. 1857 Gender: Male

.23 _____ Barton b: Abt. 1859 Gender: Male

.23 _____ Barton b: Abt. 1861 Gender: Male

.23 _____ Barton b: Abt. 1863 Gender: Male

.22 Charlotte Blakeney b: 1827 in Kerkiras, Greece d: October 31, 1906 Number of children: 3 Gender: Female

.+Marcus Wylly De la Poer Beresford, Col. (royal line) b: February 22, 1825 m: July 24, 1852 d: February 12, 1902 Number of children: 3 Father: John de la Poer Beresford Mother: Harriet Eliza Wylly Gender: Male

.23 Marcus Henry De La Paer Beresford b: Abt. November 28, 1857 in Christ Church, Barbadoes, Caribbean Number of children: 2 Gender: Male

+Margery Mary Connell b: Abt. 1860 Number of children: 2 Gender: Female

24 Marcus John de la Poer Beresford b: 1883 Gender: Male

24 Julian Walter de la Poer Beresford b: April 15, 1886 d: 1978 Gender: Male

.23 Julian Walter de la Poer Beresford b: Abt. 1860 Number of children: 1 Gender: Male

+_____ _____? b: Abt. 1862 Number of children: 1 Gender: Female

24 [6] Joseph Henry Blackhurst, Beresford b: Abt. 1890 Number of children: 2 Gender: Male

+_____ _____? b: Abt. 1892 Number of children: 1 Gender: Female

*2nd Wife of [6] Joseph Henry Blackhurst, Beresfor d:

+_____ _____? b: Abt. 1897 Number of children: 1 Gender: Female

.23 John Blakeney de la Poer Beresford Gender: Male

.22 Anne Blakeney b: 1835 in Kerkiras, Greece Gender: Female

.+G. Faught, Surgeon-Major b: Abt. 1835 m: 1858 in Corfu, Greece d: in India Gender: Male

.22 Charles Altavilla Blakeney b: January 1840 in Kerkiras, or Paxo,

THE BLAKENEYS

Greece d: January 17, 1907 in Leghorn (Livorno), Italy Number of children: 4 Gender: Male

.+Virginia Connemenos (royal line) b: Abt. 1845 in Turkey? m: in S. Maura, Ionian Islands Number of children: 4 Father: Count Nichloas Connemenos Mother: _____ _____? Gender: Female

.23 Charles Llewllyn Blakeney b: July 14, 1880 in Prevesa, Greece d: June 13, 1970 Number of children: 1 Gender: Male

+_____ _____? b: Abt. 1880 m: Abt. 1904 Number of children: 1 Gender: Female

24 Muriel Virginia Julia Blakeney b: Abt. 1905 in Athens (?), Greece Number of children: 1 Gender: Female

+_____ Spanopoulos b: Abt. 1900 in Greece? m: Abt. 1925 in Athens, Greece Number of children: 1 Gender: Male

.23 Cecilia Blakeney b: Abt. 1882 Gender: Female

.23 Mary Blakeney b: Abt. 1884 Gender: Female

.23 Sappho Blakeney b: Abt. 1885 Gender: Female

..19 Mary Blakeney b: Abt. 1692 in Lisnamult, County Roscommon (?), Ireland Number of children: 1 Gender: Female

..+Robert Ormsby b: Abt. 1690 in Gloghans, County Mayo (?), Ireland Number of children: 1 Gender: Male

..20 _____ Ormsby b: Abt. 1740 Gender: Unknown

..19 Thomas Blakeney, Judge, b: 1693 in County Galway (?), Ireland. d: May 27, 1762 in Castle Blakeney or Tuam (?), Ireland. Number of children: 9 Gender: Male Burial: Tuam Cathedral, Tuam, Ireland.

..+Sarah Burke, b: Abt. 1700 in Cornacuogh, Tyaquin, County Galway (?), Ireland m: 1715 in County Galway (?), Ireland d: February 1763 in Ireland Number of children: 9 Father: Redmond (Robert?) Burke, Esquire of Tarraquin Mother: _____ _____? Gender: Female Burial: Feb 18, 1763, Tuam Cathedral, Tuam, Ireland

..20 Edward Blakeney b: 1716 in Cornacuogh, County Galway (?), Ireland d: 1799 Gender: Male

..20 Elizabeth Blakeney b: Abt. 1718 in Dublin (?), Ireland Number of children: 1 Gender: Female

..+Thomas Waldron, Esquire b: Abt. 1715 in Drumsna, County Leitrim, Ireland Number of children: 1 Gender: Male

.21 _____ Waldron b: Abt. 1740 Gender: Unknown

..20 Thomas Blakeney b: Abt. 1720 in Feigh (County Galway) or Dublin (?), Ireland d: Abt. July 21, 1789 in Ireland Gender: Male Burial: July 23, 1789, Ireland

..+Margaret Wallace b: Abt. 1725 in Feigh, County Galway (?), Ireland m: January 29, 1760 in Dublin, Ireland (Notes: they had no children) d: Abt. April 04, 1795 in Ireland? Gender: Female Burial: April 6, 1795, Ireland (?)

..20 Robert Blakeney, Lieutenant b: Abt. 1725 d: September 20, 1762 off Havana, Cuba (in a military skirmish?) Gender: Male (Notes: he died without bearing children).

..20 George Blakeney b: Abt. 1728 in Ireland? Gender: Male (Notes: he died without bearing children).

..20 Charles Blakeney, b: 1731 in Cornacuogh (or Culliogh), County Galway, Ireland d: December 1815 in Dublin, Ireland Number of children: 7 Gender: Male

..+Bridget Gunning, b: Abt. 1735 in Ireland? m: March 06, 1761 in County Roscommon, Ireland d: September 15, 1776 in Ireland? Number of children: 7 Father: Barnaby Gunning, Esquire of Holywell Mother: Anne Staunton Gender: Female

.21 Anne Blakeney b: 1762 in Dublin (?), Ireland. d: July 19, 1809 Number of children: 1 Gender: Female

.+Richard Saint Leger, Honorable & Colonel (royal line) b: Abt. 1760 in Dublin, Ireland m: July 20, 1779 in St Peter's, Dublin, Ireland d: December 30, 1840 Number of children: 1 Father: Viscount Doneraile Mother: _____ _____? Gender: Male (Note: surname also spelled Ledger and Legier)

.22 _____ Saint Leger b: Abt. 1780 Gender: Unknown

.21 [10] John Edward Blakeney, Captain R. M. b: June 07, 1763 in Greenhall (County Roscommon)?, Ireland d: Aft. 1805 in Ireland? Number of children: 7 Gender: Male

.+Frances Bradley b: Abt. 1765 in Ireland? d: Abt. April 25, 1820 in Ireland? Number of children: 7 Father: Thomas Bradley Mother:

THE BLAKENEYS

_____ _____? Gender: Female

.22   Richard Blakeney, Lieutenant b: 1788 in Ballymurry, County Roscommon, Ireland. d: September 26, 1848 Number of children: 6 Gender: Male

. +Susan Maria Purdon b: Abt. 1800 in Lissbride, County Roscommon, Ireland. m: August 21, 1816 d: February 24, 1863 Number of children: 6 Father: John (or James) Batty Purdon Mother: Magdalene (Purdon) (de) Courcy Gender: Female

.23   John Blakeney b: Abt. 1817 d: Abt. 1818 Gender: Male (Notes: he died young).

.23   [7] Richard Paul Blakeney, Rev. & D.D. b: June 02, 1820 in County Roscommon, Ireland? d: December 31, 1884 in Bridlington, England Number of children: 10 Gender: Male

+Anne O'Connor b: Abt. 1825 in County Roscommon, Ireland? m: April 01, 1841 d: July 02, 1855 Number of children: 1 Father: Richard O'Connor, Lieutenant Mother: _____ _____? Gender: Female

24   Susan Blakeney b: Abt. 1842 in York, England or County Roscommon, Ireland? Gender: Female

+Albert Wade, Reverend b: Abt. 1840 in York, England? m: October 10, 1865 in York, England? d: December 31, 1884 in Bridlington, England Number of children: 1 Gender: Male

.*2nd Wife of [7] Richard Paul Blakeney, Rev. & D.D.:

+Elizabeth Bibby b: Abt. 1825 in Liverpool, England? m: December 02, 1856 d: September 19, 1916 in England? Number of children: 10 Father: Robert Bibby Mother: _____ _____? Gender: Female

24   Richard Blakeney, Reverend & Vicar b: October 14, 1857 in York, England? d: February 28, 1946 in England? Gender: Male (Notes: he was Vicar of Bishopthorpe).

+Alice Unwin b: Abt. 1860 in Broom Cross, Sheffield, England? m: April 16, 1884 in Oxford, England? Father: Henry Unwin Mother: _____ _____? Gender: Female

24   Elizabeth Gunning Blakeney, (twin a1) b: November 23, 1859 in England? d: February 03, 1882 in England? Gender: Female

+Arthur Penry Williams, Captain b: Abt. 1855 in England? m: July 14, 1881 in England? Gender: Male

24 Ellen St. Leger Blakeney, (twin a2) b: November 23, 1859 in England? d: August 09, 1947 in England? Gender: Female

+John Howard Deasdey, Reverend b: Abt. 1855 in England or Ireland? m: July 28, 1887 in England d: August 18, 1924 in England? Gender: Male

24 Florence Purdon Blakeney b: December 26, 1861 in England? d: January 20, 1900 in England? Gender: Female

24 Robert Bibby Blakeney, Lieut. b: February 01, 1865 in Liverpool, England? d: May 31, 1948 in Liverpool, England? Gender: Male

+Constance Eleanor Darrah b: Abt. 1865 in Liverpool, England? m: July 19, 1894 in Liverpool, England? Father: Henry Zouch Darrah, Colonel Mother: _____ _____? Gender: Female

24 John Edward Charles Blakeney, Lieutenant-Colonel b: December 20, 1866 in Cambridge, England? d: January 17, 1961 in Cambridge, England? Gender: Male

+Louisa Margaret Mosse b: Abt. 1866 in Cambridge, England? m: February 28, 1899 in Cambridge, England? d: February 20, 1946 in England? Father: Lorenzo N. Mosse, Lt-Col. Mother: _____ _____? Gender: Female

24 Constance Blakeney, twin, (b1) b: September 08, 1870 d: May 23, 1966 Gender: Female

+Walter de Sausmarez Cayley, Sir b: Abt. 1875 in Bengal, India? m: December 08, 1886 d: July 21, 1952 Father: Henry Cayley Mother: _____ _____? Gender: Male

24 Magdalene Amelia Ireland Blakeney, (twin b2) b: September 08, 1870 in England? d: September 08, 1932 in England? Number of children: 1 Gender: Female

+Lancelot Hicks Becher, Reverend b: Abt. 1865 in England? m: January 06, 1898 in England? d: May 07, 1912 in England? Number of children: 1 Father: Michael Allyn Richard Becher Mother: _____ _____? Gender: Male

24 [8] Herbert de Courcy Blakeney, Major b: December 18, 1873 in England? d: March 14, 1954 in London, England? Number of

children: 2 Gender: Male

+Edith Sara Bower b: Abt. 1875 in Whitefield, Lancashire, England? m: October 02, 1895 in England? Number of children: 2 Father: George Bower Mother: _____ _____? Gender: Female

*2nd Wife of [8] Herbert de Courcy Blakeney, Major:

+Gladys Sybella Tilley b: Abt. 1875 in London, England? m: October 09, 1915 in London, England? d: April 29, 1959 Father: Arthur Tilley, Professor Mother: _____ _____? Gender: Female

.23 Ellen Blakeney b: 1823 in County Roscommon, Ireland, or England? Gender: Female

+William Clementson, Reverend b: Abt. 1820 in England? m: 1842 Gender: Male

.23 John Edward Blakeney, Ven. b: December 07, 1824 in County Roscommon (?), Ireland d: January 12, 1895 in England? Number of children: 3 Gender: Male (Notes: he was the Archdeacon of Sheffield, England).

+Martha Darbyshire b: Abt. 1830 in Hamilton Square, Birkenhead, England m: June 03, 1856 in England? Number of children: 3 Father: Benjamin Darbyshire Gender: Female

24 Martha Susan Blakeney b: December 25, 1862 in Yorkshire (?), England d: February 25, 1941 Number of children: 1 Gender: Female

+Samuel Roberts, Right Honorable b: Abt. 1860 in Eccleshall (?), England m: December 21, 1880 in England d: June 19, 1926 Number of children: 1 Gender: Male

24 Edward Purdon Blakeney, Rev. b: October 12, 1870 in Sheffield, England? d: October 23, 1933 in England? Number of children: 5 Gender: Male

+Hilda Kate Dring b: Abt. 1870 in Sheffield, England? m: June 20, 1899 in England? d: January 21, 1935 in England? Number of children: 5 Father: William Ernest Dring, Dr. Mother: _____ _____? Gender: Female

24 John St. Leger Blakeney b: December 15, 1873 in Yorkshire (?), England d: November 10, 1967 Number of children: 2 Gender: Male

+Amy Elizabeth Lowes b: Abt. 1875 in Sharrow, Sheffield, Yorkshire (?), England m: October 19, 1909 in Yorkshire (?), England Number of children: 2 Father: John Lowes Mother: _____ _____? Gender: Female

.23 William Purdon Blakeney, Sr. b: 1834 in County Roscommon, Ireland, or England? d: January 02, 1879 Number of children: 1 Gender: Male

+Emily Clegge b: Abt. 1835 in Cheshire, England? m: 1853 Number of children: 1 Father: Thomas Clegge Gender: Female

24 William Purdon Blakeney, Jr. b: February 02, 1856 d: March 1945 Number of children: 1 Gender: Male (Notes: he was "in Holy Orders").

+Elizabeth Adaline Wilson b: Abt. 1855 in Derbyshire (?), England m: April 29, 1889 in England? Number of children: 1 Father: William John Wilson Mother: _____ _____? Gender: Female

.23 Magdalene Blakeney b: Abt. 1826 d: Abt. 1826 Gender: Female (Notes: she died young).

.22 John Blakeney, Lieutenant b: Abt. 1789 in Greenhall (County Roscommon)?, Ireland. d: 1815 in Verdun, France. Gender: Male (Notes: he died unmarried).

.22 Thomas Blakeney, Lieutenant b: Abt. 1793 in Roscommon County (?), Ireland d: 1833 Gender: Male (Notes: he had no children).

.22 Charles William Blakeney b: Abt. 1795 in Roscommon County (?), Ireland d: July 10, 1848 in Island of Mauritius Number of children: 1 Gender: Male

.+_____ _____? b: Abt. 1800 Number of children: 1 Gender: Female

.23 _____ Blakeney b: Abt. 1820 d: in Drowned Gender: Male

.22 Theophilus Blakeney b: Abt. 1796 in Roscommon County (?), Ireland d: Abt. 1797 in Roscommon County (?), Ireland Gender: Male (Notes: he died young).

.22 Edward Blakeney b: Abt. 1800 Gender: Male (Notes: he had no children).

.22 [9] Robert H. Blakeney b: Abt. June 1805 in County Roscommon (?), Ireland Number of children: 1 Gender: Male

.+[11] Magdalene (Purdon) (de) Courcy (royal line) b: Abt. 1810 in

Diocese of Elphin, Roscommon, Ireland Number of children: 2
Father: _____ de Courcy Mother: Susannah Stanley Gender:
Female

.23   Mary Anne Blakeney b: Abt. 1825 in County Roscommon (?),
Ireland Gender: Female

.*2nd Wife of [9] Robert H. Blakeney:

.+_____ _____? b: Abt. 1805 in Roscommon County (?), Ireland
Gender: Female

.*2nd Wife of [10] John Edward Blakeney, Captain R. M.:

.+[11] Magdalene (Purdon) (de) Courcy b: Abt. 1810 in Diocese of
Elphin, Roscommon, Ireland Number of children: 2 Father:
_____ de Courcy Mother: Susannah Stanley Gender: Female

.21   Thomas Blakeney, Reverend & Dean, b: 1770 in Dublin, County
Dublin, Ireland. d: January 18, 1845 in Dublin, Ireland?
Number of children: 7 Gender: Male (Notes: he was Dean of
Roscommon).

.+Alicia Newcome, b: Abt. 1775 in Dublin, Ireland? m: July 1801 in
Bath (Somerset County), England d: January 09, 1851 in
Dublin, Ireland? Number of children: 7 Father: William
Newcome, Archbishop, Mother: _____ _____?, Gender:
Female

.22   Charles William Blakeney, Judge b: Abt. July 15, 1802 in Holywell,
County Roscommon (or Dublin),? Ireland. d: January 12, 1876
in Ireland? Number of children: 1 Gender: Male

.+Ellen Francis Jeffries b: Abt. 1805 in County Cork (Blarney Castle),
Ireland. m: Abt. October 26, 1826 d: Aft. 1832 in Ireland?
Number of children: 1 Father: John Jeffries Mother: _____
_____? Gender: Female

.23   William Theophilus Blakeney b: September 09, 1832 in Malahide
(County Dublin), Ireland. d: June 26, 1898 in Ireland? Number
of children: 7 Gender: Male

+Elizabeth Louise Carr b: Abt. 1835 in Tullamore, County Carlow,
Ireland. m: March 31, 1853 in Ireland? d: April 06, 1907 in
Ireland? Number of children: 7 Father: Frederick Carr Mother:
_____ _____? Gender: Female

24   Charles William Blakeney b: February 24, 1854 in Ireland or Australia? d: March 29, 1854 in Ireland or Australia? Gender: Male

24 Ellen Frances Blakeney b: Abt. 1856 in Ireland or Australia? Number of children: 1 Gender: Female

+Thomas H. Barron, Lieutenant b: Abt. 1850 in Ireland or Australia? m: March 29, 1871 Number of children: 1 Gender: Male

24   Elizabeth Amy Augusta Blakeney b: Abt. 1857 in Ireland or Australia? d: Abt. 1858 in Ireland or Australia? Gender: Female

24 Amy Emma Blakeney b: Abt. 1859 in Ireland or Australia? Gender: Female

+Charles Ridley-Smith b: Abt. 1850 in Eaton Square, London, England? or Queensland, Australia? m: April 06, 1875 Gender: Male

24   Mabel Henrietta Blakeney b: Abt. 1861 in Ireland or Australia? Gender: Female

+George E. Elliot b: Abt. 1855 in Ireland or Australia? Gender: Male

24   Grace Louisa Blakeney b: Abt. 1863 in Ireland or Australia? d: January 30, 1940 Number of children: 1 Gender: Female

+Sydney Colen Legge b: Abt. 1850 in Bristol, England? Number of children: 1 Gender: Male

24   Gertrude Isabel Blakeney b: Abt. 1865 in Ireland or Australia? Gender: Female

+Stuart Brownrigg Leishaman (or Leishman) b: Abt. 1855 in Ireland or Australia? m: July 06, 1904 Gender: Male

.22 Thomas Blakeney, Blackney, b: 1804 in Dublin, Ireland (some say, Hazelwood, Haldimand, Canada) d: Aft. 1854 in Ottawa, Canada? Number of children: 5 Gender: Male

.+Emma Jones, b: Abt. 1810 in Killinearrick, County Wicklow (or Dublin?), Ireland. (some say, Hazelwood, Haldimand, Canada) m: 1834 in Dublin, Ireland? d: Aft. 1854 in Ottawa, Canada? Number of children: 5 Father: Charles Jones, Mother: Eleanor Palmer, Gender: Female

.23 Anne Blakeney b: 1836 in Hazelwood, Haldimand, Canada Number of children: 6 Gender: Female

+Evan Stratford Martin b: October 26, 1826 in Cayuga, Ontario,

Haldimand, Canada m: November 09, 1859 Number of children: 6 Father: Richard Martin, Colonel Mother: Emily Sylvia Kirwan Gender: Male

24 Richard Blakeney/Blackeney Martin b: August 18, 1860 in Cayuga, Ontario, Canada Gender: Male

24 Emma Sylvia Martin b: Abt. 1862 in Cayuga, Ontario, Canada Gender: Female

24 Harriet Mary Martin b: Abt. 1864 in Cayuga, Ontario, Canada Gender: Female

24 Evan Stratford Jones Martin b: April 22, 1866 in Cayuga, Ontario, Canada Gender: Male

24 Frances Anne Newcome Martin b: Abt. 1868 in Cayuga, Ontario, Canada Gender: Female

24 Thomas Barnewall Martin b: March 28, 1871 in Cayuga, Ontario, Canada Gender: Male

.23 [12] Thomas Richard Blakeney, Sr., New England Branch b: March 1841 in Dublin, County Dublin, Ireland d: August 22, 1934 in Watertown, Middlesex County, MA. Number of children: 6 Gender: Male Burial: August 24, 1934 St. Patrick's Cemetery, Watertown, MA. Won a Purple Heart serving on the Federal side during the War for Southern Independence (the "Civil War"). Note: It is the author's theory that Thomas, like thousands of other Irishmen, may have decided to fight with the Yankees because he was bribed by Abraham Lincoln with today's equivalent of a $5,000 bounty, a common ploy by the U.S. president to gain Irish-Catholic recruits at the time. Either way Thomas went against the family grain: the vast majority of American Blakeneys fought for the Confederate States of America (C.S.A.). Thomas is the progenitor of the "New England Blakeney Line."

+Mary Hassett, or Catherine _____?, b: Bet. 1815 - 1843 in (Thomond, Country Clare?) Ireland m: 1866 in (St. Patrick's Church?) Watertown, Middle Sex County, MA d: Bet. 1870 - 1880 in Watertown, Middle Sex County MA? Number of children: 4 Father: _____ Hassett Mother: _____ _____?

Gender: Female Burial: St. Patrick's Cemetery, Watertown, Middle Sex County, MA?

24 Howard Blakeney b: Abt. 1867 Gender: Male

24 John William Blakeney, I Sr., b: Bet. 1869 - 1871 in Watertown, Middlesex County, MA. d: Abt. 1942 in Newton, Middle Sex County MA Number of children: 9 Gender: Male Burial: Calvary Cemetery, Waltham, Middlesex County, MA

+Rose Aine (Ann) Lynch, b: Bet. 1866 - 1868 in Newton, Middlesex County, MA m: November 24, 1886 in Our Lady's Church, Newtonville (Newton), Middlesex County, MA d: May 21, 1946 in Newton, Middlesex County, MA Number of children: 9 Father: John Lynch, (born in Ireland) Mother: Mary Mague, (born in Massachusetts) Gender: Female Burial: Calvary Cemetery, Waltham, Middlesex County, MA

24 Margaret Blakeney b: Abt. 1871 Gender: Female

24 Albert Blakeney b: Abt. 1873 Gender: Male

.*2nd Wife of [12] Thomas Richard Blakeney, Sr., New England Branch:

+Elizabeth Giroux b: Abt. 1850 in Watertown, Middlesex County, MA? or Canada? m: Abt. 1875 Number of children: 1 Gender: Female

24 _____ Blakeney b: Abt. 1876 Gender: Male

.*3rd Wife of [12] Thomas Richard Blakeney, Sr., New England Branch:

+Ellen Murray b: Abt. 1845 in Ottawa, Canada, MA, or Ireland? m: Abt. 1878 d: Bet. 1930 - 1931 in Massachusetts? Number of children: 1 Father: _____ Murray Mother: _____ _____? Gender: Female

24 Thomas Richard Blakeney, Jr. b: Abt. 1879 in Watertown, Middlesex County, MA d: Abt. July 27, 1952 in Watertown, Middlesex County, MA Gender: Male Burial: Abt. July 29, 1952 St. Patrick's Cemetery, Watertown, MA. (Note: he never married)

.23 Henry Blakeney b: November 04, 1845 in Dublin, Ireland or Ottawa, Canada? d: July 26, 1931 in Ottawa, Canada. Number of children: 4 Gender: Male

+Rebecca Kathleen Lewis b: Abt. 1850 in Dublin, Ireland or Ottawa,

Canada? m: April 09, 1892 d: August 12, 1931 in Ottawa, Canada. Number of children: 4 Father: R. P. Lewis, Dr. Mother: _____ _____? Gender: Female

24 Thomas Lewis Blakeney b: 1896 in Ontario (?), Canada. Number of children: 2 Gender: Male

+Mary Frances Owens b: Abt. 1898 in Ontario, Canada (or Drogheda, County Louth, Ireland)? m: April 22, 1922 d: 1963 Number of children: 2 Father: Thomas P. Owens Mother: _____ _____? Gender: Female

24 Henry Newcome Blakeney b: 1898 in Ontario (?), Canada d: 1971 in Canada? Number of children: 4 Gender: Male

+Elizabeth Whitley b: Abt. 1900 in Toronto, Ontario, Canada? m: 1933 in Canada? d: Aft. 1942 in Canada? Number of children: 4 Gender: Female

24 Millicent Deane Blakeney b: 1900 in Ontario (?), Canada d: 1901 Gender: Female

24 Rebecca Kathleen Blakeney b: Abt. 1902 in Ontario (?), Canada Number of children: 3 Gender: Female

+Frederick Owen Hodgins, Lt-Col. b: Abt. 1900 in Canada? m: 1921 in Canada? Number of children: 3 Father: William Egerton Hodgins, Major-General Mother: _____ _____? Gender: Male

.23 Catherine Maria Blakeney b: Abt. 1852 in Dublin, Ireland (or Ottawa, Canada?) Number of children: 7 Gender: Female

+Frederick Oliver Martin b: Abt. 1859 in Ireland, or Derryclere, York, Canada? m: Abt. 1870 in Ireland? Number of children: 7 Father: Richard Martin, Colonel Mother: Emily Sylvia Kirwan Gender: Male

24 _____ Martin b: Abt. 1875 Gender: Female
24 _____ Martin b: Abt. 1876 Gender: Female
24 _____ Martin b: Abt. 1877 Gender: Male
24 _____ Martin b: Abt. 1878 Gender: Male
24 _____ Martin b: Abt. 1879 Gender: Male
24 _____ Martin b: Abt. 1880 Gender: Male
24 _____ Martin b: Abt. 1881 Gender: Male

.23 Arthur William Blakeney b: 1854 in Dublin, Ireland or Ottawa,

Canada? Gender: Male

+Alicia A. Sutton b: Abt. 1860 in Canada? Gender: Female

.22 Edward Blakeney b: Abt. May 24, 1805 in Sallymount, County Roscommon (?), Ireland. d: March 27, 1857 in Ireland? Number of children: 6 Gender: Male

.+Anne Garvey b: Abt. 1805 in County Roscommon, Ireland? m: August 10, 1842 in Ireland? Number of children: 6 Father: Dermot Garvey Mother: _____ _____? Gender: Female

.23 Alicia Blakeney b: October 23, 1843 in County Roscommon (?), Ireland. Gender: Female

+Henry de la Valle Smyth b: Abt. 1840 in Hollywell, County Roscommon (?), Ireland. m: June 03, 1863 in County Roscommon (?), Ireland Gender: Male

.23 Frances Blakeney b: Abt. 1845 in County Roscommon (?), Ireland d: 1874 in County Roscommon (?), Ireland Gender: Female

.23 Anne Blakeney b: Abt. 1847 Gender: Female

.23 [13] Edward Thomas Blakeney b: June 10, 1849 in County Roscommon (?), Ireland. d: September 07, 1933 in Ireland? Number of children: 2 Gender: Male

+Caroline Belinda Irwin b: Abt. 1850 in Ballymoe, County Roscommon (?), Ireland m: 1881 in Ireland d: in Ireland? Father: Andrew Irwin Mother: _____ _____? Gender: Female

.*2nd Wife of [13] Edward Thomas Blakeney:

+Josephine Mangan b: Abt. 1870 in County Roscommon (?), Ireland m: November 05, 1912 in Ireland? d: August 13, 1936 in Ireland? Number of children: 2 Gender: Female

24 Edward St. Leger Blakeney b: Abt. 1913 in County Roscommon (?), Ireland Gender: Male

24 Joan Blakeney b: Abt. 1915 in County Roscommon (?), Ireland Gender: Female

.23 Richard Henry Blakeney b: September 18, 1851 in Strawberry Hill, Dalkey, County Dublin (?), Ireland d: November 1927 in Exeter, England (or Canada?) Number of children: 3 Gender: Male

+Henrietta May Catterson-Smith b: Abt. 1855 in County Dublin (?),

Ireland m: February 14, 1894 in Ireland or England? d: January 23, 1942 Number of children: 3 Father: Stephen Catterson-Smith Mother: _____ _____? Gender: Female

24 [14] Alicia Newcome Anne (twin 1) Blakeney b: January 26, 1896 in England or Ireland? d: January 23, 1961 Number of children: 1 Gender: Female

+Russell Dickens b: Abt. 1895 in Surrey (?), England Father: F. A. Dickens Mother: _____ _____? Gender: Male

*2nd Husband of [14] Alicia Newcome Anne (twin 1) Blakeney:

+Arthur Ridgeway b: Abt. 1895 in Halifax, Yorkshire (?), England m: September 21, 1921 in England? d: June 1943 in England? Number of children: 1 Father: Henry Ridgeway Mother: _____ _____? Gender: Male

24 Edward William Charles (twin 2) Blakeney, Lieut. b: January 26, 1896 in Ireland or England? d: January 1919 in Karachi, Pakistan Gender: Male

24 Stephen Richard Blakeney, Lt-Col. b: March 31, 1898 in Ireland or England? Gender: Male

+Mary Alice Falkiner b: Abt. 1900 in Noorilim, Victoria, Australia? m: March 08, 1923 in Victoria, Australia? d: October 02, 1963 in Melbourne, Australia Father: Norman Frasier Falkiner Mother: _____ _____? Gender: Female

.23 Catherine Gunning Blakeney b: March 03, 1854 in County Roscommon (?), Ireland d: February 11, 1944 in Ireland? Number of children: 1 Gender: Female

+Henry Mark Scott b: Abt. 1850 in Castle Hollow, Inniscrone, County Sligo (?), Ireland m: November 06, 1876 in Ireland? Number of children: 1 Gender: Male

24 _____ Scott b: Abt. 1877 Gender: Unknown

.22 [15] Anne Blakeney b: Abt. May 04, 1806 in Dublin (?), Ireland d: Aft. 1832 Number of children: 3 Gender: Female

.+John Nugent b: Abt. 1800 in Lacken, County Westmeath (?), Ireland m: Abt. July 06, 1830 in Ireland d: April 25, 1835 Number of children: 2 Gender: Male

.23 _____ Nugent b: Abt. 1831 Gender: Female

.23 _____ Nugent b: Abt. 1832 Gender: Male

.*2nd Husband of [15] Anne Blakeney:

.+William Trocke, Reverend b: Abt. 1800 in Mount Ormond, County Kilkenny (?), Ireland m: Abt. August 16, 1837 Number of children: 1 Gender: Male

.23 _____ Trocke b: Abt. 1838 Gender: Unknown

.22 Robert Blakeney b: Abt. November 08, 1807 in Dublin (?), Ireland d: Abt. August 30, 1863 in Dublin (?), Ireland Number of children: 3 Gender: Male

.+Rachel Anne Stewart b: Abt. 1810 in County Antrim, Ireland m: 1846 d: October 02, 1863 Number of children: 3 Father: William Stewart, Major Mother: _____ _____? Gender: Female

.23 Stewart Blakeney b: Abt. 1847 in Dublin (?), Ireland d: October 11, 1939 in Switzerland Gender: Male

+Anne Elizabeth Bourne b: Abt. 1850 in Ireland or England? m: October 12, 1894 in Ireland? Father: William Bourne Mother: _____ _____? Gender: Female

.23 Louissa Blakeney b: Abt. 1850 Gender: Female

.23 William Newcome Blakeney b: 1854 in Dublin (?), Ireland d: December 20, 1949 in Berkshire County England? Gender: Male

.22 George Blakeney b: July 19, 1810 in Dublin, Ireland d: Aft. 1853 Gender: Male

.22 Catherine Blakeney b: Abt. November 06, 1817 d: Aft. 1842 Number of children: 1 Gender: Female

.+John Battersby b: Abt. 1815 in Bobsville, County Meath (?), Ireland m: March 16, 1841 in Ireland Number of children: 1 Gender: Male

.23 _____ Battersby b: Abt. 1842 Gender: Unknown

.21 Charles Blakeney b: Abt. November 02, 1770 in Dublin (?), Ireland d: February 1791 in Dublin (?), Ireland Gender: Male Burial: St. George's, Dublin, Ireland. (Notes: he died unmarried).

.21 Bridget Blakeney b: Abt. 1771 in Dublin (?), Ireland Gender: Female

THE BLAKENEYS

.+Thomas Henn b: Abt. 1765 in Paradise Hill, Ennis, County Clare? m: July 10, 1795 d: 1822 in Ireland? Father: William Henn Mother: _____ _____? Gender: Male

.21 Robert Blakeney b: 1774 in Dublin (?), Ireland d: Abt. 1841 Number of children: 1 Gender: Male

.+Catherine Anne Owens b: Abt. 1775 in County Roscommon (?), Ireland m: Abt. January 18, 1806 in County Roscommon (?), Ireland Number of children: 1 Father: Samuel Lee Owens Mother: _____ _____? Gender: Female

.22 Mary Anne Blakeney b: Abt. 1807 Number of children: 2 Gender: Female

.+John Henry Mitchell b: Abt. 1805 in Coolmeen, County Roscommon (?), Ireland m: 1830 in County Roscommon (?), Ireland Number of children: 2 Gender: Male

.23 _____ Mitchell b: Abt. 1830 Gender: Female

.23 _____ Mitchell b: Abt. 1831 Gender: Male

.21 William Blakeney, Lieutenant b: Abt. 1775 in Dublin (?), Ireland d: June 24, 1803 in Kandy, Ceylon Gender: Male

..20 Jane Blakeney b: Abt. 1733 in County Roscommon (?), Ireland d: Aft. 1803 in Ireland? Number of children: 1 Gender: Female

..+Francis Nesbit b: Abt. 1730 in Kilmore, County Roscommon (?), Ireland m: Abt. 1750 in Ireland? Number of children: 1 Father: Matthew Nesbit Mother: _____ _____? Gender: Male

.21 _____ Nesbit b: Abt. 1755 Gender: Unknown

..20 Deborah Blakeney b: Abt. 1735 in Ireland d: Aft. 1773 in Ireland? Number of children: 6 Gender: Female

..+Andrew Kirwan, or Kerwan, Esq. of Amanghar b: Abt. 1735 in Coraghan, County Galway (?), Ireland m: Abt. 1755 in Ireland Number of children: 6 Father: Patrick Kirwan Mother: _____ _____? Gender: Male

.21 _____ Kirwan b: Abt. 1755 Gender: Male

.21 _____ Kirwan b: Abt. 1756 Gender: Male

.21 _____ Kirwan b: Abt. 1757 Gender: Male

.21 _____ Kirwan b: Abt. 1758 Gender: Male

.21 _____ Kirwan b: Abt. 1759 Gender: Female

.21 _____ Kirwan b: Abt. 1760 Gender: Female

..20 [16] Marcella Blakeney b: Abt. 1736 in Ireland d: November 29, 1781 in Ireland? Number of children: 4 Gender: Female (Notes: Marcella and Simon were cousins).

..+[17] Simon Blakeney, Lieutenant b: Abt. 1728 in Parke or Gortgariffe (?), County Galway, Ireland m: Abt. 1755 d: 1780 Number of children: 4 Father: Robert Blakeney (son of Edward, b. 1659) Mother: Elizabeth Marshall Gender: Male Burial: 1780 Tuam Cathedral, Tuam, Ireland. (Notes: Simon and Marcella were cousins).

.21 [18] Thomas Blakeney b: Abt. 1756 in Ireland d: 1769 in Ireland Gender: Male Burial: 1769 Tuam Cathedral, Tuam, Ireland.

.21 [19] Edward Blakeney b: Abt. 1757 in Ireland d: Abt. 1758 in Ireland Gender: Male

.21 [20] Elizabeth Blakeney b: Abt. 1759 Number of children: 1 Gender: Female

.+[21] James Bertragh b: Abt. 1755 in Manin, County Mayo (?), Ireland m: 1787 in Athlone, Ireland Number of children: 1 Gender: Male

.22 [22] _____ Bertragh b: Abt. 1790 Gender: Unknown

.21 [23] Sarah Blakeney b: Abt. 1765 Gender: Female

..19 Susannah Blakeney b: Abt. 1694 Gender: Female

..+William Godwin b: Abt. 1690 in of Tuam, Ireland Gender: Male

..19 John Blakeney, Lieutenant b: Abt. 1695 in Lisnamult, County Roscommon (?), Ireland d: 1760 Number of children: 3 Gender: Male

..+_____ Lovelace b: Abt. 1695 in Ballybride, County Roscommon, Ireland m: Abt. 1715 in Ireland? Number of children: 3 Father: Arthur Lovelace Mother: _____ _____? Gender: Female

..20 George Blakeney b: Abt. 1715 Gender: Male

..20 Charles Blakeney b: Abt. 1717 Gender: Male

..20 William Blakeney b: Abt. 1719 Gender: Male

..19 William Blakeney, Blakely, South Carolina Branch b: Abt. 1710 in Newtownards, County Down (or Armagh), Northern Ireland d: 1765 in SC Number of children: 5 Gender: Male (Note: Parents not known for sure; immigrated Nov 1782 to Halifax, Nova Scotia, Canada aboard the "Earl of Donegal"; Looking for his ancestors, who some say is Edward Blakeney, born 1659; he is listed thus)

..+Elizabeth Chambers b: Abt. 1713 in Northern Ireland m: Bet. 1735 - 1738 in Northern Ireland d: 1765 in SC Number of children: 5 Gender: Female (Note: Looking for her ancestors)

..20 Elizabeth Blakeney b: Abt. 1739 in Northern Ireland Gender: Female

..20 Sarah Blakeney b: Abt. 1743 in Northern Ireland Gender: Female

..20 David Blakeney, Sr. b: 1745 in Newtown Ards, County Down, Ireland d: Aft. 1825 in Petitcodiac, Westmorland County New Brunswick, Canada Number of children: 8 Gender: Male

..+Elizabeth _____? b: 1749 in SC m: Abt. 1770 in Old 96, Granville County, SC d: in Petitcodiac, Westmorland County New Brunswick, Canada Number of children: 8 Gender: Female

.21 David Blakeney, Jr. b: 1767 in Cuffytown Creek, Granville County, SC d: in North River, Petitcodiac, Westmorland County New Brunswick, Canada Gender: Male

.21 George Blakeney b: 1767 in New Brunswick, Canada, some say Cuffytown Creek, Granville County, SC Gender: Male

.+_____ Starkey b: Abt. 1770 Gender: Female

.21 William Blakeney b: 1769 in Cuffytown Creek, Granville County, SC Number of children: 1 Gender: Male

.+Barbara Jacques b: Abt. 1775 m: September 23, 1794 in Salisbury Parish, Westmorland County New Brunswick, Canada Number of children: 1 Gender: Female

.22 Samuel Blakeney b: Abt. 1811 Number of children: 1 Gender: Male

.+_____ _____? b: Abt. 1813 Number of children: 1 Gender: Female

.23 J. Edward Blakeney b: October 09, 1866 Number of children: 1 Gender: Male

+_____ _____? b: Abt. 1868 Number of children: 1 Gender: Female

24 Dora Catherine Blakeney b: June 1898 in Upper Coverdale, Albert County, NB, Canada Gender: Female

.21 Uzziel "Uz" Blakeney b: 1771 in Cuffytown Creek, Granville

County, SC d: 1825 in Petitcodiac River, New Brunswick, Canada Number of children: 1 Gender: Male

.+Ann Watson b: Abt. 1780 m: May 18, 1815 in New Brunswick, Canada Number of children: 1 Gender: Female

.22 Thomas Blakeney b: Abt. 1816 in Woodstock, New Brunswick, Canada Gender: Male

.+Charlotte Tupper b: Abt. 1818 Gender: Female

.21 [24] Chambers Blakeney b: Bet. 1773 - 1776 in Cuffytown, Granville County, SC d: Aft. April 1852 in North River, Westmorland County, New Brunswick, Canada Number of children: 8 Gender: Male

.+Sarah Lewis b: Abt. 1777 in North River, Westmorland County, New Brunswick, Canada m: September 22, 1800 in in a farm on the North River, near her Father's home, Salisbury Parish, Westmorland County, New Brunswick, Canada d: Bef. 1816 in North River, Westmorland County, New Brunswick, Canada Number of children: 4 Father: Charles Lewis, Reverend Mother: Levinia Chambers Gender: Female

.22 Sarah Blakeney b: Abt. 1800 in New Brunswick, Canada Gender: Female

.+David Kierstead b: Abt. 1798 in New Brunswick, Canada? m: June 08, 1823 in Westmorland County New Brunswick, Canada Gender: Male

.22 Charles Blakeney b: January 22, 1803 in Petitcodiac, Westmorland County, New Brunswick, Canada d: March 22, 1876 in Elgin, Albert County, New Brunswick, Canada Number of children: 10 Gender: Male

.+Sarah Anne Colpitts b: October 04, 1807 in Pollet River, Salisbury Parish, Westmorland County, New Brunswick, Canada m: December 19, 1828 in Pollet River, Salisbury Parish, Westmorland County, New Brunswick, Canada d: March 18, 1892 in Elgin, Albert County, New Brunswick, Canada Number of children: 10 Gender: Female

.23 Charles Lewis Blakeney, b: 1839 in Elgin, Albert County, New Brunswick, Canada, d: 1936 in Elgin, Albert County, New

Brunswick, Canada, Gender: Male

..+Annie Laurie Mollins b: 1849 in Elgin, Albert County, New Brunswick, Canada?; d: December 08, 1925, in Elgin, Albert County, New Brunswick, Canada, Gender: Female

.23 Sarah Elizabeth Blakeney Gender: Female

.23 Frances A. Blakeney Gender: Female

.23 Thomas C. Blakeney Gender: Male

.23 Eunice M. Blakeney Gender: Female

.23 Benjamin R. Blakeney Gender: Male

.23 Mariner Blakeney Gender: Male

.23 Moses C. Blakeney Gender: Male

.23 Joseph Charles Blakeney Gender: Male

.23 Jerusha Jane Blakeney Gender: Female

.22 Jerusha Blakeney b: August 1804 in Sus Sex Parish, Kings County, New Brunswick, Canada d: April 03, 1871 in Kings County, New Brunswick, Canada Number of children: 1 Gender: Female

.+Charles McCready b: October 12, 1798 in Upper Settlement, Kings County, New Brunswick, Canada m: January 27, 1824 in Kings County, New Brunswick, Canada d: February 07, 1861 in Upper Sus Sex, Kings County New Brunswick, Canada Number of children: 1 Father: _____ McCready Mother: Isabella Ford Gender: Male

.23 Sarah "Sally" McCready b: October 21, 1825 in Penobsquis, Kings County, New Brunswick, Canada d: August 1890 Gender: Female (Note: She and Lewis Evans Carll are 1st cousins, once removed)

+Lewis Evans Carll b: Abt. 1823 m: March 19, 1846 in Sus Sex, Kings County, New Brunswick, Canada Gender: Male

.22 Unknown Blakeney b: Abt. 1808 in New Brunswick, Canada Gender: Female

.*2nd Wife of [24] Chambers Blakeney:

.+Ann Geldart b: Abt. 1773 in Hillsborough, Albert County, New Brunswick, Canada m: June 13, 1816 in New Brunswick, Canada d: Aft. April 1852 in Westmorland County, New Brunswick, Canada Number of children: 4 Gender: Female

.22 Robert Blakeney b: Aft. 1816 in New Brunswick, Canada Gender: Male

.22 Amelia Blakeney b: Abt. 1818 in New Brunswick, Canada Gender: Female

.22 Jonathan Blakeney b: Abt. 1820 in New Brunswick, Canada Gender: Male

.22 Joseph C. Blakeney b: 1823 in Salisbury Parish, Westmorland County, New Brunswick, Canada d: 1903 Number of children: 1 Gender: Male

.+Deborah Mills b: 1834 in New Brunswick, Canada m: March 31, 1851 in New Brunswick, Canada d: December 12, 1887 Number of children: 1 Gender: Female

.23 Amelia Ann Blakeney b: 1852 in Salisbury, Westmorland County, New Brunswick, Canada d: 1921 in Winnipeg, Manitoba, Canada Gender: Female

.21 John Blakeney b: 1775 in Cuffytown Creek, Granville, South Carolina Gender: Male

.21 [26] James Blakeney, Bleakney b: 1777 in Cuffytown Creek, Granville, SC d: Bef. 1851 in Petitcodiac, Westmorland, New Brunswick, Canada Number of children: 11 Gender: Male

.+[25] Catherine Blakeney, Blakely b: April 09, 1777 in Cuffytown Creek, SC m: Abt. 1796 d: May 28, 1863 in Petitcodiac, Westmorland, New Brunswick, Canada Number of children: 11 Father: Chambers Blakeney, Sr., Bleakney, Blakely Mother: Catherine White Gender: Female

.22 [27] Kate Blakeney b: 1797 in Petitcodiac, Westmorland, New Brunswick, Canada d: 1878 Gender: Female

.+[28] Adam King b: Abt. 1795 m: October 30, 1833 in Petitcodiac, Westmorland, New Brunswick, Canada Gender: Male

.22 [29] Lucretia Blakeney b: August 29, 1802 in Petitcodiac, Westmorland, New Brunswick, Canada d: November 03, 1867 in Butternut Ridge, New Brunswick, Canada Number of children: 2 Gender: Female

.+[30] George Marshall Price b: May 12, 1808 in New Cannan, Queens County, New Brunswick, Canada m: January 31, 1832 d:

January 13, 1882 in Butternut Ridge, Kings County, New Brunswick, Canada Number of children: 2 Gender: Male

.23 [31] Oswell Nelson Price b: November 23, 1832 Gender: Male

.23 [32] Emily Ann Price b: June 01, 1839 in Havelock, New Brunswick, Canada d: September 1904 in Havelock, New Brunswick, Canada Gender: Female

+[33] William Cusack b: April 19, 1834 in Havelock, New Brunswick, Canada m: August 16, 1857 d: October 15, 1911 Gender: Male

.22 [34] Chambers Blakeney b: 1803 in Petitcodiac, Westmorland, New Brunswick, Canada Gender: Male

.+[35] Lavina Cain b: Abt. 1805 m: December 31, 1834 Gender: Female

.22 [36] David Crandall Blakeney b: 1804 d: 1895 in Glenvale, New Brunswick, Canada Number of children: 12 Gender: Male

.+[37] Rachel Catherine Keith b: May 18, 1814 d: January 1903 Number of children: 12 Gender: Female

.23 [38] James Ainsley Blakeney b: April 1835 d: June 08, 1911 in Salisbury Parish, NB, Canada Gender: Male

+[39] Ruth Amelia Gross b: October 08, 1835 d: April 14, 1929 Gender: Female

.23 [40] Jarvis Ring Blakeney b: 1836 Gender: Male

.23 [41] George Miles Blakeney b: 1838 d: July 25, 1917 Gender: Male

.23 [42] William S. Blakeney b: 1840 d: December 04, 1915 Gender: Male

.23 [43] Uzzie Blakeney b: March 1842 d: October 26, 1909 in Portland, OR Gender: Male

.23 [44] Alida Alcha Blakeney b: 1844 d: May 22, 1916 in Springhill, NS, Canada Gender: Female

.23 [45] Sybil Blakeney b: August 19, 1845 d: January 29, 1941 in Glenvale, NB, Canada Gender: Female

.23 [46] Charles Blakeney b: 1847 d: in Maryville, NB, Canada Gender: Male

.23 [47] Saphronia Blakeney b: 1849 d: November 1926 Gender: Female

.23 [48] Eli Blakeney b: 1851 d: 1852 Gender: Male

.23 [49] Edgar Blakeney b: 1853 d: 1860 Gender: Male

.23 [50] Dwitt Blakeney b: March 16, 1854 d: May 08, 1927 Gender: Male

.22 [51] Rebecca Blakeney b: 1806 in Petitcodiac, Westmorland, New Brunswick, Canada Gender: Female

.22 [52] Uzziel Blakeney b: 1808 in Petitcodiac, Westmorland, New Brunswick, Canada Gender: Male

.22 [53] William Blakeney b: 1810 d: 1871 in Petitcodiac, Westmorland, New Brunswick, Canada Gender: Male

.22 [54] Phoebe A. Blakeney b: April 1811 in Petitcodiac, Westmorland, New Brunswick, Canada d: October 11, 1879 in Havelock Co. NB, Canada Number of children: 9 Gender: Female

.+[55] James Herrett b: January 22, 1807 d: January 26, 1885 Number of children: 9 Gender: Male

.23 [56] Millidge Herrett b: 1829 in Havelock Co. NB, Canada d: May 1925 in Aberdeen, South Dakota Gender: Female

.23 [57] Catherine B. Herrett b: 1830 Gender: Female

.23 [58] Hannah Almira Herrett b: 1830 Gender: Female

.23 [59] David M. Herrett b: 1831 Gender: Male

.23 [60] Frances Jane Herrett b: 1834 Gender: Female

.23 [61] Elizabeth Herrett b: October 21, 1836 Gender: Female

.23 [62] Margaret Amanda Herrett b: 1839 Gender: Female

.23 [63] James Herrett b: 1841 Gender: Male

.23 [64] Benjamin Coy Herrett b: May 1843 Gender: Male

.22 [65] James Blakeney b: 1816 in Petitcodiac, Westmorland, New Brunswick, Canada Gender: Male

.+[66] Abigail B. Herrett b: Abt. 1825 m: January 31, 1850 Gender: Female

.22 [67] Emily Blakeney b: 1817 in Petitcodiac, Westmorland, New Brunswick, Canada d: June 01, 1859 in Havelock Co. NB, Canada Number of children: 1 Gender: Female

.+[68] Daniel Keith b: Abt. 1815 Number of children: 1 Gender: Male

.23 [69] Barbara Ellen Keith b: May 11, 1853 Gender: Female

.22 [70] Elizabeth Blakeney b: 1818 in Petitcodiac, Westmorland, New

Brunswick, Canada Gender: Female

.21 Ruth Blakeney b: 1781 in New Brunswick, Canada, some say Cuffytown Creek, Granville, SC Gender: Female

.+John Morrison b: Abt. 1783 in New Brunswick, Canada? m: June 18, 1821 in Westmorland County New Brunswick, Canada Gender: Male

..20 Chambers Blakeney, Sr., Bleakney, Blakely b: Abt. 1749 in Newtownards, County Down (or Armagh), Northern Ireland d: Bet. 1810 - 1818 in Ship Harbour, Halifax, Nova Scotia, Canada Number of children: 7 Gender: Male

..+Catherine White b: 1753 in Old 96, SC m: June 07, 1774 in Londonderry or Charleston, SC d: Aft. 1790 in Ship Harbour, Halifax, Nova Scotia, Canada Number of children: 7 Gender: Female (Note: Looking for her ancestors)

.21 Henry Blakeney b: 1772 Gender: Male

.21 William Blakeney b: September 16, 1775 in Old 96, SC d: 1862 in Jeddore, Nova Scotia Number of children: 5 Gender: Male

.+Pauline Maskell b: Abt. 1777 m: Abt. 1800 Number of children: 5 Gender: Female

.22 George Blakeney b: Abt. 1800 Gender: Male

.22 Ann Blakeney b: Abt. 1802 Gender: Female

.22 William Blakeney b: Abt. 1804 Gender: Male

.22 Peter Blakeney b: Abt. 1805 Gender: Male

.22 David Blakeney b: Abt. 1807 Gender: Male

.21 [25] Catherine Blakeney, Blakely b: April 09, 1777 in Cuffytown Creek, SC d: May 28, 1863 in Petitcodiac, Westmorland, New Brunswick, Canada Number of children: 11 Gender: Female

.+[26] James Blakeney, Bleakney b: 1777 in Cuffytown Creek, Granville, SC m: Abt. 1796 d: Bef. 1851 in Petitcodiac, Westmorland, New Brunswick, Canada Number of children: 11 Father: David Blakeney, Sr. Mother: Elizabeth _____? Gender: Male

.22 [27] Kate Blakeney b: 1797 in Petitcodiac, Westmorland, New Brunswick, Canada d: 1878 Gender: Female

.+[28] Adam King b: Abt. 1795 m: October 30, 1833 in Petitcodiac,

Westmorland, New Brunswick, Canada Gender: Male

.22   [29] Lucretia Blakeney b: August 29, 1802 in Petitcodiac, Westmorland, New Brunswick, Canada d: November 03, 1867 in Butternut Ridge, New Brunswick, Canada Number of children: 2 Gender: Female

.+[30] George Marshall Price b: May 12, 1808 in New Cannan, Queens County, New Brunswick, Canada m: January 31, 1832 d: January 13, 1882 in Butternut Ridge, Kings County, New Brunswick, Canada Number of children: 2 Gender: Male

.23 [31] Oswell Nelson Price b: November 23, 1832 Gender: Male

.23   [32] Emily Ann Price b: June 01, 1839 in Havelock, New Brunswick, Canada d: September 1904 in Havelock, New Brunswick, Canada Gender: Female

+[33] William Cusack b: April 19, 1834 in Havelock, New Brunswick, Canada m: August 16, 1857 d: October 15, 1911 Gender: Male

.22 [34] Chambers Blakeney b: 1803 in Petitcodiac, Westmorland, New Brunswick, Canada Gender: Male

.+[35] Lavina Cain b: Abt. 1805 m: December 31, 1834 Gender: Female

.22 [36] David Crandall Blakeney b: 1804 d: 1895 in Glenvale, New Brunswick, Canada Number of children: 12 Gender: Male

.+[37] Rachel Catherine Keith b: May 18, 1814 d: January 1903 Number of children: 12 Gender: Female

.23   [38] James Ainsley Blakeney b: April 1835 d: June 08, 1911 in Salisbury Parish, NB, Canada Gender: Male

+[39] Ruth Amelia Gross b: October 08, 1835 d: April 14, 1929 Gender: Female

.23 [40] Jarvis Ring Blakeney b: 1836 Gender: Male

.23 [41] George Miles Blakeney b: 1838 d: July 25, 1917 Gender: Male

.23 [42] William S. Blakeney b: 1840 d: December 04, 1915 Gender: Male

.23   [43] Uzzie Blakeney b: March 1842 d: October 26, 1909 in Portland, OR Gender: Male

.23 [44] Alida Alcha Blakeney b: 1844 d: May 22, 1916 in Springhill, NS, Canada Gender: Female

THE BLAKENEYS

.23 [45] Sybil Blakeney b: August 19, 1845 d: January 29, 1941 in Glenvale, NB, Canada Gender: Female

.23 [46] Charles Blakeney b: 1847 d: in Maryville, NB, Canada Gender: Male

.23 [47] Saphronia Blakeney b: 1849 d: November 1926 Gender: Female

.23 [48] Eli Blakeney b: 1851 d: 1852 Gender: Male

.23 [49] Edgar Blakeney b: 1853 d: 1860 Gender: Male

.23 [50] Dwitt Blakeney b: March 16, 1854 d: May 08, 1927 Gender: Male

.22 [51] Rebecca Blakeney b: 1806 in Petitcodiac, Westmorland, New Brunswick, Canada Gender: Female

.22 [52] Uzziel Blakeney b: 1808 in Petitcodiac, Westmorland, New Brunswick, Canada Gender: Male

.22 [53] William Blakeney b: 1810 d: 1871 in Petitcodiac, Westmorland, New Brunswick, Canada Gender: Male

.22 [54] Phoebe A. Blakeney b: April 1811 in Petitcodiac, Westmorland, New Brunswick, Canada d: October 11, 1879 in Havelock Co. NB, Canada Number of children: 9 Gender: Female

.+[55] James Herrett b: January 22, 1807 d: January 26, 1885 Number of children: 9 Gender: Male

.23 [56] Millidge Herrett b: 1829 in Havelock Co. NB, Canada d: May 1925 in Aberdeen, South Dakota Gender: Female

.23 [57] Catherine B. Herrett b: 1830 Gender: Female

.23 [58] Hannah Almira Herrett b: 1830 Gender: Female

.23 [59] David M. Herrett b: 1831 Gender: Male

.23 [60] Frances Jane Herrett b: 1834 Gender: Female

.23 [61] Elizabeth Herrett b: October 21, 1836 Gender: Female

.23 [62] Margaret Amanda Herrett b: 1839 Gender: Female

.23 [63] James Herrett b: 1841 Gender: Male

.23 [64] Benjamin Coy Herrett b: May 1843 Gender: Male

.22 [65] James Blakeney b: 1816 in Petitcodiac, Westmorland, New Brunswick, Canada Gender: Male

.+[66] Abigail B. Herrett b: Abt. 1825 m: January 31, 1850 Gender:

Female

.22 [67] Emily Blakeney b: 1817 in Petitcodiac, Westmorland, New Brunswick, Canada d: June 01, 1859 in Havelock Co. NB, Canada Number of children: 1 Gender: Female

.+[68] Daniel Keith b: Abt. 1815 Number of children: 1 Gender: Male

.23 [69] Barbara Ellen Keith b: May 11, 1853 Gender: Female

.22 [70] Elizabeth Blakeney b: 1818 in Petitcodiac, Westmorland, New Brunswick, Canada Gender: Female

.21 [71] Lawrence Blakeney b: March 26, 1780 in Old 96, SC d: June 20, 1837 in Nova Scotia Number of children: 16 Gender: Male

.+Nancy Anne Day b: 1782 m: October 17, 1802 in St. Paul's, Halifax, NS, Canada d: 1822 Father: John Day Mother: _____ _____? Gender: Female

.*2nd Wife of [71] Lawrence Blakeney:

.+Mary Margaret Weeks b: 1799 m: June 15, 1824 in St. Paul's, Halifax, NS, Canada Number of children: 16 Father: David Weeks Mother: Hannah Mehl Gender: Female (Note: Lawrence & Mary probably had 19 children; 3 are missing from the records)

.22 David Blakeney b: August 21, 1803 Gender: Male

.+Frances Day b: 1816 Gender: Female

.22 Frances Blakeney b: March 06, 1805 Gender: Female

.22 Catherine Blakeney b: August 07, 1808 d: April 16, 1891 Gender: Female

.+David Weeks b: Abt. 1806 m: June 14, 1825 in St. Paul's, Halifax, NS, Canada Gender: Male

.22 James Blakeney b: August 20, 1809 Gender: Male

.22 John William Henry Blakeney b: August 08, 1811 d: March 17, 1901 in Musquodoboit Harbour, NS, Canada Number of children: 9 Gender: Male

.+Elizabeth Biggs b: May 1824 m: September 28, 1836 in St. Paul's, Halifax, NS, Canada d: December 19, 1888 Number of children: 9 Gender: Female

.23 Freelove Blakeney b: Abt. 1837 Gender: Female

+William Henry Wambolt b: Abt. 1835 m: January 24, 1872 Gender:

Male

.23 James Thomas Blakeney b: April 01, 1838 d: December 11, 1900
Gender: Male

+Elizabeth Maria Newcombe b: November 18, 1843 m: October 28,
1875 in Gerrard's Island d: April 08, 1917 Gender: Female

.23 Suzannah C. Blakeney b: 1845 d: May 24, 1913 Gender: Female

+Samuel Frederick Parker b: Abt. 1843 m: December 31, 1866 in Ship
Harbour, Halifax, Nova Scotia, Canada Gender: Male

.23 John B. Blakeney b: 1848 Gender: Male

.23 David Henry Blakeney b: August 16, 1851 d: July 07, 1912
Gender: Male

+Sarah Catherine Brunswick b: 1855 d: December 1943 Gender:
Female

.23 Robert William Blakeney b: December 23, 1855 d: June 12, 1912
Gender: Male

+Catherine R. Roast b: Abt. 1857 m: December 06, 1887 in
Musquodoboit Harbour, NS, Canada Gender: Female

.23 Angus Walter Blakeney b: December 22, 1858 Gender: Male

.23 Samuel B. Blakeney b: 1860 Gender: Male

+Eliza A. Dupee b: Abt. 1862 m: March 18, 1889 in Sheet Harbour,
NS, Canada Gender: Female

.23 Malcom W. Blakeney b: 1865 d: December 10, 1940 Gender: Male

+Phoebe Alnira Boutilier b: Abt. 1867 m: December 18, 1891 in
Musquodoboit Harbour, NS, Canada Gender: Female

.22 Lawrence Blakeney b: September 11, 1814 d: 1857 Gender: Male

.22 Benjamin Blakeney b: September 13, 1817 in Ship Harbour,
Halifax, Nova Scotia, Canada d: January 25, 1901 Number of
children: 2 Gender: Male

.+Frances " Fanny" Day b: August 1815 m: September 21, 1838 in
Brunswick Street Methodist Church, Halifax, NS, Canada d:
February 17, 1901 Number of children: 2 Gender: Female

.23 Agnes Nancy Blakeney b: 1846 Gender: Female

+Henry John Myers b: Abt. 1842 m: January 01, 1871 Gender: Male

.23 [72] Isaac Day Blakeney b: July 09, 1853 Gender: Male

+[79] Eunice Sophia Blakeney b: October 13, 1853 d: March 1926

Father: Luke Blakeney Mother: Sarah Ann Doyle Gender: Female

.*2nd Wife of [72] Isaac Day Blakeney:

+Eunice Blakeney b: October 13, 1853 m: June 10, 1882 d: March 1926 Gender: Female

.22 William Blakeney b: April 01, 1821 Gender: Male

.22 Agnes Ann Nancy Blakeney b: December 06, 1824 d: March 13, 1904 Number of children: 1 Gender: Female

.+John Henry Newcombe b: Abt. 1822 Number of children: 1 Gender: Male

.23 Isaac Ambrose Blakeney b: Abt. 1845 Gender: Male

.22 Catherine Charlotte Blakeney b: March 27, 1826 Gender: Female

.22 Peter James Blakeney b: February 19, 1828 Gender: Male

.22 Harriet Blakeney b: September 22, 1829 in Ship Harbour, Halifax, Nova Scotia, Canada d: 1909 Gender: Female

.+Swanton Whirmore b: 1796 m: November 16, 1850 in Saugus, MA d: 1868 in Lynn, MA Gender: Male

.22 Mary Matilda Blakeney b: July 04, 1831 d: 1920 Gender: Female

.+William Mason b: Abt. 1830 m: December 21, 1854 in Pope Harbour, NS, Canada Gender: Male

.22 Polly Lucretia Blakeney b: May 02, 1833 Gender: Female

.+Simon Myers b: Abt. 1830 m: January 02, 1854 in Tangier, NS, Canada Gender: Male

.22 Daniel Blakeney b: March 29, 1835 in Ship Harbour, Halifax, Nova Scotia, Canada d: 1920 Number of children: 7 Gender: Male

.+Catherine Blakeney b: Abt. 1837 m: Abt. 1865 Number of children: 7 Gender: Female

.23 Minnie Blakeney b: Abt. 1865 Gender: Female

+Harris H. Arnold b: Abt. 1863 Gender: Male

.23 Robert Blakeney b: 1867 Gender: Male

.23 Lemuel Blakeney b: April 03, 1869 d: March 11, 1889 Gender: Male

.23 Annie Collins Blakeney b: December 06, 1870 Gender: Female

.23 Mary Rose Blakeney b: February 21, 1872 Gender: Female

.23 Thomas Blakeney b: 1874 Gender: Male

The Blakeneys

+Minnie Boutillier b: Abt. 1876 Gender: Female

.23 Lewis Wilson Blakeney b: May 1879 d: April 07, 1980 Gender: Male

+Effie Hopkins b: Abt. 1881 Gender: Female

.22 George Blakeney b: March 28, 1837 Gender: Male

.21 Andrew Blakeney b: July 02, 1785 in Ship Harbour, Halifax, Nova Scotia d: 1817 in Nova Scotia Number of children: 2 Gender: Male

.+Catherine A. Day b: 1790 in Nova Scotia m: in Nova Scotia d: September 28, 1866 Number of children: 2 Gender: Female

.22 John Blakeney b: September 28, 1814 d: 1899 Number of children: 13 Gender: Male

.+Isabelle Blakeney b: Abt. 1816 m: Abt. 1830 in St. Paul's, Halifax, NS, Canada Number of children: 13 Gender: Female

.23 Isabelle Blakeney b: Abt. 1830 d: 1899 Gender: Female

+David Weeks b: Abt. 1825 Gender: Male

.23 Lawrence Blakeney b: Abt. 1832 Gender: Male

+Mart Keizer b: Abt. 1835 m: October 01, 1866 Gender: Female

.23 [73] Susannah Blakeney b: September 20, 1843 Gender: Female

+William Burgess b: Abt. 1840 Gender: Male

.*2nd Husband of [73] Susannah Blakeney:

+James T, Day b: Abt. 1845 Gender: Male

.23 [76] Robert B. Blakeney b: 1847 Gender: Male

+[75] Catherine "Rachel" Blakeney b: Abt. 1850 m: October 12, 1866 in Halifax, NS, Canada Father: Andrew Blakeney Mother: Sarah Jane Fitzgerald Gender: Female

.23 John Andrew Blakeney b: 1848 d: August 05, 1976 Gender: Male

.23 Daniel Blakeney b: 1849 Gender: Male

+Matilda Ann Webber b: Abt. 1850 Gender: Female

.23 Isabelle Blakeney b: 1851 Gender: Female

+James Fredricks b: Abt. 1850 m: March 09, 1876 Gender: Male

.23 Augusta Blakeney b: 1853 Gender: Female

.23 [74] John Andrew Blakeney b: 1854 d: August 05, 1976 Gender: Male

+Mary Ann Wambolt b: Abt. 1855 Gender: Female

.*2nd Wife of [74] John Andrew Blakeney:

+Hannah Corkum b: Abt. 1860 Gender: Female

.23 Generetta "Jane" Blakeney b: October 22, 1856 Gender: Female

+John Gibson b: Abt. 1854 m: December 09, 1881 Gender: Male

.23 Ronald Alexander Blakeney b: 1858 Gender: Male

+Emma Catherine Myers b: Abt. 1860 Gender: Female

.23 James A. Blakeney b: 1860 Gender: Male

+Sarah A. Giddings b: Abt. 1862 Gender: Female

.23 Lavina Blakeney, adopted b: Abt. 1862 Gender: Female

.22 Andrew Blakeney b: March 23, 1819 d: March 15, 1857 Number
   of children: 8 Gender: Male

.+Sarah Jane Fitzgerald b: Abt. 1820 m: Abt. 1840 Number of children:
   8 Gender: Female

.23 Andrew Blakeney b: 1841 d: 1921 Gender: Male

+Louisa Giffin b: Abt. 1843 m: April 26, 1866 Gender: Female

.23 [75] Catherine "Rachel" Blakeney b: Abt. 1850 Gender: Female

+[76] Robert B. Blakeney b: 1847 m: October 12, 1866 in Halifax, NS,
   Canada Father: John Blakeney Mother: Isabelle Blakeney
   Gender: Male

.23 Ann Melinda Blakeney b: Abt. 1852 Gender: Female

+Zebe Hewirt Giffin b: Abt. 1850 m: October 27, 1870 in Isaac's
   Harbour, NS, Canada Gender: Male

.23 Catherine Ellen Blakeney b: December 24, 1843 Gender: Female

.23 Robert John Blakeney b: 1847 Gender: Male

.23 George Blakeney b: 1849 Gender: Male

+Anne Florence Kennedy b: Abt. 1850 m: March 20, 1873 in St.
   Mary's Melrose, NS, Canada Gender: Female

.23 Levi Blakeney b: 1852 Gender: Male

.23 John Henry Blakeney b: 1854 d: April 03, 1930 Gender: Male

+Matilda Mason b: Abt. 1856 m: June 12, 1875 in Halifax, NS, Canada
   Gender: Female

.21 Chambers Blakeney, Jr. b: March 20, 1788 in Ship Harbour,
   Halifax, Nova Scotia, Canada d: December 23, 1862 in Jeddore,
   Nova Scotia, Canada Number of children: 8 Gender: Male
   Burial: Pioneers Rest Cemetery, West Jeddore, NS, Canada

.+Ann Jane Harpell b: Abt. 1788 in Ragged Islands, Shelburne County, NS, Canada m: November 28, 1811 in St. Paul's, Halifax, Nova Scotia d: May 19, 1858 in West Jeddore, Nova Scotia, Canada Number of children: 8 Father: Luke Harpell Mother: Lydia Arnold Gender: Female Burial: Pioneers Rest Cemetery, West Jeddore, Nova Scotia, Canada

.22 Catherine Blakeney b: 1812 d: 1901 Gender: Female

.22 [77] William Blakeney b: Abt. July 20, 1814 in West Jeddore, Nova Scotia, Canada d: Aft. 1891 Number of children: 1 Gender: Male

.+Eliza Rachel Hartling b: November 08, 1818 in Eastern Passage m: June 01, 1846 in Jeddore, Nova Scotia, Canada d: July 02, 1866 in Jeddore, Nova Scotia, Canada Gender: Female

.*2nd Wife of [77] William Blakeney:

.+Mary Maskell b: Abt. 1820 in West Jeddore, Nova Scotia, Canada m: December 24, 1868 in Jeddore, Nova Scotia, Canada d: October 25, 1900 Number of children: 1 Gender: Female

.23 [78] Peter James Blakeney b: Abt. 1847 in West Jeddore, Nova Scotia, Canada d: August 14, 1916 Number of children: 1 Gender: Male

+Susan Lavinia Heffler b: Abt. 1847 in Sackville, Nova Scotia, Canada m: October 21, 1872 in Sackville d: Aft. 1891 Number of children: 1 Gender: Female

24 Percy Havelock Blakeney b: Abt. 1881 in Lower Sackville, Nova Scotia, Canada Gender: Male

.*2nd Wife of [78] Peter James Blakeney:

+Grace Margaret Mitchell b: August 24, 1862 in East Jeddore, Nova Scotia, Canada m: April 24, 1882 in Jeddore, Nova Scotia, Canada Gender: Female

.22 Luke Blakeney b: March 16, 1816 d: 1901 Number of children: 7 Gender: Male

.+Sarah Ann Doyle b: Abt. 1818 m: Abt. 1838 Number of children: 7 Gender: Female

.23 Agnes Blakeney b: Abt. 1839 Gender: Female

+Charles William Heffler b: Abt. 1837 m: August 15, 1874 in Halifax,

NS, Canada Gender: Male

.23 Mary A. Blakeney b: Abt. 1841 Gender: Female

+Rufus Hawkins b: Abt. 1839 m: January 09, 1872 Gender: Male

.23 Ellen Blakeney b: Abt. 1843 Gender: Female

+Fredrick Mosher b: Abt. 1840 m: September 10, 1874 in Halifax, NS, Canada Gender: Male

.23 [81] John Atwood Blakeney b: 1846 d: 1906 Gender: Male

+[80] Elizabeth Blakeney b: 1853 m: September 09, 1873 d: 1910 Father: David Blakeney Mother: Agnes Arnold Gender: Female

.23 [79] Eunice Sophia Blakeney b: October 13, 1853 d: March 1926 Gender: Female

+[72] Isaac Day Blakeney b: July 09, 1853 Father: Benjamin Blakeney Mother: Frances " Fanny" Day Gender: Male

.23 Luke Abner Blakeney b: 1866 d: May 09, 1867 Gender: Male

.23 Silas Blakeney b: 1866 d: 1876 Gender: Male

.22 Lydia Blakeney b: March 16, 1818 Gender: Female

.+Elijah Mosher b: Abt. 1816 Gender: Male

.22 Chambers Blakeney b: November 19, 1820 d: 1907 Gender: Male

.+Jane Mosher b: Abt. 1822 d: 1899 Gender: Female

.22 John Blakeney b: 1822 d: 1844 Gender: Male

.22 Margaret Blakeney b: Abt. 1824 Gender: Female

.+Samuel MacDonald b: Abt. 1822 Gender: Male

.22 David Blakeney b: 1825 d: April 24, 1889 Number of children: 10 Gender: Male

.+Agnes Arnold b: 1829 m: July 01, 1846 in Halifax, NS, Canada d: September 24, 1895 Number of children: 10 Gender: Female

.23 Amos H. Blakeney b: Abt. 1847 Gender: Male

+Minnie Matthews b: Abt. 1849 m: May 22, 1884 in Halifax, NS, Canada Gender: Female

.23 Lydia Ann Blakeney b: December 13, 1850 d: January 12, 1914 Gender: Female

+John Henry (Jack) Mitchell b: November 1846 m: September 28, 1872 in Jeddore, NS, Canada d: June 09, 1891 Gender: Male

.23 [80] Elizabeth Blakeney b: 1853 d: 1910 Gender: Female

+[81] John Atwood Blakeney b: 1846 m: September 09, 1873 d: 1906

THE BLAKENEYS

Father: Luke Blakeney Mother: Sarah Ann Doyle Gender: Male

.23 David H. Blakeney b: 1857 d: August 14, 1916 Gender: Male

+Grace Margaret Hart Mitchell b: 1861 m: April 24, 1882 in Jeddore, NS, Canada d: 1917 Gender: Female

.23 Gidean John Blakeney b: 1857 d: 1923 Gender: Male

+Margaret Elizabeth Mitchell b: 1861 m: November 10, 1881 in Jeddore, NS, Canada d: 1917 Gender: Female

.23 Reuben Blakeney b: 1862 d: February 17, 1920 Gender: Male

+Jessie Blanche Mitchell b: September 16, 1868 m: December 05, 1905 in Oyster Pond, Nova Scotia, Canada d: 1968 Gender: Female

.23 Lemual Blakeney b: 1863 Gender: Male

+Ermina Harpell b: 1868 d: 1927 Gender: Female

.23 Benjamin Blakeney b: 1865 d: 1931 Gender: Male

+Drucilla Mitchell b: 1873 Gender: Female

.23 Caroline Blakeney b: 1868 d: October 20, 1872 Gender: Female

.23 Adelia Blakeney b: 1870 d: 1913 Gender: Female

+Albert Peter Harpell b: 1861 d: 1937 Gender: Male

.21 John Blakeney b: June 28, 1790 in Ship Harbour, Halifax, Nova Scotia d: 1814 in Nova Scotia Gender: Male

..20 Mary Blakeney b: Abt. 1763 in Northern Ireland d: in SC? Gender: Female

17 William "the Horseman" Blakeney, Lieutenant b: Abt. 1627 in Mount Blakeney (or Thomastown), County Limerick, Ireland d: March 31, 1664 in Ireland? Number of children: 8 Gender: Male Burial: Abt. April 02, 1664 Saint Peter's Church, Kilmallock, Ireland (Notes: the Norfolk Blakeney's coat-of-arms is displayed on his tomb; he purchased Thomastown, Ireland, & afterwards called it "Mount Blakeney").

+_____ _____? b: Abt. 1630 in Ireland? m: Abt. 1650 d: Aft. 1664 in Ireland? Number of children: 8 Gender: Female

18 William Blakeney, Captain b: Abt. 1650 in Mount Blakeney (or Thomastown), County Limerick, Ireland. d: Abt. 1718 in Kilmallock, Ireland. Number of children: 9 Gender: Male Burial: Abt. 1718 Saint Peter's Church, Kilmallock, Ireland.

..+Elizabeth Bowerman b: Abt. 1650 in Holywell, Roscommon,

Ireland. m: Abt. 1671 in Ireland? d: Aft. 1710 in Mt. Blakeney, Galway, Ireland Number of children: 9 Father: Cornet Henry Bowerman Mother: Katherine Purdon Gender: Female

..19 William Blakeney Blakeney, Lord Baron (royal line) b: Bet. 1672 - 1673 in Castle Blakeney, County Limerick, Ireland. d: September 29, 1761 in London, England Gender: Male Burial: September 1761 Westminster Abbey, England. (Notes: a famous statue of Lord Blakeney was erected in Dublin, but was later torn down in the 1922 IRA uprising. Since William did not have children, sadly with his death the Blakeney royal title and peerage became extinct).

..19 Hatton Blakeney b: Abt. 1675 in Ireland Number of children: 4 Gender: Female

..+Robert Armstrong b: Abt. 1750 in of Cork, Ireland m: Abt. 1775 in Ireland Number of children: 4 Gender: Male

..20 _____ Armstrong b: Abt. 1776 Gender: Female

..20 _____ Armstrong b: Abt. 1777 Gender: Female

..20 _____ Armstrong b: Abt. 1780 Gender: Female

..20 _____ Armstrong b: Abt. 1781 Gender: Male

..19 Charles Blakeney, Lieutenant b: Abt. 1677 in Ireland? Gender: Male

..+_____ _____? b: Abt. 1695 m: Abt. 1720 Gender: Female

..19 Mary Blakeney b: Abt. 1681 in Ireland? Gender: Female

..+_____ (Le) Strange b: Abt. 1750 in Ireland? Gender: Male

..19 Robert Blakeney, Esquire & MP b: Abt. 1683 in Mount Blakeney, County Limerick, Ireland d: November 18, 1763 in Abbert, County Galway, Ireland (Lived at St. Stephen's Green, Dublin, Ireland) Number of children: 6 Gender: Male (Note: Robert's brother, Lord Baron William Blakeney, bequethed his entire estate to Robert)

..+Deborah Smythe b: Abt. 1700 in Ballynatray, County Waterford, Ireland m: January 27, 1728/29 Number of children: 6 Father: Grice Smythe, Esquire of Ballynatray Mother: _____ _____? Gender: Female

..20 Esther Blakeney b: Abt. 1730 d: Abt. 1730 Gender: Female

(Notes: she died young).

..20 William Blakeney b: 1733 in Mount Blakeney, County Limerick, Ireland. d: September 15, 1811 in Ireland? Number of children: 1 Gender: Male (Notes: William & Gertrude were cousins).

..+Gertrude (or Jemima?) Smyth, Smythe b: Abt. 1735 in Ballynatray, County Waterford, Ireland. m: June 09, 1764 in St Anne's, Dublin, Ireland d: Abt. August 24, 1768 in Dublin, Ireland Number of children: 1 Father: Richard Smyth, Smythe Mother: _____ _____ ? Gender: Female Burial: August 26, 1768 St. Andrews Church, Dublin, Ireland. (Notes: Gertrude & William were cousins).

.21 Robert Blakeney, Reverend & Vicar b: 1768 in Ireland or England? d: January 12, 1825 in England Gender: Male (Notes: he was Vicar of Great Easton).

..20 [82] Gertrude Blakeney b: Abt. 1734 in Ireland? d: April 21, 1757 in Ireland? Number of children: 2 Gender: Female (Notes: Gertrude & Robert were cousins).

..+[83] Robert Blakeney, Colonel b: Abt. 1720 in Abbert, County Galway (?), Ireland m: May 28, 1752 in Ireland? d: December 30, 1762 in Ireland? Number of children: 2 Father: John Blakeney, Colonel & MP Mother: Grace Persse Gender: Male (Notes: Robert & Gertrude were cousins).

.21 [84] Grace Blakeney b: Abt. December 1755 in Abbert, County Galway (?), Ireland d: Aft. 1787 Number of children: 1 Gender: Female

.+[85] Thomas Lyon, Esquire b: Abt. 1755 in Watercastle, Queen's County (?) m: May 09, 1786 Number of children: 1 Gender: Male

.22 [86] _____ Lyon b: Abt. 1787 Gender: Female

.21 [87] John Blakeney, Lieutenant b: September 12, 1756 in Abbert, County Galway, Ireland? d: August 23, 1781 Gender: Male Burial: (Notes: he died unmarried).

..20 George Blakeney, Lieutenant b: 1735 in Ireland Gender: Male

..20 Jane Blakeney b: Abt. 1738 Gender: Female

..+Rolf Unwin, Esquire b: Abt. 1735 in of Lordbegg Gender: Male

..20 Grice Blakeney, General b: 1741 in Ireland d: November 16, 1816 Gender: Male Burial: (Notes: he died unmarried).

..19 [88] Catherine Blakeney b: Abt. 1687 in Mount Blakeney, Ireland Number of children: 1 Gender: Female

..+James Knight, b: Abt. 1694 in Ballyhoe, Cork, Ireland Father: Christopher Knight Mother: Ellen Gibbs Gender: Male Burial: April 12, 1764

..*2nd Husband of [88] Catherine Blakeney:

..+Joseph Gubbins b: Abt. 1680 in Knocklong (or Kilfrush), County Limerick, Ireland? m: Abt. 1775 Number of children: 1 Gender: Male

..20 _____ Gubbins b: Abt. 1777 Gender: Unknown

..19 George Blakeney, Lt-Col. b: Abt. 1690 in Ireland? Gender: Male

..19 John Blakeney, Lieutenant b: Abt. 1705 in Ireland? d: February 01, 1719/20 Number of children: 1 Gender: Male (Notes: According to Lochlainn Seabrook's theory, Lt. John Blakeney MAY be the Father of Captain John Blakeney (1732-1832) who immigrated to South Carolina, and so he is temporarily listed thus; NO PROOF YET).

..+_____ _____? b: Abt. 1707 in Ireland? Number of children: 1 Gender: Female

..20 John Blakeney, Captain, South Carolina Branch b: 1732 in Mt. Blakeney, County Limerick, Ireland (some say Galway, Dublin, or Castleblakeney, Ireland) d: August 18, 1832 in Chesterfield County, SC, buried in Pageland, Chesterfield County, SC (came to Granville County, NC about 1750) Number of children: 8 Gender: Male Burial: August 20, 1832 (Notes: while it is a Blakeney family tradition that John is a grandson of Capt. William Blakeney, it has not yet been proven; if true, however, it is Lochlainn Seabrook's theory that Capt. John Blakeney may be the son of John Blakeney, born about 1705).

..+Margaret (or Mary) "Peggy" Evans, b: 1740 in Galway, Ireland m: Bet. 1755 - 1757 in Galway, County Limerick, Ireland d: Aft. 1774 in Old Cheraw, SC Number of children: 8 Gender: Female

THE BLAKENEYS

.21 [89] Thomas Blakeney, Rev. War Soldier b: Abt. 1756 in Butte, Granville County NC d: 1823 in Chesterfield County, SC Number of children: 6 Gender: Male (Note: he served in the American Revolutionary War under Col. Lemuel Benton)

.+Susanna Lowry b: Abt. 1766 in SC m: Abt. 1780 in NC or SC Number of children: 1 Father: Robert Lowry Gender: Female

.22 Jane Blakeney b: Abt. 1781 in SC Gender: Female

.*2nd Wife of [89] Thomas Blakeney:

.+Mary Atkinson b: Abt. 1759 in NC m: Abt. 1785 in NC Gender: Female (Note: looking for her ancestors)

.*3rd Wife of [89] Thomas Blakeney:

.+Harriet _____? b: Abt. 1781 in VA m: Abt. 1795 in SC Number of children: 5 Gender: Female

.22 Frederick Blakeney b: April 1796 in SC d: 1870 in Corinth, Tishomingo County, MS Number of children: 7 Gender: Male Burial: 1870 Tishomingo County, MS

.+Jane _____? b: 1801 in SC d: 1871 in Corinth, Tishomingo County, MS Number of children: 7 Gender: Female Burial: 1871 Tishomingo County MS

.23 Louisa Blakeney b: 1826 in TN Gender: Female

.23 Sarah Jane Blakeney b: 1831 in TN Gender: Female

.23 David Blakeney, Blakney b: 1833 in TN Number of children: 1 Gender: Male

+Nancy Clementine Joslin b: Abt. 1835 in SC? Number of children: 1 Gender: Female

24 Samuel Blakeney b: May 20, 1867 in (Jasper or Smith Co.?) MS d: January 25, 1950 in OK? Number of children: 2 Gender: Male

+Ervilla Samantha Idabell Ford b: Abt. 1870 in Jasper or Smith County MS? m: July 24, 1896 in Tishomingo, Tishomingo County, MS d: in OK? Number of children: 2 Father: Joseph Ford Gender: Female (Note: Ervilla is the niece of the famous automobile industrialist, Henry Ford, 1863-1947)

.23 John Blakeney b: 1834 in TN Gender: Male

.23 Alvin Henry Blakeney b: August 07, 1835 in KY Gender: Male

.23 Mary Blakeney b: 1839 in MS Gender: Female

.23 William Blakeney b: 1842 in Tishomingo County MS Gender: Male

.22 John Blakeney b: January 15, 1806 in TN Gender: Male

.22 Tobias Blakeney b: December 10, 1807 in TN Gender: Male

.22 Alvin Blakeney b: Abt. 1811 in TN Gender: Male

.22 Thomas Blakeney, Jr. b: Abt. 1815 Gender: Male

.21 [90] John Blakeney, Jr., Rev. War Soldier b: January 14, 1758 in Butte/Granville County, NC d: March 30, 1848 in Chesterfield County, SC Number of children: 12 Gender: Male (Note: He has more known descendants than any other Blakeney; he served in the American Revolutionary War under Capt. Standard)

.+Nancy Lowry b: Abt. 1765 m: Abt. 1783 Number of children: 11 Father: Robert Lowry Gender: Female

.22 Mary Blakeney b: Abt. 1784 d: 1881 Number of children: 2 Gender: Female

.+Peter May b: Abt. 1782 Number of children: 2 Father: John May Gender: Male

.23 Nancy May b: Abt. 1802 Gender: Female

.23 William May b: Abt. 1805 Gender: Male

.22 Nancy Blakeney b: August 08, 1786 Number of children: 1 Gender: Female

.+David Laney b: Abt. 1785 Number of children: 1 Gender: Male

.23 Sally Laney b: Abt. 1803 Gender: Female

.22 June (or Jane) Blakeney b: February 06, 1788 Gender: Female

.+_____ Welch b: Abt. 1785 Gender: Male

.22 Susannah Blakeney b: September 12, 1789 Gender: Female

.+Archibald Laney b: Abt. 1785 Gender: Male

.22 James Blakeney b: February 06, 1794 Gender: Male

.22 Elizabeth Blakeney b: May 22, 1797 d: May 03, 1898 Number of children: 15 Gender: Female

.+Matthias Beaver, Jr. b: July 30, 1792 d: July 30, 1877 Number of children: 15 Father: Matthias Beaver, Sr. Gender: Male

.23 Louisa Beaver b: July 28, 1817 Gender: Female

.23 Jones Beaver b: October 1818 Gender: Male

.23 Fernetty Beaver b: April 24, 1820 Gender: Female

.23 James Beaver b: February 03, 1822 Gender: Male

.23 Nancy Beaver b: October 31, 1823 Gender: Female

.23 Mary Beaver b: January 1825 Gender: Female

.23 Francis Beaver b: January 01, 1827 d: September 26, 1915 Gender: Female

+John Sanders b: November 07, 1837 m: 1861 d: February 02, 1922 Gender: Male

.23 Alfred Beaver b: October 29, 1828 Gender: Male

.23 Aaron Beaver b: December 13, 1830 Gender: Male

.23 Elizabeth Beaver b: November 19, 1832 d: August 22, 1905 Gender: Female

+Wilson Threatt b: Abt. 1830 Gender: Male

.23 Nancy Beaver b: October 06, 1834 Gender: Female

.23 Sarah Beaver b: September 16, 1836 Gender: Female

.23 John Beaver b: December 01, 1838 Gender: Male

.23 Nathan Beaver b: February 27, 1841 Gender: Male

+Paralee Funderburk b: Abt. 1843 Gender: Female

.23 Elihu Beaver b: March 20, 1843 Gender: Male

.22 Frances Blakeney b: May 02, 1800 Gender: Female

.+Henry Shute b: Abt. 1798 Gender: Male

.22 Hugh Blakeney b: July 08, 1802 d: October 29, 1846 Number of children: 1 Gender: Male

.+Palestine Pore b: December 23, 1803 d: June 1856 Number of children: 1 Gender: Female

.23 John Aaron Blakeney b: July 11, 1825 d: March 18, 1851 Gender: Male

+Sarah Hough b: January 01, 1829 d: November 15, 1849 Gender: Female

.22 Michal Blakeney b: April 01, 1807 Number of children: 2 Gender: Female

.+Berry Evans b: Abt. 1805 Number of children: 2 Gender: Male

.23 John Evans b: July 02, 1844 Gender: Male

+Harriet Miller b: Abt. 1845 Gender: Female

.23 Mary Ann 'Mollie' Evans b: April 22, 1849 Number of children: 5 Gender: Female

+George Richard Sowell b: Abt. 1845 Number of children: 5 Gender:

Male

24 Belle Sowell b: August 12, 1872 in SC Gender: Female

24 Lillian Sowell b: January 20, 1874 in SC Gender: Female

24 Elizabeth 'Lizzie' Virginia Sowell b: August 29, 1876 in SC Gender: Female

+John William Ingram b: Abt. 1875 m: December 02, 1891 Gender: Male

24 Kate Sowell b: September 22, 1877 Number of children: 3 Gender: Female

+George Richard Doster b: Abt. 1875 Number of children: 3 Gender: Male

24 Henry Berry Sowell b: October 26, 1878 in SC Gender: Male

+Jessie Delena Blakeney b: Abt. 1880 m: March 02, 1902 Gender: Female

.22 William Blakeney b: March 16, 1810 Gender: Male

.22 Lewis Alexander Blakeney b: 1812 Number of children: 2 Gender: Male

.+Elizabeth Funderburk b: 1808 d: March 20, 1863 Number of children: 2 Gender: Female

.23 Melancton Leander Blakeney b: 1833 d: August 1884 Number of children: 1 Gender: Male

+Susan J. Rogers b: Abt. 1835 Number of children: 1 Gender: Female

24 Percy C. Blakeney b: 1882 in Chesterfield, South Carolina Gender: Male

.23 Lewis Columbus Blakeney b: November 07, 1851 Gender: Male

+Rachel Rebecca Vail b: Abt. 1853 Gender: Female

.*2nd Wife of [90] John Blakeney, Jr.:

.+Nancy May b: July 12, 1769 in Anson County, NC m: 1785 in Anson, NC d: August 1815 Number of children: 1 Father: John May Mother: Mary _____? Gender: Female

.22 [95] John "Jack" Blakeney III b: August 09, 1787 in Pageland, Chesterfield County, SC d: July 29, 1876 in Pageland, Chesterfield County, SC Number of children: 21 Gender: Male

.+Elizabeth Page b: Abt. 1793 in Chesterfield County, SC m: 1812 in Chesterfield, SC d: July 31, 1827 in Chesterfield County, SC

Number of children: 9 Father: _____ Page Gender: Female

.23 Albert Blakeney b: June 06, 1813 d: October 13, 1846 Number of children: 6 Gender: Male

+Anne Ray b: February 1809 Number of children: 6 Gender: Female

24 Reece Blakeney b: December 21, 1834 Gender: Male

+Caroline K. Kirkley b: Abt. 1835 m: May 12, 1854 Gender: Female

24 [91] Elizabeth Blakeney b: January 30, 1836 Gender: Female

+A. Jackson Parks b: Abt. 1835 m: October 11, 1856 Gender: Male

*2nd Husband of [91] Elizabeth Blakeney:

+John Peter Hancock b: Abt. 1836 m: Abt. 1860 Gender: Male

24 James C. Blakeney b: May 07, 1838 Gender: Male

24 Louisa Blakeney b: November 15, 1840 Gender: Female

24 [93] Eliza Blakeney b: October 12, 1843 Gender: Female

+[92] John Jackson b: 1837 m: 1865 in Sumter County, AL d: 1915 Father: James Jackson Mother: Charlotte Blakeney Gender: Male

24 John W. Blakeney b: June 26, 1847 Gender: Male

+Roberta Campbell b: September 16, 1850 m: Abt. 1869 d: December 20, 1925 Gender: Female

.23 Elender Blakeney b: February 01, 1815 Gender: Female

.23 James Blakeney b: May 10, 1816 d: in Jasper County, MS (killed by his overseer) Number of children: 1 Gender: Male

+Harriet Shelby b: 1826 Number of children: 1 Gender: Female

24 John C. ("Charles"?) Blakeney b: April 13, 1844 d: September 14, 1910 Gender: Male

+Lula Cole b: Abt. 1845 m: February 21, 1877 in Ellis County, TX Gender: Female

.23 Harriet Blakeney b: October 14, 1817 d: Abt. 1876 in Sumpter County, AL Gender: Female

+George Morris b: Abt. 1815 Gender: Male

.23 Charlotte Blakeney b: July 14, 1819 d: 1897 Number of children: 7 Gender: Female

+James Jackson b: 1804 m: 1836 d: 1867 Number of children: 7 Gender: Male

24 [92] John Jackson b: 1837 d: 1915 Gender: Male

+[93] Eliza Blakeney b: October 12, 1843 m: 1865 in Sumter County,
     AL Father: Albert Blakeney Mother: Anne Ray Gender: Female
24 Elizabeth Jackson b: Abt. 1840 Gender: Female
+Vic Tutt, Captain b: Abt. 1835 Gender: Male
24 Emma Jackson b: Abt. 1844 Gender: Female
+Alexander Wimberly b: Abt. 1842 Gender: Male
24 Allison Jackson b: 1847 Gender: Female
24 Harriet Jackson b: Abt. 1850 Gender: Female
+James Barton b: Abt. 1845 Gender: Male
24 James Blakeney Jackson b: September 06, 1857 Gender: Male
+Mollie B. Jenkins b: Abt. 1860 Gender: Female
24 Andrew L. Jackson b: 1862 Gender: Male
+Annie Wylie b: Abt. 1865 m: in Ft. Worth, TX Gender: Female
.23 William W. Blakeney b: March 04, 1821 Number of children: 11
     Gender: Male
+Eliza Ann Evans b: 1832 m: in Hill County TX Number of children: 11
     Gender: Female
24 Albert Blakeney b: 1849 in White Plains, SC Gender: Male
+Annice Massey b: Abt. 1850 Gender: Female
24 Martha Jane Blakeney b: 1851 in White Plains, SC Gender: Female
+D. A. Johnston b: Abt. 1850 m: in Harrisburg, NC Gender: Male
24 John Stephen Blakeney b: 1852 in White Plains, SC Gender: Male
24 Mary Blakeney b: 1854 in White Plains, SC Gender: Female
+O. C. Curlee b: Abt. 1850 m: in Monroe, NC Gender: Male
24 Cornelia Blakeney b: 1857 in White Plains, SC Gender: Female
+C. C. McCauley b: Abt. 1855 m: in Monroe, NC Gender: Male
24 James Calhoun Blakeney b: 1861 in White Plains, SC Gender: Male
+Annie C. Redner b: 1865 m: 1887 in Ladonia, TX Gender: Female
24 Cora Virginia Blakeney b: 1864 in White Plains, SC Gender: Female
+A. W. Baird b: Abt. 1861 m: in Cleburne, TX Gender: Male
24 William Thomas Blakeney b: 1866 in Monroe, NC Gender: Male
+Lillian Newton b: Abt. 1868 m: in Cleburne, TX Gender: Female
24 Benjamin Franklin Blakeney b: 1868 in Monroe, NC Gender: Male
24 Charles O'Connor Blakeney b: 1871 in Monroe, NC Gender: Male
+Alice McGaughey b: Abt. 1874 m: in Brownwood, TX Gender:

Female

24 Virginia Blakeney b: 1876 Gender: Female

+J. H. Lee b: Abt. 1875 m: in Fort Worth, TX Gender: Male

.23 Matilda Blakeney b: September 24, 1822 Gender: Female

+John Shelby b: Abt. 1820 m: Abt. 1840 in Hill County, TX Gender: Male

.23 Elizabeth Blakeney b: June 14, 1824 d: September 1875 Number of children: 7 Gender: Female

+George Brewer b: Abt. 1822 m: Abt. 1845 Number of children: 7 Gender: Male

24 John Brewer b: Abt. 1845 Gender: Male

24 Mary Brewer b: Abt. 1847 Gender: Female

24 Rosa Brewer b: Abt. 1849 Gender: Female

24 Louisa Brewer b: Abt. 1851 Gender: Female

24 Eliza Brewer b: Abt. 1853 Gender: Female

24 Emma Brewer b: Abt. 1855 Gender: Female

24 Ella Brewer b: Abt. 1857 Gender: Female

.23 [94] Elizabeth (Betty) Blakeney b: June 1827 in SC d: in Smith County, MS Number of children: 5 Gender: Female

+Jackson Benison b: Abt. 1825 in MS m: Abt. 1850 Number of children: 3 Gender: Male

24 Margarette Benison b: 1849 Gender: Female

24 Richard Jackson Benison b: Abt. 1851 Gender: Male

24 Nancy "Nannie" Benison b: Abt. 1854 Gender: Female

.*2nd Husband of [94] Elizabeth (Betty) Blakeney:

+George Emmanuel (Manuel) Ainsworth b: Abt. 1825 m: Abt. 1858 Number of children: 2 Gender: Male

24 Lucy Vance Ainsworth b: 1859 Gender: Female

24 Mary Elizabeth (Betty) Ainsworth b: November 1860 Number of children: 2 Gender: Female

+Matthew A. Russell b: June 25, 1864 d: October 05, 1898 (Murdered) Number of children: 2 Father: Frank Absolum Russell Mother: Lucinda Vann Gender: Male Burial: Mt. Zion Cemetery, Smith County, MS

.*2nd Wife of [95] John "Jack" Blakeney III:

.+Sallie Evans b: Abt. 1810 in Pageland, Chesterfield County, SC m: August 03, 1833 in Pageland, Chesterfield County, SC d: July 27, 1847 in Pageland, Chesterfield County, SC Number of children: 7 Father: William Evans Gender: Female

.23 [96] Franklin Blakeney b: December 14, 1833 d: in TX Number of children: 3 Gender: Male

+Susanna Blakeney b: Abt. 1835 in Sumpter County, AL? m: Abt. 1853 Number of children: 3 Father: Hugh Blakeney Gender: Female

24 Albert Blakeney b: Abt. 1854 Gender: Male

24 Annie Blakeney b: Abt. 1856 Gender: Female

24 Benjamin Franklin Blakeney b: Abt. 1858 in Bonham, TX Gender: Male

.*2nd Wife of [96] Franklin Blakeney:

+[105] Mary Blakeney b: Abt. 1818 m: Abt. 1855 Father: Alfred Blakeney Mother: Margaret McIntosh Gender: Female

.23 Mary Jane Blakeney b: May 16, 1836 Number of children: 7 Gender: Female

+Robert James Blakeney b: December 24, 1836 m: 1856 d: December 24, 1878 Number of children: 7 Father: Hugh Blakeney Gender: Male

24 [97] Mary Louisa Blakeney b: January 31, 1858 d: January 03, 1911 Gender: Female

+Polk Rushing b: Abt. 1855 Gender: Male

*2nd Husband of [97] Mary Louisa Blakeney:

+Richard Tillery b: Abt. 1857 Gender: Male

24 Opheilia Davis Blakeney b: August 18, 1860 Gender: Female

+Fred Stringfellow b: Abt. 1858 m: in Athens, TX Gender: Male

24 Fannie Morgan Blakeney b: February 09, 1862 d: April 05, 1883 Gender: Female

+John Dave Butcher b: Abt. 1860 Gender: Male

24 Temperance Ann Blakeney b: September 18, 1865 Gender: Female

+Thomas Brown b: Abt. 1863 m: in Ft. Worth, TX Gender: Male

24 Sallie Eugenia Blakeney b: July 12, 1867 Gender: Female

+Thomas J, Swansonackson b: Abt. 1865 m: in Malikoff, TX Gender: Male

THE BLAKENEYS

24 Robert James Blakeney b: May 03, 1870 Gender: Male
+Carrie Rushing b: Abt. 1872 m: in Athens, TX Gender: Female
24 John R. Blakeney b: December 16, 1874 d: August 22, 1893
     Gender: Male
.23 Peter Blakeney b: November 17, 1838 in Chesterfield, SC d:
     November 08, 1936 Number of children: 4 Gender: Male
+Mary Evans b: February 06, 1846 in Chesterfield, SC m: Abt. 1855 in
     Chesterfield, SC d: June 30, 1915 in SC Number of children: 4
     Father: John Evans Gender: Female
24 Hugh Blakeney b: Abt. 1855 Gender: Male
24 Frank Blakeney b: Abt. 1857 Gender: Male
24 James Blakeney b: Abt. 1861 Gender: Male
24 John Blakeney b: March 05, 1873 Number of children: 1 Gender:
     Male
.23 John C. ("Charles"?) Blakeney b: December 05, 1841 d: 1910
     Number of children: 3 Gender: Male
+Sallie Bennett b: Abt. 1845 in Monroe, NC? m: 1870 Number of
     children: 3 Gender: Female
24 Frank Blakeney b: 1872 Gender: Male
24 Bennett Blakeney b: 1874 Gender: Male
24 [98] Mary Blakeney b: 1880 Gender: Female
+C. D. Meacham b: Abt. 1878 m: 1905 Gender: Male
*2nd Husband of [98] Mary Blakeney:
+C. E. Ransom b: Abt. 1880 m: 1922 Gender: Male
.23 Lewis Blakeney, Civil War Soldier b: June 04, 1843 d: 1863 in Civil
     War (unmarried) Gender: Male
.23 Hugh Blakeney, Civil War Soldier b: July 08, 1845 d: 1864 in Civil
     War (unmarried) Gender: Male
.23 George Whitefield Blakeney b: February 09, 1846 d: March 13,
     1915 Number of children: 4 Gender: Male
+Nancy Weldon b: Abt. 1848 in Ladonia, TX? m: December 19, 1871
     in Ladonia, TX Number of children: 4 Father: C. W. T.
     Weldon Gender: Female
24 Frank W. Blakeney b: November 18, 1872 d: March 11, 1921
     Gender: Male

+Myrtle Pickens b: Abt. 1875 m: August 29, 1896 Gender: Female

24 Marvin M. Blakeney b: January 07, 1877 Gender: Male

+Dell Perry b: Abt. 1880 m: January 30, 1910 Gender: Female

24 George Hooks Blakeney b: January 24, 1881 Gender: Male

+Lena Stovall b: Abt. 1884 m: 1902 in Hugo, OK Gender: Female

24 Leonard Blakeney b: January 27, 1887 Gender: Male

+Tesla Pearce b: Abt. 1890 m: 1926 in Dallas, TX Gender: Female

.*3rd Wife of [95] John "Jack" Blakeney III:

.+Rosanna "Rosa" Vick b: Abt. 1829 in Pageland, Chesterfield County, SC m: August 03, 1854 in Chesterfield, SC d: 1903 in Chesterfield County, SC Number of children: 5 Gender: Female

.23 [99] Rochel E. Blakeney, Sr. b: February 07, 1855 Number of children: 7 Gender: Male

+Margaret Ann Houston b: Abt. 1858 m: February 25, 1891 Number of children: 7 Gender: Female

24 Susan Amelia Blakeney b: November 29, 1891 Gender: Female

+W. O. Baucum b: Abt. 1890 Gender: Male

24 Rosa May Blakeney b: June 24, 1893 Gender: Female

+Benjamin Carl Parker b: Abt. 1890 m: 1919 Gender: Male

24 Alice Louise Blakeney b: February 19, 1895 Gender: Female

+Herrington Williams, Dr. b: Abt. 1893 m: 1921 Gender: Male

24 Martha Elizabeth Blakeney b: September 12, 1897 Gender: Female

+Luther Hartwell Hodges b: Abt. 1895 m: 1922 Gender: Male

24 Nellie Covington Blakeney b: February 28, 1900 Gender: Female

+Lester Leonedas Parker b: Abt. 1898 m: 1926 Gender: Male

24 Margaret Houston Blakeney b: August 03, 1903 Gender: Female

+James Seaborn Blair b: Abt. 1900 m: 1922 Gender: Male

24 Rochel Edward Blakeney, Jr. b: February 20, 1906 Gender: Male

.*2nd Wife of [99] Rochel E. Blakeney, Sr.:

+Rosa Venable b: Abt. 1900 m: December 10, 1921 Gender: Female

.23 [100] Preston Brooks Blakeney b: April 07, 1856 Number of children: 18 Gender: Male

+Wincy L. Wadsworth b: Abt. 1858 m: November 16, 1875 Number of children: 18 Gender: Female

24 Carl Thomas Blakeney b: September 13, 1876 Gender: Male

+Jessie Nelson b: Abt. 1878 Gender: Female
24 Basil H. Blakeney b: July 30, 1878 Gender: Male
+Maud Cowden b: Abt. 1880 Gender: Female
24 Brooks Blakeney b: July 30, 1878 Gender: Male
+_____ _____? b: Abt. 1880 m: in New Smyrna, FL Gender: Female
24 Rosa Etta Blakeney b: January 06, 1881 Gender: Female
+R. K. Helms b: Abt. 1880 Gender: Male
24 John Preston Blakeney b: February 15, 1883 Gender: Male
24 Kate May Blakeney b: December 03, 1884 Gender: Female
24 Mary Wadsworth Blakeney b: December 22, 1886 Gender: Female
24 Winnie Fay Blakeney b: February 16, 1889 Gender: Female
+J. A. Nelson b: Abt. 1886 Gender: Male
24 Henry C. Blakeney b: September 27, 1891 Gender: Male
24 S. Lillian Blakeney b: March 06, 1894 Gender: Female
+Albert C. Johnston b: Abt. 1892 Gender: Male
24 Annie L. Helms Blakeney b: January 27, 1895 Gender: Female
24 Fannie Louise Blakeney b: January 01, 1896 Gender: Female
24 William Wade Blakeney b: December 19, 1898 Gender: Male
24 Gladys Blakeney b: September 20, 1901 Gender: Female
24 Annie Elizabeth Blakeney b: June 11, 1904 Gender: Female
24 Fannie Helms Blakeney b: October 25, 1905 Gender: Female
24 Prestine Blakeney b: July 28, 1907 Gender: Female
24 Frances Blakeney b: September 08, 1909 Gender: Female
.*2nd Wife of [100] Preston Brooks Blakeney:
+Annie L. Helms b: Abt. 1876 m: January 27, 1895 Gender: Female
.*3rd Wife of [100] Preston Brooks Blakeney:
+Fannie H. Helms b: Abt. 1887 m: October 25, 1905 Gender: Female
.23 Sarah Victoria Blakeney b: July 20, 1859 Number of children: 3
        Gender: Female
+E. B. Sloan, Dr. b: Abt. 1855 m: Abt. 1877 Number of children: 3
        Gender: Male
24 Edna Birdie Sloan b: Abt. 1878 Gender: Female
24 Isabel Sloan b: Abt. 1880 Gender: Female
24 Rosa Sloan b: Abt. 1882 Gender: Female
.23 Alice Louise Blakeney b: June 29, 1861 d: 1888 Number of

children: 1 Gender: Female

+James E. Stack b: Abt. 1860 m: 1881 in Monroe, NC Number of children: 1 Gender: Male

24 Ervin Blakeney Stack, Sr. b: 1882 Number of children: 2 Gender: Male

+Iona Miller b: Abt. 1885 Number of children: 2 Gender: Female

.23 Whiteford Smith Blakeney, Sr. b: May 04, 1865 in on his Father's farm in Pageland, SC Number of children: 3 Gender: Male

+Virginia May Cole b: Abt. 1880 in Rockingham, NC m: December 28, 1905 Number of children: 3 Gender: Female

24 Whiteford Smith Blakeney, Jr. b: September 29, 1906 Gender: Male

24 Virginia Cole Blakeney b: October 21, 1907 Gender: Female

24 Jack Cole Blakeney b: August 26, 1911 Gender: Male

.21 Jane Blakeney b: Abt. 1760 Gender: Female

.+_____ Welch b: Abt. 1755 Gender: Male

.21 Robert Blakeney, Rev. War Soldier b: Abt. 1760 in Chesterfield County, SC? Gender: Male (Note: served in American Revolutionary War under Col. Lemuel Benton)

.+_____ _____? b: Abt. 1762 in Chesterfield County, SC? Gender: Female

.21 [103] William Blakeney b: Abt. 1763 in Granville, NC d: Abt. 1825 Number of children: 4 Gender: Male

.+Mary Jackson b: Abt. 1767 in Chesterfield County, SC m: Abt. 1785 in Chesterfield, SC Number of children: 2 Gender: Female

.22 [110] James Thomas Blakeney b: 1788 in Chesterfield County, SC d: 1870 in Ashley County, AR Number of children: 9 Gender: Male (Note: James and his wife and three oldest children, moved to Mississippi Territory sometime between 1825 and 1826, just prior to Smith County, MS. being established December 23, 1833)

.+[111] Martha Matilda Page b: 1788 m: Abt. 1817 d: 1870 Number of children: 9 Father: _____ Page Gender: Female

.23 [112] Hugh Blakeney b: 1820 in SC d: 1867 in MS? Number of children: 15 Gender: Male Burial: Old Nebo Church, Smith or Jasper County, MS

+[113] Nancy Yelverton b: September 10, 1818 in SC d: April 27, 1892 in Smith County, MS Number of children: 15 Father: Zadok Yelverton, Jr. Mother: Susan Powell Gender: Female Burial: Ditched Graveyard, Smith County, MS

24 [114] Albert Blakeney b: Abt. 1843 in Smith County, MS d: 1863 in Vicksburg, MS in Civil War Gender: Male

24 [115] Elizabeth Parcenia Blakeney b: 1845 in Smith County, MS Gender: Female

24 [116] William Blakeney b: 1846 in Smith County, MS Gender: Male

+[117] Zilla Ann Mathis b: Abt. 1848 Gender: Female

24 [118] Alfred T. Blakeney b: 1847 Gender: Male

24 [119] Mary Ann Blakeney b: Abt. 1849 Gender: Female

24 [120] Simeon Dave Blakeney b: 1851 in Jasper County, MS Gender: Male

+[121] Edna Williams b: 1872 Gender: Female

24 [122] Lovick Blakeney b: 1850 Gender: Female

24 [101] Susan Caroline Blakeney b: 1854 Number of children: 3 Gender: Female

+[123] John Paul Norris b: Abt. 1850 d: 1881 Number of children: 3 Gender: Male

*2nd Husband of [101] Susan Caroline Blakeney:

+[124] Elias Shorter (Short) Russell b: Abt. 1852 m: 1882 Father: Frank Absolum Russell Mother: Lucinda Vann Gender: Male

24 [125] Martha Mathilda Blakeney b: 1856 Gender: Female

24 [126] Thomas Lafayette Blakeney b: October 26, 1856 d: 1879 Number of children: 4 Gender: Male

+[127] Louise M. Mayfield b: Abt. 1858 m: Abt. 1875 Number of children: 4 Gender: Female

24 [128] Jefferson Davis "Jeff" Blakeney b: 1858 Gender: Male

+[129] Ellen Morris b: Abt. 1860 Gender: Female

24 [130] John Blakeney b: 1860 Gender: Male

+[131] Nancy Bryant b: Abt. 1862 Gender: Female

24 [132] Adelaide Alabama Blakeney b: May 26, 1862 Gender: Female

+[133] George Washington "Babe" Jones b: September 18, 1860 Gender: Male

24 [134] Hugh Blakeney b: October 20, 1863 in Smith County, MS d: October 04, 1937 Gender: Male

+[135] Emma Adelaide McLaurin b: Abt. 1865 m: December 25, 1886 Gender: Female

24 [136] Nancy Catherine Blakeney b: 1865 Gender: Female

.23 [137] Matilda Arabella Blakeney b: 1817 in SC d: 1850 Number of children: 4 Gender: Female

+[138] Arlow (or Aslou) Ainsworth b: Abt. 1797 in KY Number of children: 4 Gender: Male

24 [139] Arthenia Ainsworth b: Abt. 1837 Gender: Female

24 [140] Harrison Ainsworth b: 1839 Gender: Male

24 [102] Elmira (Almina) Ainsworth b: 1841 Number of children: 9 Gender: Female

+[141] Joseph Guess b: Abt. 1840 Gender: Male

*2nd Husband of [102] Elmira (Almina) Ainsworth:

+[142] Moses Stamps b: Abt. 1833 in Gwinnett County, GA m: Abt. 1865 in Newton County Mississippi Number of children: 9 Gender: Male

24 [143] Nancy Matilder "Nan" Ainsworth b: Abt. 1843 Gender: Female

.23 [144] Jacob Blakeney, C.S.A., b: 1825 in SC Number of children: 13 Gender: Male, Confederate soldier in Lincoln's War

+[145] Eliza Jernigan b: Abt. 1827 Number of children: 13 Gender: Female

24 [146] Steven Erasmus Blakeney b: April 13, 1849 Gender: Male

+[147] Amanda Balentine b: Abt. 1850 Gender: Female

24 [148] James Marion Blakeney, C.S.A. b: May 05, 1850 Number of children: 10 Gender: Male, Confederate soldier in Lincoln's War

+[149] Keziah Elizabeth Walters b: May 04, 1850 m: February 11, 1873 Number of children: 10 Gender: Female

24 [150] Terry Blakeney b: November 23, 1852 Gender: Male

+[151] Pattie Ainsworth b: Abt. 1855 Gender: Female

24 [152] Benjamin Franklin Blakeney b: January 22, 1854 Gender: Male

+[153] Margaret Nichols b: Abt. 1856 Gender: Female

24 [154] Matilda Blakeney b: 1855 Gender: Female

+[155] Bill Windham b: Abt. 1853 Gender: Male

24 [156] Ellen Blakeney b: April 09, 1857 Gender: Female

+[157] Alvin Stringer b: Abt. 1855 Gender: Male

24 [158] Lucy Blakeney b: June 20, 1858 Gender: Female

24 [159] Robert Blakeney b: November 21, 1859 Gender: Male

+[160] Armathia Ainsworth b: Abt. 1860 Gender: Female

24 [161] Mary Blakeney b: August 03, 1862 Gender: Female

+[162] Joel Laird b: Abt. 1860 Gender: Male

24 [163] Martha "Matt" Blakeney b: June 30, 1864 Gender: Female

+[164] Jesse Sylvanus "Sibbie" Laird, C.S.A. b: 1852 d: 1942 Gender:
  Male; Confederate soldier in Lincoln's War

24 [165] Albert Blakeney b: November 25, 1865 Gender: Male

+[166] Ellen Nichols b: Abt. 1867 Gender: Female

24 [167] Ransom Lafayette Blakeney b: November 10, 1866 Gender:
  Male

+[168] Sarah Nichols b: Abt. 1868 Gender: Female

24 [169] Floyd Blakeney b: February 20, 1871 Gender: Male

+[170] Parcenia Blackwell b: Abt. 1873 Gender: Female

.23 [171] Robert Blakeney b: 1826 Number of children: 1 Gender:
  Male

+[172] Anne Blair b: Abt. 1828 Number of children: 1 Gender: Female

24 [173] Robert James Blakeney b: Abt. 1860 Gender: Male

.23 [174] Mathilda Blakeney b: 1829 in MS Gender: Female

+[175] Felix Blackwell b: Abt. 1825 Gender: Male

.23 [176] Eleanora Blakeney b: 1831 in MS Gender: Female

.23 [177] Alvin Blakeney b: 1833 in MS Number of children: 2 Gender:
  Male

+[178] Lucy Ann Jernigan b: Abt. 1835 in MS? m: in (Note: they had 7
  children) Number of children: 2 Gender: Female

24 [179] William Penn Blakeney b: July 15, 1859 d: 1935 in
  Taylorsville, MS Gender: Male Burial: Fellowship Cemetery,
  Taylorsville, MS

+[180] Mary Josephine Hardin b: 1866 d: July 29, 1942 in Taylorsville,
  MS Gender: Female Burial: Fellowship Cemetery, Taylorsville,

MS

24 [181] Laura Blakeney b: Abt. 1865 in Smith County, MS Gender: Female

+[182] Ringo McLaurin b: Abt. 1862 Gender: Male

.23 [183] Lucy S. Blakeney b: 1839 in MS Gender: Female

.23 [184] William T. Blakeney b: 1844 in MS Gender: Male

.22 Mary Blakeney b: Abt. 1791 Gender: Female

.+Peter Boggan b: Abt. 1790 Father: John Boggan Mother: Mary _____? Gender: Male

.*2nd Wife of [103] William Blakeney:

.+Leah Shehorn b: Abt. 1770 m: Abt. 1818 Number of children: 2 Gender: Female

.22 Frances Blakeney b: July 07, 1819 d: July 26, 1881 Gender: Female

.+James M. Miller b: 1816 d: 1865 Gender: Male

.22 Charlotte Blakeney b: August 21, 1821 d: August 18, 1889 Number of children: 12 Gender: Female

.+Travis Evans, Sr. b: October 03, 1819 m: July 28, 1839 d: June 12, 1896 Number of children: 12 Father: William Evans Mother: Cynthia Morning Diggs Gender: Male

.23 Harriet Evans b: August 17, 1840 Gender: Female

+Charles Clark b: Abt. 1838 Gender: Male

.23 Benjamin Franklin Evans, Civil War Soldier b: April 30, 1842 d: Abt. 1864 in Civil War (unmarried) Gender: Male

.23 Frances Evans b: April 21, 1844 Gender: Female

+Nathan Courtney b: Abt. 1842 Father: _____ Courtney Gender: Male

.23 Louise Evans b: August 16, 1846 d: January 28, 1922 Gender: Female

+William Courtney b: September 16, 1838 d: July 29, 1893 Father: _____ Courtney Gender: Male

.23 Travis Evans, Jr. b: February 14, 1849 Gender: Male

+Marilda Robertson b: Abt. 1850 Gender: Female

.23 Mary Ann Evans b: September 04, 1851 Gender: Female

+Bynum Funderburk b: Abt. 1850 Gender: Male

.23 Thomas Evans b: December 22, 1853 Gender: Male

+Nettie McManus b: August 08, 1866 m: October 12, 1884 Gender:

Female

.23 Susan Ellen Evans b: May 07, 1856 Gender: Female

+William Hicks b: Abt. 1855 Gender: Male

.23 George W. Evans b: July 18, 1858 d: August 02, 1884 Gender: Male

+Rilda Hasty b: Abt. 1860 Gender: Female

.23 Laura Jane Evans b: July 29, 1859 Gender: Female

+Jerry Knight b: Abt. 1855 Gender: Male

.23 Queen Victoria Evans b: November 14, 1861 Gender: Female

.23 Lotta B. Evans b: August 09, 1864 Gender: Female

+Roachel Arant b: Abt. 1862 Gender: Male

.21 [108] James Blakeney, Honorable b: November 12, 1765 in Granville, NC d: October 1819 Number of children: 8 Gender: Male Burial: Cartarrh on Lynch's Creek

.+Susanna Haile b: January 31, 1766 in Granville, NC m: April 01, 1788 in Cheraw, Lancaster County, SC Number of children: 8 Father: Benjamin Haile, Sr. Mother: Kate Ferguson Gender: Female

.22 Mary May Blakeney b: May 13, 1789 Number of children: 4 Gender: Female

.+Henry A. Jackson b: Abt. 1785 m: 1807 Number of children: 4 Gender: Male

.23 Stephen Jackson b: Abt. 1810 d: November 16, 1887 Gender: Male

+Roxanna Timmons b: Abt. 1810 Gender: Female

.23 Henrietta Jackson b: February 28, 1806 Gender: Female

+Alfred M. Lowry b: Abt. 1804 Gender: Male

.23 Benjamin A. Jackson, Civil War Solder b: Abt. 1810 d: Abt. 1864 in VA in Civil War Gender: Male

+Mary C. Blakeney b: Abt. 1831 m: Abt. 1848 in Pulaski County, AR Father: Benjamin Blakeney Gender: Female

.23 Susannah Jackson b: August 07, 1812 d: April 18, 1875 Gender: Female

+Alexander May b: Abt. 1810 m: September 30, 1838 Gender: Male

.22 Benjamin Blakeney b: May 12, 1793 d: 1854 Number of children: 2 Gender: Male Burial: at his farm near Cabot, AR (Note:

served in the War of 1812 as a Sergeant under Capt. John McNeill, 3rd Reg., S.C. Infantry.)

.+Eliza Ferguson b: Abt. 1800 m: 1821 in Lancaster County SC Number of children: 2 Father: James Ferguson Mother: Abigail _____? Gender: Female

.23 [104] James Madison Blakeney b: October 26, 1822 d: September 1887 in OR Gender: Male

+Martha Evans b: July 20, 1826 m: October 12, 1845 d: 1867 Gender: Female

.*2nd Wife of [104] James Madison Blakeney:

+Eunice Brown b: Abt. 1845 m: October 31, 1867 Gender: Female

.23 Catherine Mary Carolina Blakeney b: Abt. 1831 Gender: Female

+Benjamin A. Jackson b: Abt. 1829 m: Abt. 1848 Gender: Male

.22 John Goodloe Blakeney b: February 20, 1795 in Chesterfield County, SC d: December 14, 1870 in Des Arc, Arkansas Number of children: 9 Gender: Male Burial: Des Arc, AL (Note: He owned plantations in Clark County, MS and Choctaw County, AL, and had a large number of African slaves, many who probably took Blakeney as their surname; his plantations were lost during the Civil War)

.+Isabella McLendaon b: 1804 m: 1822 d: March 08, 1882 Number of children: 9 Gender: Female

.23 [106] James Blakeney b: January 06, 1825 d: January 26, 1862 Gender: Male

+[105] Mary Blakeney b: Abt. 1818 m: Abt. 1848 Father: Alfred Blakeney Mother: Margaret McIntosh Gender: Female

.23 Sarah Ann Blakeney b: February 22, 1826 d: January 11, 1892 Gender: Female

+Charles Wesley Moody b: 1820 m: September 1846 d: 1886 Gender: Male

.23 Benjamin Blakeney b: October 16, 1827 d: May 13, 1873 Gender: Male

+Mary Elizabeth Quaries b: October 08, 1831 m: October 01, 1851 d: October 07, 1895 Gender: Female

.23 William R. Blakeney b: April 22, 1829 Gender: Male

.23 Columbia I. Blakeney b: August 28, 1832 Gender: Unknown

.23 Lousia Blakeney b: September 14, 1835 Gender: Female

.23 Susan Blakeney b: April 29, 1838 d: 1869 Gender: Female

+Amon A. Stallworth, Dr. b: Abt. 1835 Gender: Male

.23 Alfred A. Blakeney b: January 09, 1840 Gender: Male

.23 John C. ("Charles"?) Blakeney b: October 28, 1841 Gender: Male

.22 William Blakeney b: February 22, 1796 d: Drowned in Miss. River Gender: Male (Note: He had no children)

.22 Alfred Blakeney b: October 25, 1796 d: Bef. 1850 Number of children: 6 Gender: Male

.+Margaret McIntosh b: Abt. 1800 in AL m: in Choctaw County, AL Number of children: 6 Gender: Female

.23 [105] Mary Blakeney b: Abt. 1818 Gender: Female

+Altus Hinson b: Abt. 1810 m: Abt. 1837 Gender: Male

.*2nd Husband of [105] Mary Blakeney:

+[106] James Blakeney b: January 06, 1825 m: Abt. 1848 d: January 26, 1862 Father: John Goodloe Blakeney Mother: Isabella McLendaon Gender: Male

.*3rd Husband of [105] Mary Blakeney:

+[96] Franklin Blakeney b: December 14, 1833 m: Abt. 1855 d: in TX Number of children: 3 Father: John "Jack" Blakeney III Mother: Sallie Evans Gender: Male

.23 Ann Blakeney b: Abt. 1820 Gender: Female

+_____ Morrison b: Abt. 1818 Gender: Male

.23 James Martin Blakeney b: 1832 Gender: Male

.23 Margaret Blakeney b: 1833 Gender: Female

.23 Elizabeth Blakeney b: 1833 Gender: Female

+_____ Horn b: Abt. 1830 in TN? Father: Jere Horn Gender: Male

.23 Henrietta Blakeney b: 1840 Gender: Female

.22 Louisa Blakeney b: Abt. 1799 d: in AL? Gender: Female

.+_____ Perkins b: Abt. 1795 Gender: Male

.22 Calvin James Blakeney b: September 21, 1802 d: October 09 Gender: Male

.+[109] Mary White b: Abt. 1770 Gender: Female

.22 James White Blakeney, Sr., General & Attorney b: October 08,

1809 in Cheraw, Chesterfield, South Carolina d: December 27, 1863 in Pageland, Chesterfield County, South Carolina Number of children: 6 Gender: Male Burial: St. David's Cemetery, Cheraw, SC (Note: fought in the Seminole War in Florida)

.+Virginia DuBose b: September 13, 1822 m: July 16, 1846 d: May 22, 1901 Number of children: 6 Gender: Female

.23 Henrietta Julia Blakeney b: January 06, 1848 Gender: Female

+Henry M. DuBose b: Abt. 1845 m: June 24, 1868 Gender: Male

.23 Mary Grizzella Blakeney b: April 21, 1850 d: December 04, 1926 Gender: Female

+Eugene Capers Zemp b: October 27, 1854 m: May 02, 1876 Gender: Male

.23 Elizabeth DuBose Blakeney b: July 24, 1852 d: October 01, 1853 Gender: Female

.23 Louise Blakeney b: July 11, 1856 d: July 05, 1875 Gender: Female

.23 James White Blakeney, Jr. b: July 14, 1858 d: April 18, 1897 Gender: Male

+Sallie Kennedy b: Abt. 1860 m: February 16, 1888 Gender: Female

.23 [107] Eugene DuBose Blakeney b: January 03, 1862 Gender: Male

+Lillian M. Kennedy b: Abt. 1865 m: November 29, 1882 d: January 12, 1896 Gender: Female

.*2nd Wife of [107] Eugene DuBose Blakeney:

+Rosa Pearce b: August 27, 1879 m: January 18, 1898 Gender: Female

.*2nd Wife of [108] James Blakeney, Honorable:

.+[109] Mary White b: Abt. 1770 m: Abt. 1790 Gender: Female

.21 Mary Blakeney b: Abt. 1768 Gender: Female (Note: she married and moved to Georgia, where she and her entire family was murdered by Indians)

.21 (William) Hugh Blakeney b: Abt. 1774 in Chesterfield County SC d: 1842 in Montgomery County, TN Number of children: 6 Gender: Male

.+Nancy Ann Welch b: Abt. 1780 m: Abt. 1796 d: Abt. 1817 in SC Number of children: 6 Father: William Welch, Welsh Mother: _____ _____? Gender: Female

.22 Thomas Blakeney b: 1794 in Pee Dee River, Cheraw District, SC d:

1876 Number of children: 1 Gender: Male

.23 Hugh Blakeney b: 1820 Gender: Male

.22 Eleanor Blakeney b: Abt. 1798 Gender: Female

.22 Jane Blakeney b: Abt. 1800 Gender: Female

.22 Nancy Ann Blakeney b: Abt. 1803 Gender: Female

.22 Mary Blakeney b: 1806 Gender: Female

.22 [110] James Thomas Blakeney b: 1788 in Chesterfield County, SC d: 1870 in Ashley County, AR Number of children: 9 Gender: Male (Note: James and his wife and three oldest children, moved to Mississippi Territory, sometime between 1825 and 1826, just prior to Smith County, MS. being established December 23, 1833)

.+[111] Martha Matilda Page b: 1788 m: Abt. 1817 d: 1870 Number of children: 9 Father: _____ Page Gender: Female

.23 [112] Hugh Blakeney b: 1820 in SC d: 1867 in MS? Number of children: 15 Gender: Male Burial: Old Nebo Church, Smith or Jasper County, MS

+[113] Nancy Yelverton b: September 10, 1818 in SC d: April 27, 1892 in Smith County, MS Number of children: 15 Father: Zadok Yelverton, Jr. Mother: Susan Powell Gender: Female Burial: Ditched Graveyard, Smith County, MS

24 [114] Albert Blakeney b: Abt. 1843 in Smith County, MS d: 1863 in Vicksburg, MS in Civil War Gender: Male

24 [115] Elizabeth Parcenia Blakeney b: 1845 in Smith County, MS Gender: Female

24 [116] William Blakeney b: 1846 in Smith County, MS Gender: Male

+[117] Zilla Ann Mathis b: Abt. 1848 Gender: Female

24 [118] Alfred T. Blakeney b: 1847 Gender: Male

24 [119] Mary Ann Blakeney b: Abt. 1849 Gender: Female

24 [120] Simeon Dave Blakeney b: 1851 in Jasper County, MS Gender: Male

+[121] Edna Williams b: 1872 Gender: Female

24 [122] Lovick Blakeney b: 1850 Gender: Female

24 [101] Susan Caroline Blakeney b: 1854 Number of children: 3 Gender: Female

+[123] John Paul Norris b: Abt. 1850 d: 1881 Number of children: 3
    Gender: Male

*2nd Husband of [101] Susan Caroline Blakeney:

+[124] Elias Shorter (Short) Russell b: Abt. 1852 m: 1882 Father: Frank
    Absolum Russell Mother: Lucinda Vann Gender: Male

24 [125] Martha Mathilda Blakeney b: 1856 Gender: Female

24 [126] Thomas Lafayette Blakeney b: October 26, 1856 d: 1879
    Number of children: 4 Gender: Male

+[127] Louise M. Mayfield b: Abt. 1858 m: Abt. 1875 Number of
    children: 4 Gender: Female

24 [128] Jefferson Davis "Jeff" Blakeney [his parents' were supporters of
    the Southern Confederacy during Lincoln's War] b: 1858
    Gender: Male

+[129] Ellen Morris b: Abt. 1860 Gender: Female

24 [130] John Blakeney b: 1860 Gender: Male

+[131] Nancy Bryant b: Abt. 1862 Gender: Female

24 [132] Adelaide Alabama Blakeney b: May 26, 1862 Gender: Female

+[133] George Washington "Babe" Jones b: September 18, 1860
    Gender: Male

24 [134] Hugh Blakeney b: October 20, 1863 in Smith County, MS d:
    October 04, 1937 Gender: Male

+[135] Emma Adelaide McLaurin b: Abt. 1865 m: December 25, 1886
    Gender: Female

24 [136] Nancy Catherine Blakeney b: 1865 Gender: Female

.23 [137] Matilda Arabella Blakeney b: 1817 in SC d: 1850 Number of
    children: 4 Gender: Female

+[138] Arlow (or Aslou) Ainsworth b: Abt. 1797 in KY Number of
    children: 4 Gender: Male

24 [139] Arthenia Ainsworth b: Abt. 1837 Gender: Female

24 [140] Harrison Ainsworth b: 1839 Gender: Male

24 [102] Elmira (Almina) Ainsworth b: 1841 Number of children: 9
    Gender: Female

+[141] Joseph Guess b: Abt. 1840 Gender: Male

*2nd Husband of [102] Elmira (Almina) Ainsworth:

+[142] Moses Stamps b: Abt. 1833 in Gwinnett County, GA m: Abt.

1865 in Newton County, Mississippi Number of children: 9
Gender: Male

24   [143] Nancy Matilder "Nan" Ainsworth b: Abt. 1843 Gender:
Female

.23   [144] Jacob Blakeney b: 1825 in SC Number of children: 13
Gender: Male

+[145] Eliza Jernigan b: Abt. 1827 Number of children: 13 Gender:
Female

24   [146] Steven Erasmus Blakeney b: April 13, 1849 Gender: Male

+[147] Amanda Balentine b: Abt. 1850 Gender: Female

24   [148] James Marion Blakeney b: May 05, 1850 Number of children:
10 Gender: Male

+[149] Kizar Elizabeth b: May 04, 1850 m: February 11, 1873 Number
of children: 10 Gender: Female

24   [150] Terry Blakeney b: November 23, 1852 Gender: Male

+[151] Pattie Ainsworth b: Abt. 1855 Gender: Female

24   [152] Benjamin Franklin Blakeney b: January 22, 1854 Gender: Male

+[153] Margaret Nichols b: Abt. 1856 Gender: Female

24   [154] Matilda Blakeney b: 1855 Gender: Female

+[155] Bill Windham b: Abt. 1853 Gender: Male

24   [156] Ellen Blakeney b: April 09, 1857 Gender: Female

+[157] Alvin Stringer b: Abt. 1855 Gender: Male

24   [158] Lucy Blakeney b: June 20, 1858 Gender: Female

24   [159] Robert Blakeney b: November 21, 1859 Gender: Male

+[160] Armathia Ainsworth b: Abt. 1860 Gender: Female

24   [161] Mary Blakeney b: August 03, 1862 Gender: Female

+[162] Joel Laird b: Abt. 1860 Gender: Male

24   [163] Matthew Blakeney b: June 30, 1864 Gender: Male

+[164] Sibbie Laird b: Abt. 1866 Gender: Female

24   [165] Albert Blakeney b: November 25, 1865 Gender: Male

+[166] Ellen Nichols b: Abt. 1867 Gender: Female

24   [167] Ransom Lafayette Blakeney b: November 10, 1866 Gender:
Male

+[168] Sarah Nichols b: Abt. 1868 Gender: Female

24   [169] Floyd Blakeney b: February 20, 1871 Gender: Male

+[170] Parcenia Blackwell b: Abt. 1873 Gender: Female

.23 [171] Robert Blakeney b: 1826 Number of children: 1 Gender: Male

+[172] Anne Blair b: Abt. 1828 Number of children: 1 Gender: Female

24 [173] Robert James Blakeney b: Abt. 1860 Gender: Male

.23 [174] Mathilda Blakeney b: 1829 in MS Gender: Female

+[175] Felix Blackwell b: Abt. 1825 Gender: Male

.23 [176] Eleanora Blakeney b: 1831 in MS Gender: Female

.23 [177] Alvin Blakeney b: 1833 in MS Number of children: 2 Gender: Male

+[178] Lucy Ann Jernigan b: Abt. 1835 in MS? m: in (Note: they had 7 children) Number of children: 2 Gender: Female

24 [179] William Penn Blakeney b: July 15, 1859 d: 1935 in Taylorsville, MS Gender: Male Burial: Fellowship Cemetery, Taylorsville, MS

+[180] Mary Josephine Hardin b: 1866 d: July 29, 1942 in Taylorsville, MS Gender: Female Burial: Fellowship Cemetery, Taylorsville, MS

24 [181] Laura Blakeney b: Abt. 1865 in Smith County, MS Gender: Female

+[182] Ringo McLaurin b: Abt. 1862 Gender: Male

.23 [183] Lucy S. Blakeney b: 1839 in MS Gender: Female

.23 [184] William T. Blakeney b: 1844 in MS Gender: Male

..19 Elizabeth Blakeney b: 1710 in Ireland d: 1744 Number of children: 1 Gender: Female

..+Francis Creed b: Abt. 1710 in Ballygrenane, Uregare, County Limerick, Ireland Number of children: 1 Gender: Male

..20 _____ Creed b: Abt. 1743 Gender: Unknown

18 George Blakeney, Lt.-Col b: Abt. 1655 in Mount Blakeney (or Thomastown), County Limerick, Ireland d: Abt. 1728 Gender: Male Burial: (Notes: he died unmarried).

18 John Blakeney b: Abt. 1657 Gender: Male

18 Charles Blakeney b: Abt. 1660 Gender: Male

18 Henry Blakeney b: Abt. 1661 Gender: Male

18 Hatton Blakeney b: Abt. 1662 Gender: Female

The Blakeneys

..+_____ Pepper b: Abt. 1660 in Drogheda, Ireland Gender: Male

18 _____ Blakeney b: Abt. 1663 Number of children: 1 Gender: Female

..+_____ Lovelace b: Abt. 1660 in Ireland Number of children: 1 Gender: Male

..19 _____ Lovelace b: Abt. 1685 Gender: Unknown

18 _____ Blakeney b: Abt. 1664 in Ireland? Number of children: 1 Gender: Female

..+J. Gardner b: Abt. 1660 in Ireland? m: Abt. 1685 in Ireland? Number of children: 1 Gender: Male

..19 _____ Gardner b: Abt. 1690 Gender: Unknown

17 _____ Blakeney b: Abt. 1629 Gender: Female

+_____ Pepper b: Abt. 1625 in of Drogheda, Ireland Gender: Male

17 John "the Gentleman" Blakeney b: Abt. 1633 Gender: Male

17 George "the Farmer" Blakeney b: Abt. 1635 Number of children: 2 Gender: Male

+_____ _____? b: Abt. 1640 Number of children: 2 Gender: Female

18 Hatton Blakeney b: Abt. 1660 Number of children: 2 Gender: Male

..+_____ Gardiner b: Abt. 1665 Number of children: 2 Gender: Female

..19 _____ Blakeney b: Abt. 1685 Gender: Male (Notes: he was an officer in the Army).

..19 _____ Blakeney b: Abt. 1690 Gender: Male (Notes: he was an officer in the Army).

18 _____ Blakeney b: Abt. 1665 Gender: Female

..+J. Gardiner, Esquire b: Abt. 1660 Gender: Male

17 Charles "the Strongman" Blakeney b: Abt. 1637 Gender: Male

17 Henry "the Clown" Blakeney b: Abt. 1640 Gender: Male

16 Henry Blakeney b: 1586 in Sparham, Norfolk County, England. Gender: Male

.15 Charles Blakeney b: Abt. 1557 Number of children: 2 Gender: Male

.+Dionysia _____? b: Abt. 1560 Number of children: 2 Gender: Female

16 Charles Blakeney b: 1585 Gender: Male

16 William Blakeney b: 1598 Gender: Male

.15 John Blakeney b: Abt. 1559 Gender: Male

.+Elizabeth Green b: Abt. 1560 m: 1574 Gender: Female

.7 Nicholas Blakeney, Lord of Galthorpe Hall Manor b: Abt. 1305 in Norfolk?, England Number of children: 1 Gender: Male (Notes: his full title was the Lord of the Manor of Galthorpe Hall, in 1351).

.+_____ _____? b: Abt. 1310 Number of children: 1 Gender: Female

.8 Bartholemew Blakeney, Bailiff of Norwich b: Abt. 1340 in Norfolk?, England Gender: Male (Notes: he may have spelled his last name "de Blakeney"; he was Bailiff of Norwich in 1400).

END OF BLAKENEY FAMILY TREE

Illustrations

Figure 1 The ancestors of the Norman Blakeneys were Danish Viking raiders who made the initial voyage to England in the 8th Century on a ship similar to this.

Figure 2 Medieval tapestry portraying the Norman Invasion of England in the year 1066. The earliest known (recorded) Blakeneys were Normans who entered England a second time during this period.

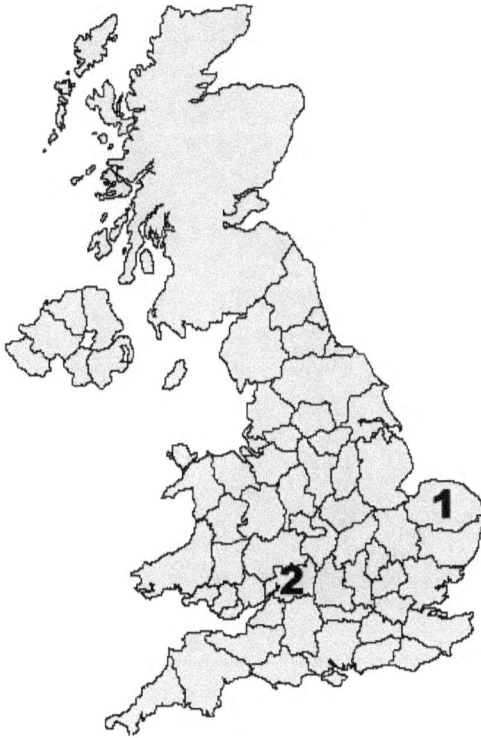

Figure 3 Map of England showing the counties in which the towns of 1) Blakeney, Norfolk , and 2) Blakeney, Gloucestershire, are located (image copyright ©).

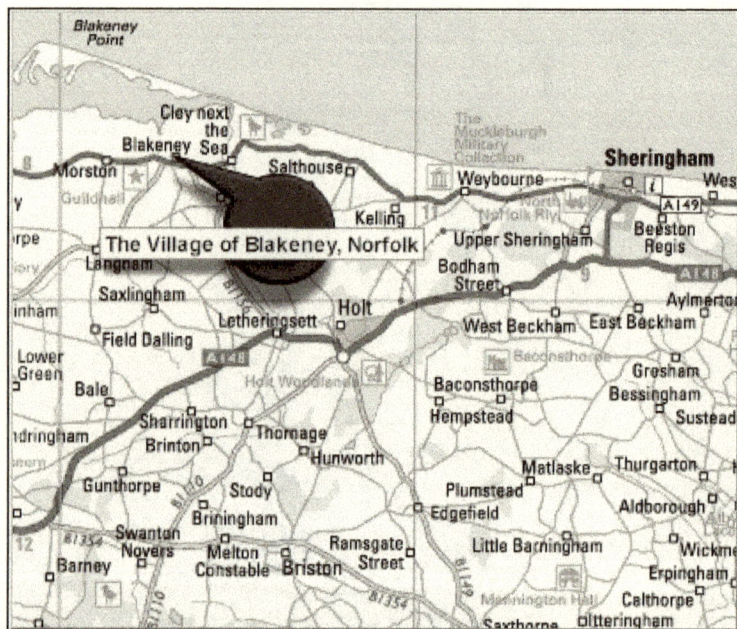

Figure 4 A modern map showing the location of the town of Blakeney, Norfolk County, England, first known as Snitterly in the Middle Ages. Blakeney is situated on the northern edge of East Anglia, on the mid-eastern central side of England. Note Blakeney Point in the upper left (image copyright ©).

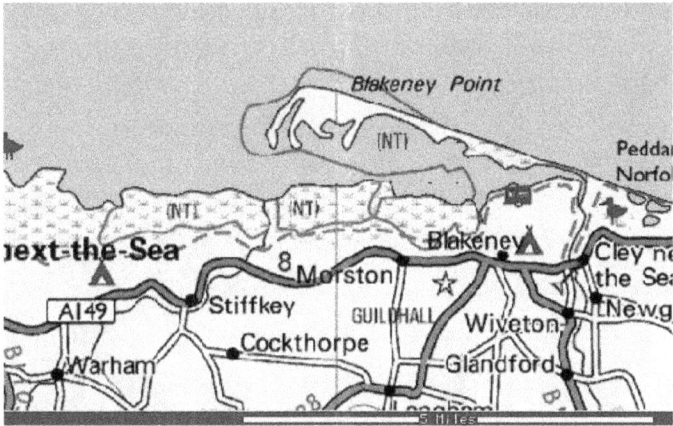

Figure 5 A close-up map showing the location of the town of Blakeney, and also Blakeney Point, Norfolk County, England.

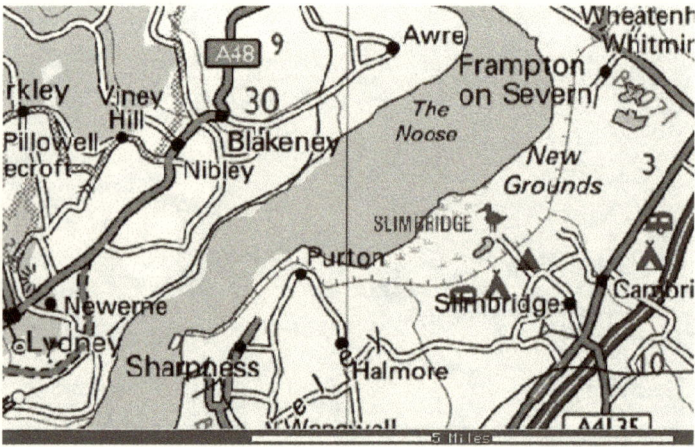

Figure 6 Map showing the location of the town of Blakeney near the River Severn, Gloucestershire County, England.

Figure 7 An aerial view of the town of Blakeney, Norfolk County, England, showing some of the colorless fens (lower right) that were seen by our invading Danish Blakeney ancestors in the 8th Century. The "bleakness" of the fens is apparent even in this black and white image. My theory is that the name "Blakeney," a modern anglicization of *blaekno* and *ey* (the Old Norse words for "bleak" and "island"), originated here (image copyright ©).

Figure 8 The tomb of Strongbow (d. 1176) at Christ Church Cathedral in Dublin, Ireland. The first English Blakeneys to enter Ireland may have come in 1170 as soldiers in Strongbow's army, which defeated Dublin shortly thereafter. Note: This is not Strongbow's original tomb, which was destroyed when the roof of the Cathedral collapsed in 1562. Later, fine 14th-Century statuary (shown here) was used to replace it. The small figure next to the tomb is believed to be a fragment from the original monument.

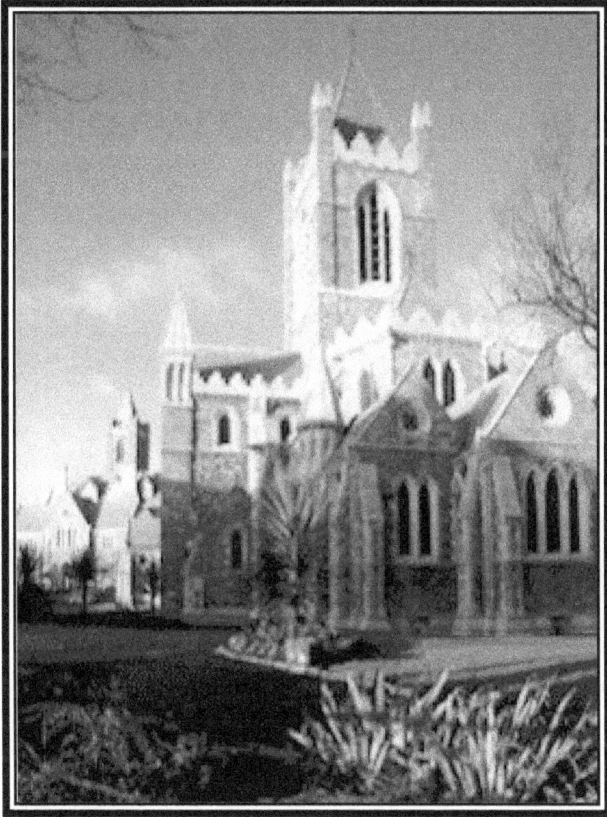

Figure 9 Christ Church, Dublin, Ireland, burial site of Strongbow, d. 1176 (image copyright ©).

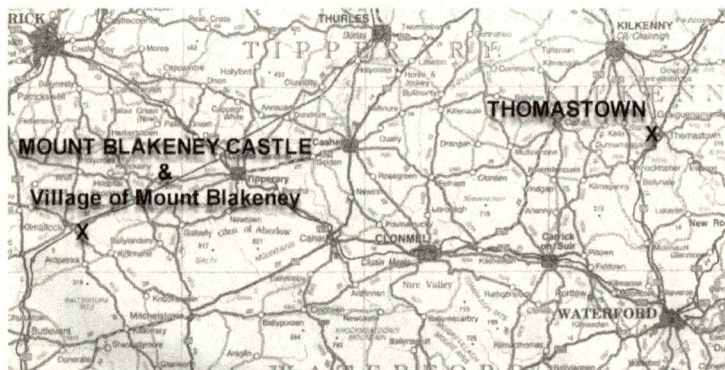

Figure 10 Modern map showing the locations of the village of Mount Blakeney, near Kilmallock, County Galway, Ireland, and Thomastown, County Kilkenny, Ireland, which was named after Thomas Blakeney (son of Launcelot Blakeney), situated just north of Waterford (image copyright ©).

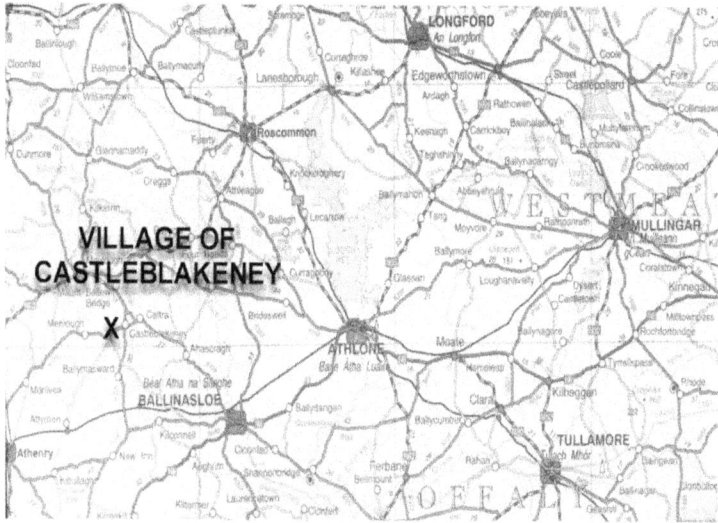

Figure 11 Modern map showing location (circle to the right of the X) of the village of Castleblakeney, County Galway, Ireland (image copyright ©).

Figure 12 An aerial photo of the village of Castleblakeney (earlier known as Killasoolan, or Gallagh), County Galway, Ireland. It is located about 30 miles northeast of Galway, near the crossroads of Route 358 and Route 359. Photo taken circa 1997 (?). Note the Parish Church of Castleblakeney in the lower left foreground, which is now undergoing renovation, thanks to the efforts of the Castleblakeney Community Development Association (image copyright ©).

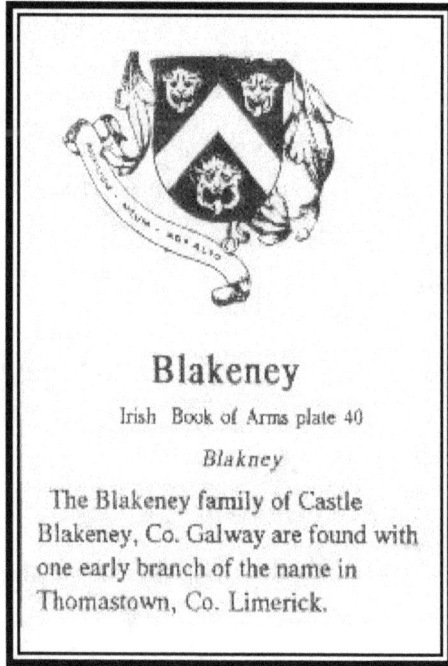

Blakeney

Irish Book of Arms plate 40

Blakney

The Blakeney family of Castle Blakeney, Co. Galway are found with one early branch of the name in Thomastown, Co. Limerick.

Figure 13 The Irish Blakeney Family Coat of Arms (or crest). On the banner is the Blakeney motto in Latin: *Auxilium Meum Ab Alto*: "My Help Comes From Above".

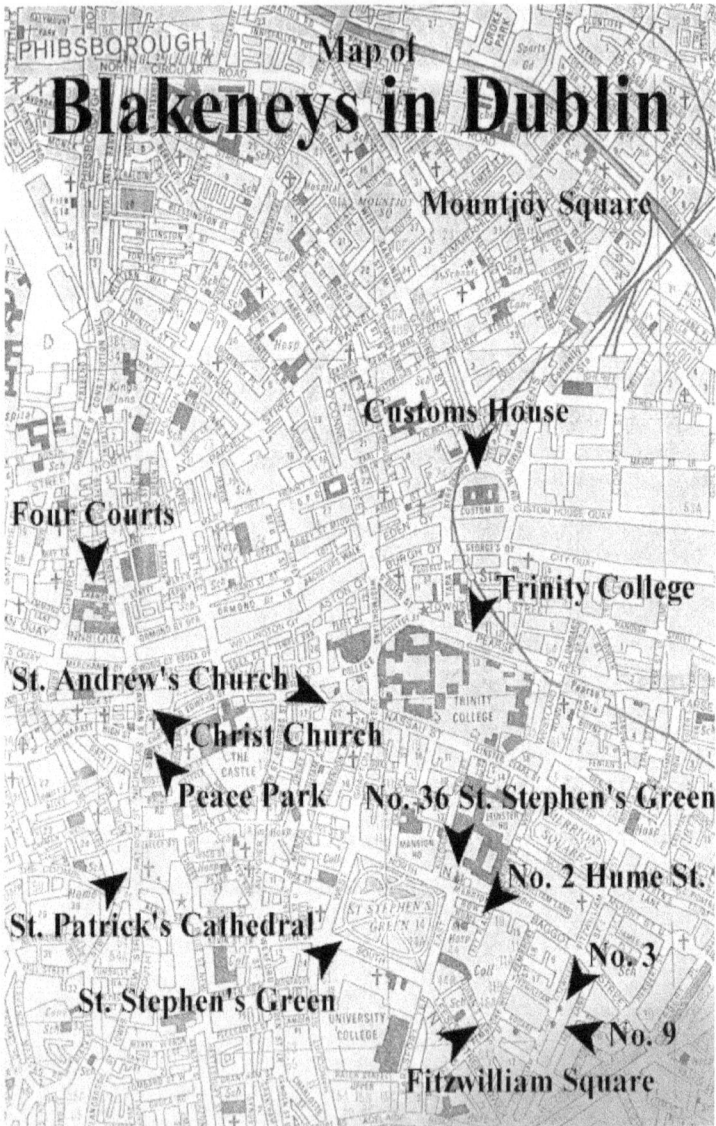

Figure 14 Map showing a few of the old Irish Blakeney residences, and also some of the sites and places with which they were occupationally involved, in Dublin, Ireland (image copyright ©).

THE BLAKENEYS

Figure 15 Notable views of Dublin, a city founded in 988 by the Vikings, and the probable original home of the English Blakeneys in Ireland. Clockwise, from top left-hand corner:

1) The Dublin Four Courts. The numerous lawyers, sheriffs, and judges among our Blakeney ancestors would have spent much time here.

2) Trinity College, where many Blakeneys have been educated.

3) Civic Offices, Christ Church Cathedral, and bridge over the River Liffey.

4) Door: An example of Georgian elegance in Fitzwilliam Square, where many of our well-to-do Blakeney ancestors were born and resided.

5) St. Patrick's Cathedral (lower right corner).

6) St. Stephen's Green, another section of Dublin where many of our Blakeney ancestors resided (lower left corner).

7) The River Liffey at twilight.

8) Statue of the famous Molly Malone, in front of the Provost House, Trinity College.

9) Center: Dublin Customs House, where no doubt many of our Blakeney ancestors conducted business.

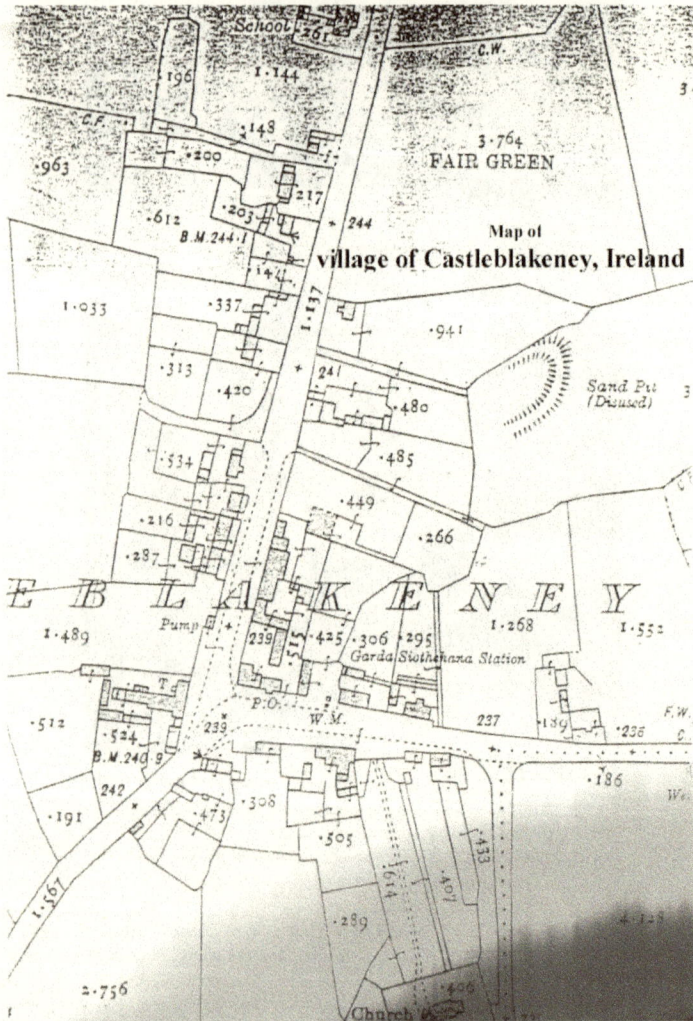

Figure 16 Surveyor's map of the village of Castleblakeney, County Galway, Ireland. Note the Parish Church at bottom center (image copyright ©).

Figure 17 Beautiful Fitzwilliam Square, Dublin, Ireland. Once the residential area of 17th- and 18th-Century nobility, it is now occupied primarily by commercial businesses, such as law, architectural, and doctors' offices. Fitzwilliam Square was the birthplace and home of many of our Irish Blakeney ancestors, including Thomas R. Blakeney, Sr., the progenitor of the New England Blakeney Line (photo copyright © - courtesy Michael Nelson).

Figure 18 The Blakeney manor in Abbert (near Castleblakeney), Ireland. Known as "Blakeney's House," sadly, it is now rubble (image copyright ©).

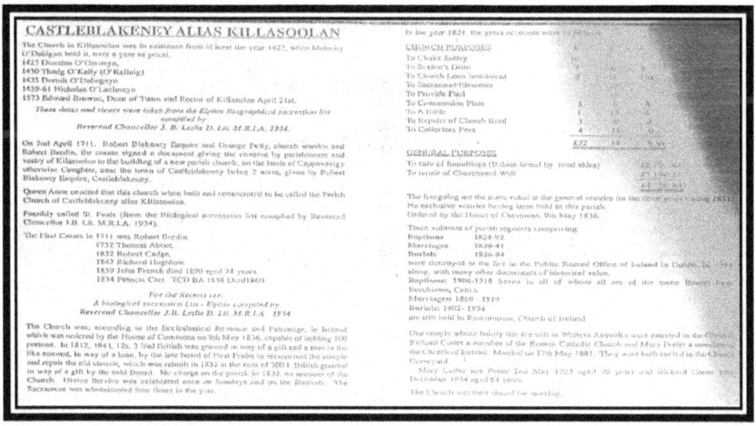

Figure 19 A brief history of the Castleblakeney Parish Church (also known as St. Pauls), County Galway, Ireland. Note the name of Robert Blakeney, Esquire. It is not known which Robert this is. It is probable though that this is Captain Robert Blakeney (circa 1657-1731), a son of Major Robert Blakeney (circa 1625-circa 1660), the first known Blakeney in County Galway, and also the instigator of the line from which the New England Blakeney Branch descends. Robert Blakeney, Esquire, a well-to-do and influential gentleman in the area, served as Deputy Governor, Mayor, and High Sheriff of Galway in the early 1700s. According to this document, on 2 April, 1711, Robert Blakeney gave two acres of land to the parishioners of Castleblakeney on which to build a new church (image copyright ©).

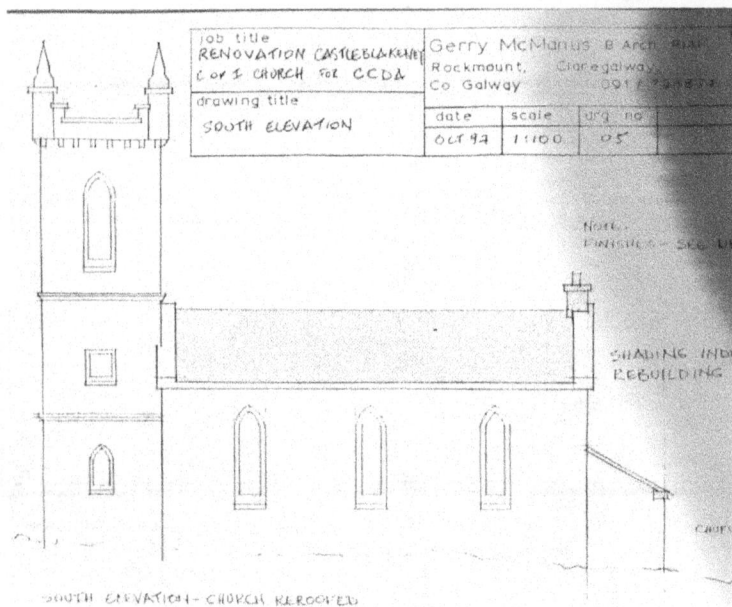

Figure 20 Some of the renovation plans for the Church in the village of Castleblakeney, County Galway, Ireland. Note: The Renovation Committee welcomes your donations for this worthy cause (image copyright ©).

Figure 21 St. Andrews Church, St. Andrew Street, Dublin, Ireland. Gertrude Smyth (d. 1768), the wife of William Blakeney (1733-1811), was buried here in 1768. The cemetery that was once associated with the Church has been paved over. Note: In the Middle Ages the Danes sailed up the River Liffey into Dublin and built a Temple to their Mother-Goddess Frig on this site. Only later did Christians construct their own sacred building here, St. Andrews Church (photo copyright © - courtesy Michael Nelson).

The History of the
Parish Church

of

Castleblakeney

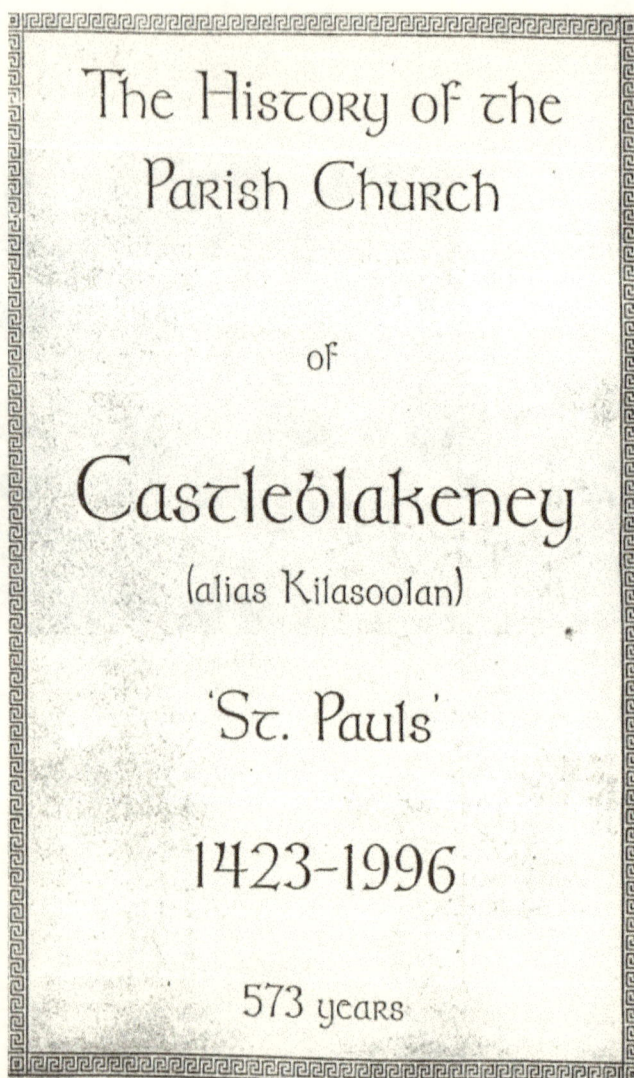

(alias Kilasoolan)

'St. Pauls'

1423-1996

573 years

Figure 22 Cover of a book focusing on the history of the Parish Church at Castleblakeney, County Galway, Ireland, 1996 (image copyright ©).

```
from:

            TUAM TITLE BOOK 1711 - 1755

                                (held in the Representative
                                 Church Body library, Dublin)


'The Parish Church of Killasoolan' to be moved to Castleblakeney.
Two acres of Land having been given for the building of the new
Church by Robert Blakeney.
In the year of the reign of Queen Anne.

'Killasoolan Church is in a ruinous condition in a place "onbironod"
with boggs and the road is impassable.'

'Remove all the material of the old Church to the new Church.'
                                              9th February 1711


'Timber and stone from the said old Church' to be brought to
Castleblakeney 'but to be used to no other use whatsoever than
for the Church in Castleblakeney.'
                                             26th February 1711
                John, Lord Archbishop of Tuam and Elphin.


From the above, one could conclude that it is very possible that
the stone from Killasoolan Church was possibly 15th century stone,
or possibly older, and was transferred up to Castleblakeney by
carts and horses.


THE MEMBERS OF THE VESTRY AND CHURCH WARDENS - FEBRUARY 1711:

Robert Blakeney
George Petty                   Edward Blakeney.
Gilbert Miller                 Loghlin Frow
James Budd                     Thomas Ffinn
John Concanen                  James Joyce
Edmond Guiffe                  Cormuck Nugent
John Masterton                 John Connollan
David Hors                     Hugh Kelly
John Gardivs                   John Ffarrell
Roger Luhune                   John Cook
William Porver                 James Guiffe
Daniel Quin
Robert Cardiff
```

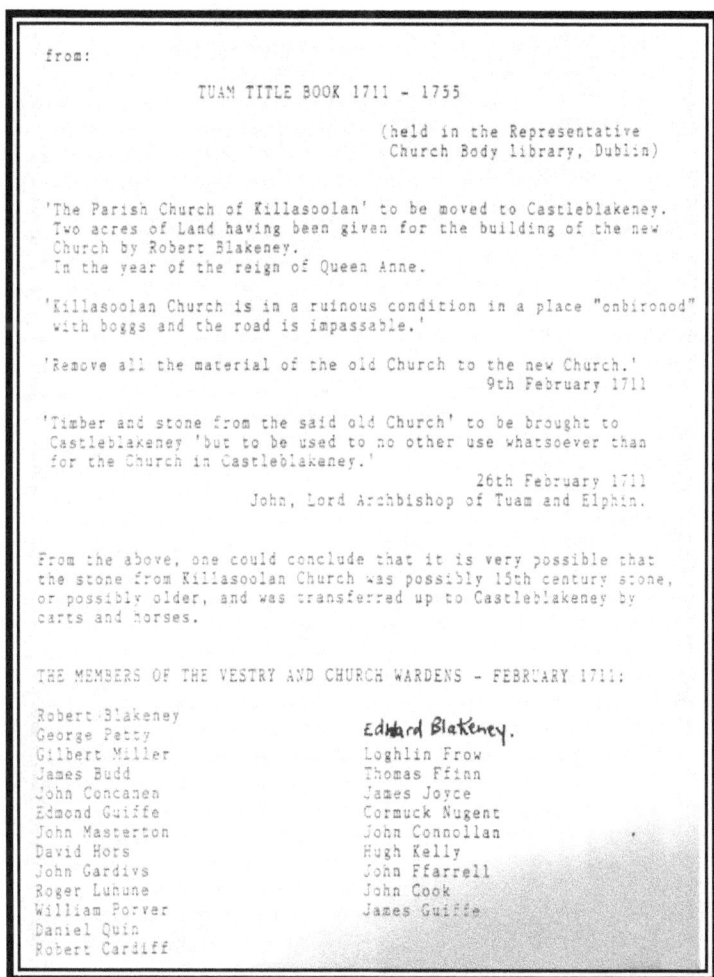

Figure 23 Reconstructed page from the Tuam Title Book (February 1711) discussing moving of the Parish Church of Killasoolan to the village of Castleblakeney, County Galway, Ireland, onto land donated by Colonel and MP, Robert Blakeney (d. 5 May, 1733). (The town of Tuam is just northwest of Castleblakeney.) Note the names of Robert Blakeney and Edward Blakeney among the members of the vestry and church wardens (image copyright ©).

THE CASTLEBLAKENEY CHURCH OF IRELAND

To be used as a Central Point for over 2,500 years of history on the Walking Trail around Castleblakeney. All material in hand from the British Museum and the National Museum of Ireland and Scotland.

1. **MUSEUM**

150 - 500 B.C.	The Gallagh Bog Man
	Ringforts and sutterains
1500's	The O'Kellys
1700's	The Blakeneys and "Bonnie Prince Charles"
	The Church in "Killasoolen" 1423 - 1711
	The Church in Castleblakeney 1711 - 1997
	The Village life of Castleblakeney
	Horsefairs - over 200 years
	Carnivals
	Mummers
	The old thatched cottage of the Ryan Family, Crannagh with a wattle chimney, circa 1690

2. **A GARDEN OF REMEMBRANCE AND PEACE**

For those people who have relatives buried in the graveyard

Ormbys	Bourns
Potters	Bowmans
Cotters and others	

For relatives of those who were married or baptised in the Church and are still alive in Galway and Ireland.

3. **CRAFT CENTRE**

Local Ladies Crafts - Croquet, Knitting, Liquid Embroidery, i.e. pictures, tablecloths, cushion covers and fire screens.
County Galway Arts and Crafts
Paintings, Pottery, China and Chrystal

4. **LIBRARY**

For two Secondary schools and one Vocational school and six National schools within a three mile radius
Library for Educational use i.e. Adult Night Classes, European Languages, Culture, History.

5. **TEA / COFFEE SHOP**

Home Baking - soda bread, scones, cakes, etc
Local Cookery Book for sale from the Kitchens of the Ladies and Gentlemen of Castleblakeney 1997

Figure 24 An information sheet from the National Museum of Ireland and Scotland, which uses the Church at Castleblakeney as a starting point on its "Walking Trail." Note the mention of "The Blakeneys and Bonnie Prince Charles" (image copyright ©).

Figure 25 There are many puzzles surrounding the Blakeneys. The identity of this gentleman, for example, is not known. It is thought that he may be John Blakeney, Sr. (circa 1765 -circa 1831). If so, he served in the British Army between 1780 and 1790, and had a son named John Blakeney, Jr. Other than these few paltry facts, his life story (and that of his son) remains a perplexing mystery (image copyright ©).

Figure 26 Miniature portrait of Dr. John Theophilus Blakeney (1774-1856), son of Colonel Walter Blakeney and Sarah Shield, by the Irish artist Walter Robertson (circa 1820). John was a surgeon, and also a barrister at the Inner Temple in 1801. He never married and died without issue (photo copyright © - courtesy Claudia Hill).

Figure 27 Irish Parliament, 1780. MP John Blakeney is near the center.

Figure 28 Detail from painting on previous page of MP John Blakeney (center).

Figure 29 The Old Blakeney Cemetery on Captain John Blakeney's plantation, located between the towns of Dudley and Pageland in Chesterfield County, South Carolina, USA. The cemetery is in a remote area on an unnamed road. Directions: From Pageland head southwest on Route 601/9. After about 2-3 miles turn right on Dudley Road (also known as State Road S-13-105). You are now traveling northwest. Go about 1 mile and turn left on an unnamed dirt road, which leads to the cemetery (located at the end). If you pass John Blakeney Lane (on the left) while driving on Dudley Road, you have gone too far (image copyright ©).

THE BLAKENEYS

Figure 30 Captain John Blakeney's memorial headstone, Old Blakeney Cemetery, South Carolina (image copyright ©).

Figure 31 A memorial headstone listing Captain John Blakeney's children and their spouses, Old Blakeney Cemetery, South Carolina (image copyright ©).

Figure 32 Full text of Captain John Blakeney's memorial headstone, Old Blakeney Cemetery, South Carolina (image copyright ©).

Figure 33 Captain John Blakeney's actual grave with headstone, Old Blakeney Cemetery, South Carolina (image copyright ©).

Figure 34 The headstone of Margaret "Peggy" (surname unknown; possibly Evans), the wife of Captain John Blakeney, Old Blakeney Cemetery, South Carolina (image copyright ©).

Figure 35 Fitzwilliam Square, Dublin, Ireland. Our Blakeney ancestors would have been very familiar with these beautiful Georgian doorways (image copyright ©).

Figure 36 Thomas Richard Blakeney, Sr. (second from left), born in Dublin, Ireland, in 1841, is a descendant of the Castle Blakeney line. The son of Thomas Blakeney (b. 1804) and Emma Jones (b. circa 1810), he and his family lived at 3 Fitzwilliam Square. They emigrated to the U.S., probably through Canada, around 1847. Thomas appears to have married three times and had at least six children between these marriages. During the American War for Southern Independence he fought for the Union in Company 1, 11th Regiment Massachusetts Infantry. He was wounded three times and was later awarded the Purple Heart. Thomas died in Watertown, Massachusetts, August 22, 1934, and was buried at Saint Patrick's Cemetery. Like thousands of other Irishmen, Thomas may have decided to fight with the Yankees because he was bribed by Abraham Lincoln with today's equivalent of a $5,000 bounty, a common ploy by the U.S. president to gain Irish-Catholic recruits at the time. While Thomas sided with socialistic, big-government Lincoln and the liberal North, he was in the minority: most of the American Blakeneys fought for small-government President Jefferson Davis and the conservative South. This is something the English Blakeneys would have been very proud of, for the majority of Britons, in particular the upper classes, enthusiastically supported the Confederacy. England was finally only prevented from openly sending ships, guns, ammunition, and supplies to President Davis because tragically, and illegally, Lincoln threatened war against any nation who attempted to aid the South (image copyright ©).

THE BLAKENEYS

Figure 37 John William Blakeney, Jr. (1896-1978), and his wife
Sarah "Sadie" Wing (1897-1978). Photo probably taken about 1918. John
is the grandson of Thomas R. Blakeney, Sr. (previous page) and the father
of Jean M. (Blakeney) King (following page). Born in Watertown,
Massachusetts, John is a member of the New England Blakeney family and
a descendant of the Castle Blakeney line. He served in World War I,
attended law school at Boston University, became a successful attorney,
and was a popular playwright, singer, and storyteller. John's wife Sadie,
an excellent seamstress with a beautiful singing voice, descends from the
Wing family of Banbury, Oxfordshire, England. Sadie's father Paul
Wrightington Wing, Sr. (1851-1918) was a New England whaler, while
her mother Rosée D. Croteau (1871-1935) of Quebec, was a Canadian of
French heritage. The early Wings were English Puritans and Quakers who
helped settle Cape Cod, Massachusetts. I am related to the Blakeneys
through various lines. Some of my early ancestors, the Wrights of North
Carolina, for example, married into the Southern Blakeney branch, while
I have mutual European royal ancestors with the New England Blakeney
branch (image copyright ©).

Figure 38 Jean Marilyn (Blakeney) King, a New England Blakeney, great-granddaughter of Thomas Richard Blakeney, Sr., and a descendant of the Castle Blakeney line. Jean is of English, Irish, and French-Canadian heritage, and descends from European royalty. The wife of Donald Thomas King, Sr. and the mother of seven children, she attended Regis College in Weston, Massachusetts, and was the organist and pianist at St. Bernard's Catholic Church in Concord, Massachusetts. Her husband's King family descends from Princess Diana Spencer's family, an American clan that includes Charles King (president of Columbia College), Cyrus King (U.S. congressman), James Gore King (Revolutionary War general), Edward King (founder of the Cincinnati Law School), William King (first governor of Maine), and Rufus King (signer of the U.S. Constitution and presidential candidate in 1816). After his death Rufus' farm in Queens, New York, was turned into what is now known as "King Park," and his home, "King Manor," became a public museum. The Rufus King School in Fresh Meadows, New York, was named after him, as was Rufus King Hall at CUNY, Queens, New York. The earliest known Kings have been traced to Ugborough Parish, Devonshire, England, where they lived in the great Kynge family castle known as "Fowlescomb" (now a bed and breakfast). Jean is a cousin of numerous other individuals of French-Canadian ancestry, such as Angelina Jolie, Madonna Louise Ciccone ("Madonna"), the Duchess of Cornwall Camilla Parker Bowles (wife of Prince Charles), Hillary Rodham Clinton, and Celine Dion (image copyright ©).

Bibliography

Alexander, Henry. *The Story of Our Language.* 1940. Canada: Thomas Nelson and Sons, Ltd (1962 Dolphin Books ed.).

Anderson, John M. *The Grammar of Names.* Oxford, UK: Oxford University Press, 2007.

Arnold, Martin. *The Vikings: Wolves of War.* Lanham, MD: Rowman and Littlefield, 2006.

Ashwin, Trevor. *Historical Atlas of Norfolk.* Andover, UK: Phillimore and Co., 2005.

Ayto, John. *Dictionary of Word Origins.* New York, NY: Arcade, 1990.

Bede. *Ecclesiastical History of the English People.* 731. London, UK: Penguin, 1955, 1990 ed.

Blakeney / Blakley Family Association Newsletters. Various editions. Nova Scotia, Canada.

Ball, Catherine N. Personal correspondence. Washington, D.C.

Barnhart, Robert K. *The Barnhart Concise Dictionary of Etymology.* New York, NY: HarperResource, 1995.

Barnhart, Robert K., and Sol Steinmetz. *Chambers Dictionary of Etymology.* 1988. Edinburgh, Scotland: Chambers Harrap, 2006 ed.

Baugh, Albert C. *A History of the English Language.* 1957. Englewood Cliffs, NJ: Prentice-Hall, 1963 ed.

Blair, Peter Hunt. *Roman Britain and Early England: 55 B.C.-A.D. 871.* 1963. New York, NY: W. W. Norton, 1966 ed.

Blakeney, Amy. Personal correspondence. Novato, California.

Blakeney, John Oscar. *The Blakeneys in America and Some Collaterals, With Some Reference to English-Irish Families.* 1927. Self-Published, Little Rock, AR, 1928.

Blakeney, Ray H. *My Help Comes From Above: Blakeney and Blakely - The History of Chambers Blakely and David Bleakney and their Neighbours in the 18th Century.* Dartmouth, Nova Scotia, Canada: self-published, 2000.

——. Personal correspondence.

Boïelle, James. *Heath's French and English Dictionary.* Boston, MA: D. C. Heath and Co., 1903.

Brewer, Paul (ed.). *Ireland; History, People, Culture.* London, UK: Salamander, 2001.

Bridges, E. M. *Classic Landforms of the North Norfolk Coast.* Sheffield, UK: Geographical Association, 1998.

Briffault, Robert Stephen. *The Mothers: The Matriarchal Theory of Social Origins.* 1927. New York, NY: Macmillan, 1931 (single volume, abridged) ed.

Brooks, Peter. *Have You Heard About Blakeney?* Cromer, Norfolk, UK: Poppyland Publishing, 1981.

Bryson, Bill. *The Mother Tongue: English and How It Got That Way.* New York, NY: William Morrow, 1990.

Burke, John. *Burke's Peerage: Genealogical and Heraldic History of the Baronetage and Knightage* (104th ed.). 1826. London, UK: Waterlow and Sons, 1967 ed.

Caesar, Julius. *The Gallic War.* 1st Century B.C. Oxford, UK: Oxford University Press, 1996, 2008 ed.

Cahill, Thomas. *How the Irish Saved Civilization.* New York, NY: Anchor, 1995.

Carpenter, David. *The Struggle for Mastery: The Penguin History of Britain 1066-1284.* 2003. London, UK: Penguin, 2004 ed.

Christiansen, Eric. *The Norsemen in the Viking Age.* Oxford, UK: Blackwell, 2002.

Clements, Jonathan. *A Brief History of the Vikings: The Last Pagans or the First Modern Europeans?* New York, NY: Carroll and Graf, 2005.

Coohill, Joseph. *Ireland: A Short History.* 2000. Oxford, UK: Oneworld, 2005 ed.

Cullen, Kathryn E. Jones. Personal correspondence. Stoughton, MA.

Currie, Robin. *Britain and Ireland: A Visual Tour of the Enchanted Isles.* Washington, D.C.: National Geographic, 2010.

Curtis, Edmund. *A History of Ireland: From the Earliest Times to 1922.* 1936. London, UK: Routledge, 2002 ed.

Davies, John. *The Land of Boudica: Prehistoric and Roman Norfolk.* Great Dunham, UK: Heritage Marketing and Publications, 2009.

Davis, William, and Martha Blakeney Davis. Personal correspondence.

Domesday Book: A Survey of the Counties of England. Compiled by direction of King William I: Winchester, 1086. Chichester, UK: Phillimore and Co., 1984.

Dorward, David. *Scottish Surnames: A Guide to the Family Names of Scotland.* Glasgow, Scotland: HarperCollins, 1995.

Downham, Clare. *Viking Kings of Britain and Ireland: The Dynasty of Ívarr to A.D. 1014.* Edinburgh, Scotland: Dunedin Academic Press, 2007.

Dunmore, Charles, and Rita M. Fleischer. *Studies in Etymology.* Newburyport,

MA: Focus, 2008.

Durkin, Philip. *The Oxford Guide to Etymology*. Oxford, UK: Oxford University Press, 2009.

Encyclopedia Britannica: A New Survey of Universal Knowledge. 1768. Chicago, IL/London, UK: Encyclopedia Britannica, 1955 ed.

Ewing, Thor. *Gods and Worshippers: In the Viking and Germanic World*. Charleston, SC: The History Press, 2008.

Farmer, David Hugh. *The Oxford Dictionary of Saints*. 1978. Oxford, UK: Oxford University Press, 1992 ed.

Fellows-Jensen, Gillian. Personal correspondence.

Forte, Angelo, Richard Oram, and Frederik Pedersen. *Viking Empires*. Cambridge, UK: Cambridge University Press, 2005.

Fraser, Rebecca. *The Story of Britain: From the Romans to the Present: A Narrative History*. 2003. New York, NY: W. W. Norton, 2005 ed.

Gerrad, David (ed.). *The Hidden Places of Norfolk: Including the Norfolk Broads*. Plymouth, UK: Travel Publishing, 1998.

Gimbutas, Marija Alseikaitè. *The Civilization of the Goddess: The World of Old Europe* (Joan Marler, ed.). New York, NY: HarperCollins, 1991.

——. *The Goddesses and Gods of Old Europe: Myths and Cult Images*. 1974. Berkeley, CA: University of California Press, 1992 ed.

Glyn, Anthony. *The British: Portrait of a People*. New York, NY: G. P. Putnam's Sons, 1970.

Geoffrey of Monmouth. *The History of the Kings of Britain*. Circa 1136. London, UK: Penguin, 1966 ed.

Graves, Robert. *The Greek Myths*. 1955. Harmondsworth, UK: Penguin, 1992 combined ed.

——. *The White Goddess: A Historical Grammar of Poetic Myth*. 1948. New York, NY: Noonday Press, 1991 ed.

Green, John Richard. *A Short History of the English People* (Vol. 1). London, UK: Macmillan and Co., 1892.

Farrell, Deborah, and Carole Presser. *The Herder Symbol Dictionary*. 1978. Wilmette, IL: Chiron, 1990 ed.

Hall, John Richard Clark. *A Concise Anglo-Saxon Dictionary*. 1894. Toronto, Canada: University of Toronto Press, 1960 ed.

Harrison, Mark. *The Vikings: Voyagers of Discovery and Plunder*. Oxford, UK: Osprey, 2006.

Haywood, John. *The Penguin Historical Atlas of the Vikings*. London, UK: Penguin, 1995.

———. *Encyclopedia of the Viking Age*. London, UK: Thames and Hudson, 2000.

Herm, Gerhard. *The Celts: The People Who Came Out of the Darkness*. New York, NY: St. Martin's Press, 1976.

Hoad, T. F. (ed.). *The Concise Oxford Dictionary of English Etymology*. 1996. Oxford, UK: Oxford University Press, 2003 ed.

Holm, Deanna Adams. Personal correspondence.

Hooton, Jonathan. *The Glaven Ports: A Maritime History of Blakeney, Cley, and Wiveton in North Norfolk*. Norwich, Norfolk, UK: Blakeney History Group, 1996.

James, Montague Rhodes. *Suffolk and Norfolk: A Perambulation of the Two Counties with Notices of their History and their Ancient Buildings*. Cambridge, UK: Cambridge University Press, 2010.

Johnston, Rev. James B. *Place-names of England and Wales*. London, UK: John Murray, 1915.

Jones, Gwyn. *A History of the Vikings*. 1968. Oxford, UK: Oxford University Press, 1984 ed.

Jones, Prudence, and Nigel Pennick. *A History of Pagan Europe*. London, UK: Routledge, 1995.

Kearney, Hugh. *The British Isles: A History of Four Nations*. 1989. Cambridge, UK: Cambridge University Press, 2006 ed.

Kee, Robert. *Ireland: A History*. 1980. London, UK: Abacus, 2004 ed.

Kettridge, J. O. *Kettridge's French-English Dictionary*. New York, NY: David McKay Co., n.d.

King, Jean M. (Blakeney). Personal correspondence. Concord, MA.

Kinsella, Valerie (Treasurer of the Castleblakeney Development Committee). Personal correspondence. Castleblakeney, Ireland.

Kirkland, Don, and Michael Walsh. *White Cargo: The Forgotten History of Britain's White Slaves in America*. 2007. New York, NY: New York University Press, 2008 ed.

Laird, Charlton. *The Miracle of Language*. 1953. New York, NY: Premier, 1963 ed.

Langendonck, Willy Van. *Theory and Typology of Proper Names*. Berlin, Germany: Mouton de Gruyter, 2007.

Larousse Encyclopedia of Mythology, New. 1959. London, UK: Hamlyn Publishing Group, 1976 ed.

Lauer, Gregorio F., Esq. Personal correspondence. Rio Rancho, NM.

Lawrence, Richard Russell. *Roman Britain*. Colchester, UK: Shire, 2010.

Logan, F. Donald. *The Vikings in History*. 1983. London, UK: Routledge,

2003 ed.

McCaffrey, Carmel. *In Search of Ireland's Heroes: The Story of the Irish from the English Invasion to the Present Day*. Chicago, IL: Ivan R. Dee, 2006.

McCaffrey, Carmel, and Leo Eaton. *In Search of Ancient Ireland: The Origins of the Irish from Neolithic Times to the Coming of the English*. Chicago, IL: New Amsterdam, 2002.

Mackay, Charles. *The Gaelic Etymology of the Languages of Western Europe, and More Especially of the English and Lowland Scotch*. London, UK: N. Trübner and Co., 1877.

Mackie, J. D. *A History of Scotland*. 1964. London, UK: Penguin, 1991 ed.

MacLean, Fitzroy. *Scotland: A Concise History*. 1970. London, UK: Thames and Hudson, 2000 ed.

MacLysaght, Edward. *The Surnames of Ireland*. 1985. Dublin, Ireland: Irish Academic Press, 1999 ed.

MacManus, Seumas. *The Story of the Irish Race: A Popular History of Ireland*. New York, NY: Cosimo, 2005.

Mathias, Peter. *The First Industrial Nation: The Economic History of Britain, 1700-1914*. 1969. London, UK: Routledge, 2001 ed.

Mattingly, David. *An Imperial Possession: Britain in the Roman Empire, 54 BC-AD 409*. 2006. London, UK: Penguin, 2007 ed.

McArthur, Tom (ed.). *The Oxford Companion to the English Language*. Oxford, UK: Oxford University Press, 1992.

Mills, A. D. *Oxford Dictionary of English Place-names*. 1991. Oxford, UK: Oxford University Press, 1998 ed.

Monaghan, Patricia. *The Book of Goddesses and Heroines*. 1990. St. Paul, MN: Llewellyn, 1991 ed.

Moreton, C. E. *The Townshends and Their World: Gentry, Law, and Land in Norfolk circa 1450-1551*. Oxford, UK: Oxford University Press, 1992.

Morgan, Kenneth O. *The Oxford History of Britain*. 1984. Oxford, UK: Oxford University Press, 2010 ed.

Nelson, Michael. Personal correspondence. Dublin, Ireland.

Neumann, Erich. *The Great Mother: An Analysis of the Archetype* (Ralph Manheim, trans.). New York, NY: Pantheon, 1955.

Nyland, Edo. *Linguistic Archaeology: An Introduction*. Victoria, B.C., Canada: Trafford, 2001.

O'Brien, Maire and Conor Cruise. *Ireland: A Concise History*. 1972. New York, NY: Thames and Hudson, 1999 ed.

Oliver, F. W. *Blakeney Point, Norfolk: Topography and Vegetation*. Charleston,

SC: BiblioLife: 2009.

Onions, C. T. (ed.). *The Oxford Dictionary of English Etymology.* Oxford, UK: Oxford University Press, 1966.

Oxford English Dictionary, The (compact edition, 2 vols.). 1928. Oxford, UK: Oxford University Press, 1979 ed.

Page, R. I. *Chronicles of the Vikings: Records, Memorials and Myths.* Toronto, Canada: University of Toronto Press, 1995.

Parry, Melanie (ed.). *Chambers Biographical Dictionary.* 1897. Edinburgh, Scotland: Larousse Kingfisher Chambers, 1998 (centenary) ed.

Raftery, Barry. *Pagan Celtic Ireland: The Enigma of the Irish Iron Age.* London, UK: Thames and Hudson, 1994.

Ramondino, Salvatore (ed.). *The New World Spanish-English and English-Spanish Dictionary.* New York, NY: Signet, 1969.

Reaney, P. H. and R. M. Wilson. *A Dictionary of English Surnames.* 1958. Oxford, UK: Oxford University Press, 1997 ed.

Rufus, Anneli S., and Kristan Lawson. *Goddess Sites: Europe.* New York, NY: HarperCollins, 1991.

Rule, Lareina. *Name Your Baby.* 1963. New York, NY: Bantam, 1978 ed.

Sawyer, Peter. *The Oxford Illustrated History of the Vikings.* 1997. Oxford, UK: Oxford University Press, 1999 ed.

Scally, Robert. *The End of Hidden Ireland: Rebellion, Famine, and Emigration.* 1995. Oxford, UK: Oxford University Press, 1996 ed.

Schama, Simon. *A History of Britain, Vol. 1: At the Edge of the World?, 3000 BC-AD 1603.* New York, NY: Hyperion, 2000.

———. *A History of Britain, Vol. 2: The Wars of the British, 1603-1776.* New York, NY: Hyperion, 2001.

Seabrook, Lochlainn. *The Goddess Dictionary of Words and Phrases: Introducing a New Core Vocabulary for the Women's Spirituality Movement.* 1999. Franklin, TN: Sea Raven Press, 2010 ed.

———. *Britannia Rules: Goddess-Worship in Ancient Anglo-Celtic Society: An Academic Look at the United Kingdom's Matricentric Spiritual Past.* 1999. Franklin, TN: Sea Raven Press, 2010 ed.

———. *The Book of Kelle: An Introduction to Goddess-Worship and the Great Celtic Mother-Goddess Kelle, Original Blessed Lady of Ireland.* 1999. Franklin, TN: Sea Raven Press, 2010 ed.

———. *The Caudills: An Etymological, Ethnological, and Genealogical Study.* 2000. Franklin, TN: Sea Raven Press, 2010 ed.

——. *The McGavocks of Carnton Plantation: A Southern History - Celebrating One of Dixie's Most Noble Confederate Families and Their Tennessee Home*. Franklin, TN: Sea Raven Press, 2007.

——. *Abraham Lincoln: The Southern View - Demythologizing America's Sixteenth President*. Franklin, TN: Sea Raven Press, 2007.

——. *Nathan Bedford Forrest: Southern Hero, American Patriot*. 2007. Franklin, TN: Sea Raven Press, 2009 ed.

——. *A Rebel Born: A Defense of Nathan Bedford Forrest, Confederate General, American Legend*. Franklin, TN: Sea Raven Press, 2010.

——. *Aphrodite's Trade: The Hidden History of Prostitution Unveiled*. Franklin, TN: Sea Raven Press, 2010.

——. *Everything You Were Taught About the Civil War is Wrong: Ask a Southerner! - Correcting the Errors of Yankee "History."* Franklin, TN: Sea Raven Press, 2010.

——. *The Way of Holiness: The Evolution of Religion—From the Cave Bear Cult to Christianity*. Franklin, TN: Sea Raven Press, unpublished manuscript.

——. *The Goddess Encyclopedia of Secret Words, Names, and Places*. Franklin, TN: Sea Raven Press, unpublished manuscript.

Shipley, Joseph Twadell. *The Origins of English Words: A Discursive Dictionary of Indo-European Roots*. Baltimore, MD: John Hopkins University Press, 2001.

Skeat, Walter W. *A Concise Etymological Dictionary of the English Language*. 1882. New York, NY: Capricorn, 1963 ed.

Skelton, Robin, and Margaret Blackwood. *Earth, Air, Fire, Water: Pre-Christian and Pagan Elements in British Songs, Rhymes and Ballads*. Harmondsworth, UK: Arkana, 1990.

Sluis, Pieter. *Dublin: Official Guide and Maps*. 1966. Dublin, Ireland: The Irish and Overseas Publishing Co., Ltd.

Smith, Philip D. Jr. *Tartan For Me! Suggested Tartans for 13,695 Scottish, Scotch-Irish, Irish, and North American Names with Lists of Clan, Family and District Tartans*. Bruceton Mills, WV: Scotpress, 1990.

Sprague, Martina. *Norse Warfare: The Unconventional Battle Strategies of the Ancient Vikings*. New York, NY: Hippocrene, 2007.

Strong, Roy. *The Story of Britain: A People's History*. London, UK: Pimlico, 1998.

Sykes, Bryan. *Saxons, Vikings, ands Celts: The Genetic Roots of Britain and Ireland*. New York, NY: W. W. Norton, 2006.

Timpson, John. *Timpsons' Norfolk Notebook*. London, UK: Thorogood, 2002.

Traupman, John C. *The New College Latin and English Dictionary*. 1966. New York, NY: Bantam, 1988 ed.

——. *The Bantam New College German and English Dictionary*. 1981. New York,, NY: Bantam, 1986 ed.

Visser, G. J. *Nederlands Engels Woordenboek (Netherlands English Dictionary)*. Antwerp, Belgium: Uitgeverij Het Spectrum N.V., 1970.

Walker, Barbara G. *The Woman's Encyclopedia of Myths and Secrets*. San Francisco, CA: Harper and Row, 1983.

Watkins, Calvert (ed.). *The American Heritage Dictionary of Indo-European Roots*. Boston, MA: Houghton Mifflin, 2000.

Way, George, and Romilly Squire. *Scottish Clan and Family Encyclopedia*. Glasgow, Scotland: Harper Collins, 1994.

Webster's Biographical Dictionary. Springfield, MA: G. and C. Merriam Company, 1943.

Webster's Ninth New Collegiate Dictionary. 1898. Springfield, MA: Merriam-Webster, 1984 ed.

Weisser, Henry. *England: An Illustrated History*. New York, NY: Hippocrene, 2000.

——. *Wales: An Illustrated History*. New York, NY: Hippocrene, 2002.

Wilson, Bill. *Norfolk 1: Norwich and North-East*. New Haven, CT: Yale University Press, 1997.

——. *Norfolk 2: North-West and South*. New Haven, CT: Yale University Press, 1999.

Index

NOTES: *1) This index was compiled using a computer indexer, which may produce various peculiarities. 2) Most of the individuals in the Blakeney Family Tree are not included in this index.*

The Blakeneys

THE BLAKENEYS

About the Author

Lochlainn Seabrook is an unreconstructed Southern author and traditional agrarian of Scottish, English, Irish, Welsh, and German extraction. An encyclopedist and lexicographer, a musician, artist, graphic designer, and photographer, and an award-winning poet, songwriter, and screenwriter, he has a twenty-five year background in the various fields of the American Civil War, thealogy (female-based religion), anthropology, etymology, and comparative mythology and religion. Due to similarities in their works, themes, styles, theories, and beliefs, Lochlainn is sometimes referred to as the "American Robert Graves," after the prolific English writer, poet, and author of the classic work *The White Goddess*.

The grandson of an Appalachian coal-mining family, Lochlainn is a seventh generation Kentuckian, a professional genealogist, co-chair of the Jent/Gent Family Committee (Kentucky), founder and director of the Blakeney Family Tree Project, and a board member of the Friends of Colonel Benjamin E. Caudill. Lochlainn's literary works have been endorsed by leading authorities, bestselling authors, celebrities, noted scientists, esteemed Southern organizations, and well respected academicians from around the world.

As a professional writer Lochlainn has authored some thirty popular adult books ranging in scope from pro-South studies, the anthropology of religion, historical biographies, genealogical monographs, and Goddess-worship, to ghost stories, family histories, etymological dictionaries, a comparative analysis of the origins of Christmas, and cross-cultural studies of the family and marriage.

Lochlainn's eight children's books include a dictionary of religion and myth, a rewriting of the King Arthur legend (which reinstates the original pre-Christian motifs), bedtime stories for preschoolers, a naturalist's guidebook to owls, a worldwide look at the family, a scientific investigation of UFOs and aliens, and an examination of the Near-Death Experience.

THE BLAKENEYS

Of blue-blooded Southern stock through his Kentucky, Tennessee, Virginia, West Virginia, and North Carolina ancestors, Lochlainn is a direct descendant of European royalty via his 6th great-grandfather, the Earl of Oxford, after which London's famous Harley Street is named. Among his celebrated male Celtic ancestors is Robert the Bruce, King of Scotland, Lochlainn's 22nd great-grandfather. The 21st great-grandson of Edward I "Longshanks" Plantagenet (1239-1307), King of England, Lochlainn is also a thirteenth-generation descendant of the colonists of Jamestown, Virginia (1607).

Lochlainn, a member of the multiracial organization Sons of Confederate Veterans (SCV), is a descendant of over a dozen Confederate soldiers and a cousin of numerous notable Confederates, among them: Robert E. Lee, Nathan Bedford Forrest, Stonewall Jackson, John S. Mosby, James Longstreet, John Hunt Morgan, Jeb Stuart, States Rights Gist, George W. Gordon, Arthur M. Manigault, John Bell Hood, P. G. T. Beauregard, John H. Winder, Gideon J. Pillow, Stephen D. Lee, John C. Breckinridge, Leonidas Polk, William Giles Harding (of Belle Meade Plantation, Nashville, TN), Zebulon Vance, George Wythe Randolph (Thomas Jefferson's grandson), Felix K. Zollicoffer, Fitzhugh Lee, Benjamin E. Caudill, Nathaniel F. Cheairs (of Rippavilla Plantation, Spring Hill, TN), Jesse James, Frank James, Robert Brank Vance, Richard Taylor, Charles Sydney Winder, John W. McGavock (of Carnton Plantation, Franklin, TN), Carrie (Winder) McGavock (of Ducros Plantation, Houma, LA), David Harding McGavock (of Two Rivers Plantation, Nashville, TN), Lysander McGavock (of Midway Plantation, Brentwood, TN), James Randal McGavock (of Riverside Plantation, Franklin, TN), Randal William McGavock (of the Deery Family Home, Allisona, TN), William Henry F. Lee, Lucius E. Polk, Louisa Minor Meriwether (wife of William Andrew Charles), Sarah Knox Taylor (first wife of President Jefferson Davis), Ellen Bourne Tynes (the wife of Forrest's Chief of Artillery, Captain John W. Morton), and famed South Carolina diarist Mary Chesnut.

Lochlainn's modern day cousins include: Rebecca Gayheart (Kentucky-born actress), Shelby Lee Adams (Letcher County, Kentucky, portrait photographer), Bertram Thomas Combs (Kentucky's fiftieth governor), Edith Bolling (wife of President Woodrow Wilson), and actors Robert Duvall, Lee Marvin, and Tom Cruise.

400

THE BLAKENEYS

Born with music in his blood, Seabrook is an award-winning, multi-genre, Nashville songwriter and lyricist who has composed some 3,000 songs (250 albums). A musician, producer, multi-instrumentalist, and renown performer—whose keyboard work has been variously compared to pianists from Hargus Robbins and Vince Guaraldi to Elton John and Leonard Bernstein—Seabrook has opened for groups such as the Earl Scruggs Review, Ted Nugent, and Bob Seger, and has performed privately for such luminaries as President Ronald Reagan, Burt Reynolds, and Senator Edward W. Brooke.

His cousins in the music business include: Johnny Cash, Elvis Presley, Billy Ray and Miley Cyrus, Patty Loveless, Dolly Parton, Pat Boone, Lee Ann Womack, Naomi, Wynonna, and Ashley Judd, Ricky Skaggs, the Sunshine Sisters, Martha Carson, and Chet Atkins.

Lochlainn, who is related to both the Southern Blakeneys and the New England Blakeneys, lives with his family in historic Middle Tennessee, the heart of the Confederacy, where many of his conservative Southern ancestors fought valiantly against liberal Lincoln and the progressive North in defense of Jeffersonianism, constitutional government, and personal liberty.

LOCHLAINNSEABROOK.com

Luke 17:21

King James Bible

www.ingramcontent.com/pod-product-compliance
Lightning Source LLC
Chambersburg PA
CBHW020817270326
41928CB00006B/377